Rediscovering the American Midwest

Series Editors: Jon K. Lauck and Patricia Oman

The Midwestern Moment — Jon K. Lauck, ed.
The Forgotten World of Early Twentieth-Century Midwestern Regionalism, 1880–1940

A Scattering Time — Sara Kosiba, ed.
How Modernism Met Midwestern Culture

Pieces of the Heartland — Andy Oler, ed.
Representing Midwestern Places

Making the Midwest — Jon K. Lauck, ed.
The Formation of Midwestern Identity, 1787–1900
   Forthcoming

Pieces of the Heartland

Pieces of the Heartland

Representing Midwestern Places

Edited by
Andy Oler

Hastings College Press | Hastings, Nebraska

© 2018 by Hastings College Press

All rights reserved. No part of this book may be used or reproduced in any manner whatsoever without permission from the publisher, except in the case of brief quotations embodied in critical articles and reviews.

Copy Editors
Kit Grode
Patricia Oman

Proofreader
Bruce Batterson

Book Design
Patricia Oman

Paperback   ISBN-10: 1942885547   ISBN-13: 978-1-942885-54-2

Hardback   ISBN-10: 1942885539   ISBN-13: 978-1-942885-53-5

Manufactured in the United States of America.

Contents

Andy Oler	Introduction Landscape, Visibility, and the Scope of the Midwest	ix
Nora Pat Small	Preserving a Midwestern Moment A Case Study of New Harmony, Indiana	1
Camden Burd	In the Land of Hiawatha Conservation and Literary Sociability in Michigan	23
Jim O'Loughlin Jordan Lea Ludwig	The Midwest Below Me James Hearst's Poetry and Prose	39
Owen Cantrell	"Ya Got Trouble" River City, Main Street, U.S.A., and Nostalgia in the Imagined Midwest	53
Wayne Anderson	"Beautiful Land of Make-Believe" Rural Iowa in 1930s Hollywood	69
Jonathon Josten	Migratory Bodies Failed Commemoration in Richard Powers's *The Echo Maker* and *Gain*	89
Seretha D. Williams Michelle Story-Stewart Patrick C. Riley	Gary, Indiana, on the Cusp of Greatness Richard G. Hatcher and the National Black Political Convention of 1972	107
Kimberly Wilmot Voss	Midwest Feminism Kay Clarenbach and the Origin of the National Organization for Women	125

Yi-chin Shih	Speaking from the Middle West Susan Glaspell's Critique of Nation in *Inheritors*	139
Bob Mellin	Moses of the Midwest Gene Stratton-Porter's Populist, Unsustainable Ecofeminism	157
Sally E. Parry	Iron George Myths of Masculinity in Sinclair Lewis's *Babbitt* and *Mantrap*	169
Kelly Hanson	Performing Haitian History on the Midwestern Stage The World Premiere of Clarence Cameron White's Modernist Opera *Ouanga*	183
Kerry Alcorn	Saskatchewan's Midwestern Moment Education in a Continental, Borderlands Context	205
Contributors		225

Andy Oler

Introduction

Landscape, Visibility, and the Scope of the Midwest

Since at least the "Revolt from the Village," emptiness, evacuation, and loss have been preoccupations of midwestern literature. Carl Van Doren saw "decay" in Spoon River, "dulness" in Gopher Prairie, tedium in Warbleton, and the inclination to escape Winesburg.[1] While the revolt is often thought to be utterly negative, Van Doren ends his book with this thought: "If American fiction cannot long escape the village, at least here is a village of a sort hardly thinkable before the revolt began. No matter what a flood of angry truth *Spoon River Anthology* let in, beauty survives. Many waters cannot quench beauty. What truth extinguishes is the weaker flames."[2] Van Doren's closing suggests that the revolt from the village may be, in the end, more about clarifying something about the village that was there but unseen—that the "flood of angry truth" doesn't make us think of the village as an ugly place, but asks us to see it more clearly. In this reading, those critiques—those feelings of loss and emptiness—become more plainly about seeing the full scope of the Midwest rather than the "sentimental affection" Van Doren found in the fifty years prior.[3]

Using questions of absence and loss to explore what we know about the Midwest continues from the literature of the 1920s throughout the twentieth century up to the present day. For instance, Gwendolyn Brooks's "We Real Cool" (1959) accepts early death as a precondition of African American life. Toni Morrison's *Sula* (1973) tells the story of a town that, from the very first page of the novel, we know only used to be there. In "The Stone Kitchen" (1996), Wendell Mayo describes a Chicago boy's attempt to learn about his mother's life growing up in Corpus Christi, Texas, but she refuses to tell him, instead making up fantastical stories about life in Guatemala, Italy, China, and Vermont. Celeste Ng's *Everything I Never Told You* (2014) is an extended meditation on the felt presence of a young Ohio woman who committed suicide. And in Alexander Weinstein's short story "Ice Age" (2016), glaciers have overtaken much of North America, and a small community of people find themselves living in igloos and hunting elk on the ice above now-empty Michigan. This sustained interest in loss also becomes visible in accounts of the rural "brain drain" as well as the methamphetamine and opioid epidemics.[4] In all of these stories—both fiction and nonfiction—there is tension between what's visible and what's not, and we use that to reconsider what we know of the region and what we know of ourselves. By investigating a range of midwestern places—different pieces of the heartland, as it were—this volume contributes to a conversation about regional identity by articulating the different ways those spaces have been constructed, used, and changed.

Because *Pieces of the Heartland* is an interdisciplinary collection, it addresses the concept of place in the Midwest from multiple perspectives. Similarly, Wright Morris's *The Inhabitants* (1946), a combination of photographs and written text about life in the Great Plains, uses its multimedia structure to both deepen and defamiliarize its subject.[5] *The Inhabitants* begins with the premise that you learn something about the people who inhabit—or inhabited—a place by looking at how the structures have developed. Morris contends that such "Inhabitants" never leave. On the first page of the book, he writes, "In all my life I've never been in anything so crowded, so full of something, as the rooms of a vacant house."[6] Rather than a standard story of people interacting with each other in a place, the book traces the theme of inhabitation through a multi-part structure that amplifies questions of vacancy and visibility. *The Inhabitants* opens with an epigraph from Henry David Thoreau. On each succeeding spread, the book continues in three parts. On the left-hand side, at the top, there is a running response to Thoreau. This is in bold type. In regular type in the center of the verso, below the response to Thoreau, there is a caption that accompanies the photo found on the recto. The photographs, set in rural spaces and small towns, have no border and continue to the very edge of the page. Although the written text retains a level of continuity based on its unfolding response to Thoreau, the captions, which read like short anecdotes or snippets of conversation, bear no apparent relation to each other and only implied relation to the photos. As a result, the book as a whole (and each spread individually) reads like a fragmented, multimedia prose poem.

Andy Oler   xi

The photographs are mostly of buildings, though some have an entire building and its landscape, while others zoom closer to focus on geometric shapes. Perhaps the most famous image from *The Inhabitants* is the Gano grain elevator from the plains of western Kansas.[7] Built during a time of intense competition for wheat storage, the elevator's bright white sides would have been visible for miles on the plains.[8] It towers over everything else in the frame, dwarfing the train, two-story building, and telephone poles located just behind the elevator. It would be easy to overlook the barbed wire fence and scrubby grass in the foreground, even though those fill a quarter of the photo's composition. Another representative photo, found on the preceding spread, is of a single-story house with boarded-up windows. The house fills the image from left to right, its edges cropped just out of the frame. While the house's wood siding appears to be whitewashed and in good shape, though perhaps worn, there is no evidence of occupation. This photo also shares unkempt grass in the foreground. The boards themselves are in poor shape and do not cover the entire windows, suggesting that this was either a hasty job or one done with scarce materials, which is unsurprising given that Morris took these photos on the plains in 1940. A third photo zooms even closer to its main subject. Judging from the chimney, this is also likely to be a house, but that is hard to confirm because the photograph represents only part of the building. Instead of showing this structure as a dwelling place, this photograph highlights the lines and angles created by the bare wood siding and tin roof.

In terms of their content and tone, there are several clear similarities between these photos. For instance, many of them are bright or overexposed, highlighting the small details and textures of the siding, roofing, and vegetation. The photographs similarly reveal such textural details. They also all conceal the same thing: The only humans pictured in the entire book are illustrations on a Vitalis hair tonic advertisement. According to Morris scholar Joseph Wydeven, this absence was intentional: "Morris almost never photographed people, wanting to avoid at all costs the invasion of personal privacy."[9] Morris avoids representing people even when it is technically difficult to do so. In what appears to be a direct frontal shot of a glass door, Morris keeps his body out of the reflection. As a result, Morris develops a consistent underlying tension caused by the absence of people in personal spaces such as houses and barns, and even familiar local places such as a drugstore or grain elevator.

These photographs represent the scales of visibility in *The Inhabitants*. For example, the grain elevator shows a recognizable location and some contextual details, while the boarded-up house is clearly a dwelling place but the photo's framing omits much identifiable context. The photograph of siding and roofing, while probably also a house, has amplified Morris's abstract concerns partly by its close-up framing. Alan Trachtenberg argues that these photos add another dimension to Morris's prose: "photography has given Morris a rich sense of the technical and symbolic possibilities of sight in fiction."[10] In this book, Morris does not attempt to represent a local place in its entirety or develop a nuanced understanding of specific histories. Instead, he generates meaning by creating tension between the different elements of *The Inhabitants*, juxtaposing photographs that are devoid of people with writing that focuses on human habitation: "Everywhere you look there is a man leaving something—or something that a man left. And everywhere you look you see that nobody left anything." Part of the project of *The Inhabitants* is to ask what remains visible even in places that appear to be empty. Tight framing limits the context of these photographs and creates a more abstract image. Morris's formal choices thus emphasize that these are types of spaces more than places with clear local or communal histories.[11]

Other photographs in *The Inhabitants* generally fit along this spectrum from recognizable local places to abstracted personal spaces, and each photo corresponds with national narratives of rural and regional identity. An image from late in the book, of a mailbox and country road (see Figure 1), slots easily into both sides of this spectrum. On the one hand, the photo includes a rural mailbox, a newspaper box, and a road that proceeds from the left side of the frame to the horizon line. Each of these suggests a specific location, especially the mailbox. Given that Morris suppresses context throughout *The Inhabitants*, it is no surprise that there is not a visible number on this mailbox, which makes it more or less a symbol of rural free delivery.[12] In this sense, mail and newspaper delivery become part of a narrative of rural places being connected to the modern world through information and commercial networks. Similarly, the road links this space to worlds beyond, and the electric lines show evidence of

Figure 1. Mailboxes, Western Nebraska ca. 1946/47. Photograph by Wright Morris. Collection Center for Creative Photography. ©2003 Center for Creative Photography, Arizona Board of Regents.

a material connection to national and regional power grids.[13] The horizon, too, could come from almost anywhere in the Midwest or Great Plains, as could the treads from trucks, tractors, and wagons that indicate an active agricultural economy. These details suggest the photo will reiterate the region's pastoral image, which James Shortridge claims was in place since before the term "Middle West" was invented in the late nineteenth century.[14] The tire treads, however, might offer an image of rural life more along the lines of William Barillas's argument that midwestern pastoralism is a dynamic combination of romanticism and utilitarianism.[15]

While these details correlate with the imagery of midwestern pastoralism, other aspects of the photograph indicate that Morris resists this version of the plains. There is very little romanticism in this photo, beginning with the sparse vegetation. In the stereotypical image of a rural landscape, lines of crops stretch to the horizon. In this photo, however, the only vegetation is some scrubby grasses and a lone tree, for which only the bark is visible. This is not breadbasket nostalgia. There is no picturesque barn and silo in the distance, no wagons of grain headed to market, and no heroic farmers tending the fields. Instead, on the facing page, Morris leaves this comment: "There never was a people who tried so hard—and left so little behind as we do. There never was a people who traveled so light—and carried so much." As part of Morris's response to Thoreau, these lines develop the tension between emptiness and inhabitation. When paired with the photograph, they underscore the many ways this image provides evidence of human influence—the road, the power lines, the mailbox—but removes the people themselves. The photos in *The Inhabitants*, then, call attention to their absences. But while men and women are both missing, the exclusive focus on exterior scenes suggests that this is a masculinist Midwest.[16] And while the photos lack both white and non-white people, they further marginalize only one of those groups.[17]

It's essential to note these omissions and the tensions they create because otherwise the image seems very open. Except for the five parallel vertical lines created by the power lines, tree, and the mailbox and newspaper posts, the horizon line is unbroken across the photograph, clear and straight from the left side of the image to the right—the landscape seems to guarantee uninterrupted farming. The landscape's promise of visibility, openness, and productivity is central to the way this book thinks about the Midwest. According to geographer Tim Cresswell, the concept of landscape "combined a focus on the material topography of a portion of land (that which can be seen) with the notion of vision (the way it is seen). Landscape is an intensely visual idea. In most definitions of landscape the viewer is outside of it. This is the primary way in which it differs from place. Places are very much things to be inside of."[18] Using Cresswell's terms highlights the way that this photograph promises openness and then breaks that promise. The image feels open because of the flat horizon in the distance. But the photograph is shot from a low angle, so there appears to be a slight rise of the land before the horizon, reducing visibility. That limit to the image's openness is therefore alienating, not least because Morris initially seems to offer a wide-open, pastoral image of the plains.

In *The Production of Space*, Henri Lefebvre argues that this sort of tension is an inherent part of looking at a landscape. According to Lefebvre, this apparent contradiction allows the viewer to claim a personal connection to the landscape before them: "The power of a landscape does not derive from the fact that it offers itself as a spectacle, but rather from the fact that, as mirror and mirage, it presents any susceptible viewer with an image at once true and false of a creative capacity which the subject (or Ego) is able, during a moment of marvelous self-deception, to claim as his own."[19] There are two related oppositions in this quotation: mirror and mirage, true and false. For Lefebvre, considering the landscape as a mirror shows how it reflects something back to the viewer, suggesting that any meaning derived from the landscape actually comes from the viewer. Then, if the landscape is a mirage, it appears to have qualities that it does not actually have; it is an illusion but also a natural phenomenon. In this relationship—personal reflection and naturally occurring illusion—Lefebvre finds the landscape's "creative capacity." The landscape seems to have an inherent meaning, though filtered through a mirage and claimed by viewers who see something of themselves in it. This act of claiming reveals how the landscape's meaning is both true and false at that moment. While the mirage offers part of the meaning, the mirror confirms how that meaning is only partially revealed, depending on the predilections of the individual viewer.

For Lefebvre, while the individual viewer only partially determines the landscape's meaning, the viewer is essential in the process, not least because the landscape is a spectacle. In that respect, it's worth noting that there's very little in Figure 1 that is *spectacular*. Even the sky, often featured in images of the plains, is uninteresting, smaller than it might be, the clouds indistinct. The terrain is flat, the horizon straight across the middle of the frame, and the photo promises openness but declines to make much actually visible. As viewers, we are given, in Lefebvre's words, "the impression of transparency,"[20] but it is a false impression. Or, rather, an impression that is at once true and false. While this photograph does not deliver on its promises, it shows something else: the interesting parts of this photo lie in its extended middleground—in the textures of the grass, the bark, and the tire tracks—those things that might usually be overlooked or plowed under. This book suggests that *textural* is a way to think about the Midwest and midwestern homeplaces. It may not be as open as it originally appears, but it does provide a multitude of details, textures, clues, each of which must be interpreted or, in Lefebvre's words, claimed. Removing people from these homes and landscapes thus facilitates the act of storytelling—it allows us to take what exists and to make meaning from it, both out of its actual, material existence and out of our experience of it.

The essays in this collection begin to do this very thing. They take the histories and the stories of particular places and make meaning from them, both for those places and people and—in the accumulated texture of a field of study—for the region as a whole. *Pieces of the Heartland* is organized roughly according to each essay's scale of visibility. The collection opens with the chapter that most carefully examines the history of a specific place, Nora Pat Small's case study of efforts to commemorate "radical religious and secular socialist" histories of New Harmony, Indiana. The second essay explores attachments to a different kind of place, as Camden Burd demonstrates how northern Michigan conservationists used Henry Wadsworth Longfellow's *The Song of Hiawatha* to connect to their landscape and, therefore, to guide preservation efforts. The poet James Hearst also linked literature and the land, but Jim O'Loughlin and Jordan Lea Ludwig argue that he was somewhat less celebratory of the Midwest, finding that Hearst both embraced his background as a Midwesterner and resisted the concept of regionalism.

A second set of essays articulates the relationship between the Midwest and the nation—or, more precisely, the relationship between stories told about them. Owen Cantrell examines another way an aspect of the Midwest is both universalized and idealized, finding a dangerous strain of nostalgia in representations of the small town. Wayne Anderson then analyzes a related kind of myth-making, arguing that several films set in Iowa in the 1930s self-consciously create a pastoral image of the Midwest in order to conceal hard times behind the camera. Jon Josten similarly contextualizes his essay within a period of national struggle, showing how two contemporary Richard Powers novels use their midwestern setting to demonstrate a fragmented national identity. The following essay shows how another midwestern space—in this case, Gary, Indiana—was used to articulate problems within national political structures. Seretha D. Williams, Michelle Story-Stewart, and Patrick C. Riley recount the history of Richard Hatcher—Gary, Indiana's first black mayor—showing how he struggled to improve life in the city but still helped create the conditions for Gary to host the first National Black Political Convention in 1972.

While the next four essays continue to explore the relationship between regional and national myth-making, they specifically turn to questions of gender. The first of these deals with another Midwesterner who influenced national politics, as Kimberly Wilmot Voss describes Wisconsinite Kay Clarenbach's contributions to founding the National Organization for Women and considers some of the reasons Midwesterners are often omitted from women's political history. Yi-chin Shih studies a similar phenomenon in Susan Glaspell's play *Inheritors*, arguing that Glaspell's construction of women's contributions offers a feminist critique of the very concept of nation. Much like *Inheritors* portrays a family's pursuit of the American Dream, Gene Stratton-Porter's novel *A Girl of the Limberlost* tells the story of a woman who works her way up in the world. While Stratton-Porter was celebrated for her representations of and relationship to the Limberlost swamp, Bob Mellin complicates its image as an ecofeminist haven. Similarly, Sally Parry shows how the wilderness does not bestow the primitive masculinity that Sinclair Lewis's midwestern characters hope it will, though it does offer a perspective that they did not have before.

Notably, Lewis's characters leave the Midwest to gain that perspective, and the final two essays further extend the scope of this collection by taking a transnational turn. First, Kelly Hanson examines *Ouanga*, an opera about the Haitian Revolution written by two African American professors, and its inaugural performance, which took place in South Bend, Indiana. According to Hanson, *Ouanga* is an instance of bringing global black modernism to the Midwest, asking midwestern audiences to relate to outside stories and thereby reinforcing links to broader cultural and historical networks. The closing essay of this collection reverses that flow. Kerry Alcorn studies how Canadian officials integrated midwestern educational ideals into the primary and higher education system of the Saskatchewan province. By challenging the customary east-to-west direction of U.S. and Canadian cultural history, Alcorn extends the boundaries of the Midwest and suggests some ways that writing about midwestern places is dependent on perspective and scope. Whether these essays study life in a specific town, the stories told about an entire state, or events linking the Midwest to other places, they show how accounting for the seemingly insignificant details within pieces of the heartland can provide a fuller, more textured view of regional culture.

Notes

1. Carl Van Doren, *Contemporary American Novelists, 1900–1920* (New York: MacMillan, 1923), 150, 62.
2. Ibid., 176.
3. Ibid., 146.
4. See Nick Reding, *Methland: The Death and Life of an American Small Town* (New York: Bloomsbury, 2009); William Campbell Garriott, *Policing Methamphetamine: Narcopolitics in Rural America* (New York: New York University Press, 2011); Robert Wuthnow, *Remaking the Heartland: Middle America since the 1950s* (Princeton, NJ: Princeton University Press, 2011).
5. *The Inhabitants* is Morris's first book-length photo-text, though an earlier version was published in *New Directions* in 1940. It includes several of the same photographs as the book-length version, though it is in a smaller format and some of the images are reversed. The accompanying anecdotes are often similar, but they are headed by names rather than the book-length version's response to Thoreau. See Wright Morris, "The Inhabitants," in *New Directions in Prose & Poetry*, ed. James Laughlin (Norfolk, CT: New Directions, 1940).
6. *The Inhabitants* (New York: C. Scribner's Sons, 1946). *The Inhabitants* has no page numbers, perhaps to "avoid any indication of strict sequence," as suggested by David Madden, *Wright Morris* (New York: Twayne, 1964), 49.
7. The Gano Grain Company (and its predecessor, the Rock Milling and Elevator Company) owned several country grain elevators in the early to mid-twentieth century; see Gail E. Balman, "George E. Gano: Kansas Grainman" (MA thesis, Wichita State University, 1965).
8. Robert W. Schoeff calls such elevators "Cathedrals of the Plains" in "The Grain Elevator," in *The Rise of the Wheat State: A History of Kansas Agriculture, 1861–1986*, ed. George E. Ham and Robin D. S. Higham (Manhattan, KS: Sunflower University Press, 1987), 123. Ham and Higham's collection also includes several essays on the history of wheat prices, competition for farmers' grain, and methods of transportation. For links to markets outside the plains, see William Cronon, *Nature's Metropolis: Chicago and the Great West* (New York: W. W. Norton, 1991). For the history and construction style of grain elevators, see Barbara Krupp Selyem and Bruce Selyem, "The Legacy of Country Grain Elevators: A Photo Essay," *Kansas History* 23, no. 1 (2000).
9. Joseph J. Wydeven, *Wright Morris Revisited* (New York: Simon & Schuster Macmillan-Twayne, 1998), 59.
10. Alan Trachtenberg, "The Craft of Vision," *Critique* 4, no. 3 (1961): 42.

11. The way that Morris uses abstraction to make national claims about inhabitation puts him somewhat at odds with other midwestern landscape artists. According to Tom Lutz, rather than elaborating specific place-based concepts or identities, landscape painters often focused on geometry: "In their responses to questions about politics and representation, the artists repeatedly returned to formal, artistic considerations." Tom Lutz, *Cosmopolitan Vistas: American Regionalism and Literary Value* (Ithaca: Cornell University Press, 2004), 9.
12. Rural Free Delivery was established across the country in the first five years of the twentieth century; it is credited with decreasing the isolation of farmers and other rural people. See Wayne Edison Fuller, *RFD: The Changing Face of Rural America* (Bloomington: Indiana University Press, 1964); Winifred Gallagher, *How the Post Office Created America: A History* (New York: Penguin, 2016).
13. For the history of rural electrification, see D. Clayton Brown, *Electricity for Rural America: The Fight for the REA* (Westport, CT: Greenwood, 1980); Ronald R. Kline, *Consumers in the Country: Technology and Social Change in Rural America* (Baltimore: Johns Hopkins University Press, 2000); Katherine Jellison, *Entitled to Power: Farm Women and Technology, 1913–1963* (Chapel Hill: University of North Carolina Press, 1993).
14. James R. Shortridge, *The Middle West: Its Meaning in American Culture* (Lawrence: University Press of Kansas, 1989).
15. William David Barillas, *The Midwestern Pastoral: Place and Landscape in Literature of the American Heartland* (Athens, OH: Ohio University Press, 2006).
16. For the history of farm women in the Midwest and Great Plains, see Katherine Jellison, *Entitled to Power: Farm Women and Technology, 1913–1963* (Chapel Hill: University of North Carolina Press, 1993); Janet Galligani Casey, *A New Heartland: Women, Modernity, and the Agrarian Ideal in America* (New York: Oxford University Press, 2009); Marilyn Irvin Holt, *Linoleum, Better Babies, and the Modern Farm Woman, 1890–1930* (Albuquerque: University of New Mexico Press, 1995).
17. The story of the Midwest and Great Plains frequently removes people of color or diminishes their contributions to the region. A great body of scholarship seeks to correct this, including Himanee Gupta-Carlson, *Muncie, India(na): Middletown and Asian America* (Urbana: University of Illinois Press, 2018); Sujey Vega, *Latino Heartland: Of Borders and Belonging in the Midwest* (New York: New York University Press, 2015); Gregory D. Smithers, *Native Diasporas: Indigenous Identities and Settler Colonialism in the Americas* (Lincoln, NE: University of Nebraska Press, 2014); Bruce A. Glasrud and Charles A. Braithwaite, *African Americans on the Great Plains* (Lincoln, NE: University of Nebraska Press, 2009); Linda Allegro and Andrew Grant Wood, eds., *Latin American Migrations to the U.S. Heartland: Changing Social Landscapes in Middle America* (Urbana, IL: University

of Illinois Press, 2013); Arnoldo De León, *Racial Frontiers: Africans, Chinese, and Mexicans in Western America, 1848–1890* (Albuquerque, NM: University of New Mexico Press, 2002); Theresa Delgadillo, "Exiles, Migrants, Settlers, and Natives: Literary Representations of Chicano/as and Mexicans in the Midwest," *Midwestern Miscellany* 30, no. 1 (2002); Michael K. Johnson, *Black Masculinity and the Frontier Myth in American Literature* (Norman, OK: University of Oklahoma Press, 2002); Arif Dirlik and Malcolm Yeung, *Chinese on the American Frontier* (Lanham, MD: Rowman & Littlefield, 2001); and Donald Lee Parman, *Indians and the American West in the Twentieth Century* (Bloomington: Indiana University Press, 1994).

18. Tim Cresswell, *Place: A Short Introduction* (Malden, MA: Blackwell, 2004), 10.
19. Henri Lefebvre, *The Production of Space*, trans. Donald Nicholson-Smith (Cambridge: Blackwell, 1991), 189.
20. Ibid.

Nora Pat Small

Preserving a Midwestern Moment

A Case Study of New Harmony, Indiana

New Harmony, Indiana, owes its existence to its founding in 1814 as a communitarian religious community, and its reputation to its very brief life as a secular socialist utopian town between 1825 and 1828. In its 200 years, New Harmony has been, in addition to the site of those two transient communal utopias, a farm town, oil boomtown, cultural mecca, state memorial, and state historic site. Parts of all of these identities remain, some consciously preserved or restored, others surviving through continued use or benign neglect. A turning point in the history of historic preservation in New Harmony occurred in 1936, at a gathering of local and state leaders to discuss the memorializing of New Harmony's particular and peculiar history. It occurred just as the field of historic preservation was professionalizing, and just as "public intellectuals sought to rediscover America" through the study and promotion of regionalism.[1] That moment, its immediate aftermath, and its historic context will be examined here, to come to a better understanding both of the stories that Midwesterners told about themselves and of the cultural landscapes they preserved in order to tell those stories.

Aside from studies of Henry Ford's Greenfield Village, little scholarship exists about the preservation movement as a whole in the Midwest, which is surprising for a region that loomed so large in the national consciousness in the early twentieth century.[2] The field of historic preservation was professionalizing just as the Mississippi Valley Historical Association was coming into its own. As in the MVHA, amateurs and trained professionals worked together in the first half of the twentieth century and contributed to their respective fields; and as was the case at the MVHA, tensions developed between the groups.[3] In New Harmony we glimpse this moment when the romantic aspirations of experienced amateurs met the rational planning of the preservation professionals. Between 1936 and 1942, multiple players, all of them amateurs, attempted to translate New Harmony's sense of place and identity into a publicly accessible memorial, more a place reborn than a place preserved.

The New Harmony Memorial Commission officially came into being in March 1939, created by an act of the Indiana legislature. Unofficially, a proto-commission, composed of local and state leaders, had been operating since December 1936. For decades prior to that moment, New Harmony and its adherents had been reshaping and memorializing the place and its legacy. But the New Harmony Memorial Commission's efforts to create a state memorial marked the first time in New Harmony's 122-year history that a group of people had attempted to enshrine elements of the town's past in a way that would remove those elements from the haphazard care of private ownership and reweave them, in their new capacity as publicly owned and maintained shrines or memorials, into the fabric of the town's daily life. The values and physical remnants they sought to honor in New Harmony's past had long been recognized locally and regionally as the town's legacy. But their proposal to revive that legacy as a model for the present to build a future was an altogether different idea.

The communitarian millenialists (German Pietists, also known as Rappites after their leader Father George Rapp) who established New Harmony on the Indiana frontier in 1814 departed en masse in 1824, leaving behind a remarkable infrastructure of over 100 single-family homes (one- and two-story, brick and frame), four community houses, a massive church, schools, a granary, distilleries, breweries, artisan shops of every sort—including shoemaker, saddler, blacksmith, watchmaker, cooper, tanner—ice houses, greenhouses, soap factory, lime and brick kilns, pottery ovens, and more.[4] The Community of Equality proposed for the site by Robert Owen, who purchased the entire town in 1825, built little and failed by 1828 but left a legacy of scientific inquiry, educational reform, and cultural pursuits that remains to this day sustained, in part, by the persistence of Owenite community member descendants into the twenty-first century.

These pasts—the radical religious and secular socialist—were combined and commemorated in various ways in the last decades of the long nineteenth century. In 1881, for example, John Holliday, an Indianapolis newspaperman, revised an essay he wrote in 1869 for presentation to the Indianapolis Literary Club. After observing that the "tastes of the grandsons of Robert Owen seem to run to business rather than to natural or social sciences," he described the remnants of the original Harmonist experiment, noting that many of the frame and brick buildings of the pioneers still stood but had been altered and *improved* beyond recognition. He characterized the village as a still potent democracy, where "[t]here is no aristocracy, no higher and lower class. The people move on the same plane, the individual is judged more by his merits than most places. There is much general intelligence, much love of books and amusements," and attributed this condition to the character of the founders.[5] He did not contemplate preservation; the town seemed to be already a place out of time, changing little over the decades. In a fashion familiar to boosters of small midwestern towns he noted, "The village is slowgoing and conservative in comparison with most of our towns. Comparatively isolated as it has always been by not being on any direct line of travel, it has retained many old-fashioned notions and customs, and there is a freedom and restfulness about its existence that is fascinating when contrasted with the hurry and hustle of city life."[6] What some might call stagnation, in this narrative, became the quiet confidence of a place that believed it had long ago put the principles of democracy into action and continued to adhere to them.

As the first generation of Owenites and so-called Afterglow residents died off at the end of the nineteenth century, New Harmonists engaged in self-conscious remembering and memorializing. In 1890 Dr. J. Schnack offered, in a paper read at the county seat's scientific society and then published as a pamphlet, a brief New Harmony history interspersed with personal reminiscences of growing up in a landscape still littered with remnants of the Harmonist experiment. He did not bemoan the loss of some of those structures. Instead, in the appendix to his pamphlet he noted that the causes for New Harmony's present success could be found in the groundwork laid by those esteemed ancestors, in the "maintenance of an excellent public library ever since Mr. W. Maclure's [Robert Owen's co-founder of the Community of Equality] first donation," and in "the excellence of the schools, especially during the past twenty years." He concluded with praise for the local citizens and the surrounding farmland, as well as an enumeration of the businesses the town supported.[7]

E.S.L. Thompson of Muncie, Indiana, memorialized New Harmony in 1894 by celebrating the town's intellectual and artistic "storied past" in a poem dedicated to the memory of Robert Owen, his sons Robert Dale Owen, David Dale Owen, and Richard Owen, and their collaborators, published in the *New Harmony Times*. He concluded his paean thus:

> Learning for thee hath service done,
> And set thee where the Princes be,
> (Who hew the Corner Stone of thought,)
> Who weave the mighty tracery
> And spin the gold of Good To-Be
> New Harmony! New Harmony![8]

This celebration of New Harmony as an economically stable center of learning and democracy, devoid of the ills of modern industrial life, continued into the twentieth century. In 1902 historian George B. Lockwood commented, "The vandal hand of business enterprise has not been heavily laid upon this place." He emphasized instead the town's quiet streets shaded by "a veritable forest of maple and gate trees" and noted the presence of a public library before moving on to the history and influence of this small midwestern town.[9] (See Figure 1.)

History, religion, and progressivism all played important roles in the town's week-long centennial celebration in June 1914. Per usual, the town's residents celebrated the intangible heritage of the two sets of founders and their successors rather than the architectural remnants. Father Rapp and his followers and Robert Owen and his experiment each had their own days, separated by "Devotional Day," which one can imagine might have been less disturbing to Rapp, even though the sermon was delivered by a Methodist, than to Owen, who had scandalized people with his insistence that his new social system had no room for religion of any sort, declaring religion to be one of the three "most monstrous evils that could be, combined to inflict mental and physical evil upon [Man's] whole race."[10] In a further jolt to Owen's spirit, former president William Howard Taft, in his keynote address on

Figure 1. Rappite Community House 4, rear facade. Photo pre-1914, copied by Lester Jones, photographer, May 1940, HABS IND 65-NEHAR 5-1.

Owen Day, observed that of course such socialist experiments must fail, because private property was what motivated people. Nevertheless, the centennial provided occasion to celebrate progressivism in the form of speeches from housing reformer Albion Fellows Bacon and from "Fola" La Follette, daughter of U.S. Senator Robert La Follette and an activist in the women's suffrage movement in her own right. In addition, speakers lauded the work of various Owenites who were instrumental in bringing public education to Indiana, and on Fraternal Day waxed eloquent on the important role clubs and associations played in American society, a point of pride in New Harmony, which claimed the distinction of being the site of the first women's club in Indiana, the Old Fauntleroy Home.[11]

Although proud of the historic and modern structures that embodied their notions of New Harmony's celebrated past, residents had rarely, with the exception of one determined woman, consciously preserved the town's physical remnants. In 1890, for instance, Rappite Community House No. 2 was being used as a storeroom, dwelling, printing office, and agricultural hall. Community House No. 3 served as a hotel, and No. 4 was used as a public hall, ballroom, and sometimes theater. Dr. Schnack recalled at the time that the south wing of the massive Rappite church, formerly used as a theater, was being used as a slaughter-house in his childhood:

> In this part the walls were beautifully frescoed and painted. The work was done by Mr. C. A. Lesueur; it was a series of Swiss scenes, prepared for the play of William Tell. In my boyhood days this part was used as a pork-packing house. Within these sacred and ornamented walls thousands of hogs were quartered and salted down ... During the slaughtering season this room, with its painted walls, presented a weird scene; one that I surely shall never forget.[12]

The remnants of that church were taken down in 1874, and the bricks used to construct a wall around the Harmonist cemetery.[13] By 1936, when the proto-memorial commission met, Community House No. 3 still served as a hotel, renamed The Old Tavern; and No. 4 had become a garage in 1913, remaining so into the 1960s (Figure 2).

The only conscious and self-proclaimed attempts at preservation occurred at the Old Fauntleroy Home and Community House No. 2. Miss Mary Emily Fauntleroy purchased the former in 1911 and the latter in 1929. Ross Lockridge noted that "the story of her efforts in reviving the historic prestige of the Old Fauntleroy Home is an epic of a woman's fortitude" and informed his readers that Community House No. 2 also had been restored under her direction for use by the Tri Kappas, Daughters of the American Revolution, and Woman's Library Club, as well as for a tea room and Rappite museum (Figure 3).[14]

Among the five men and five women who sat down to a dinner at New Harmony's Old Tavern on December 17, 1936, to plan the work of a proposed New Harmony Memorial Commission were an assortment of statewide and local leaders, including the president of the New Harmony Commercial Club, an Indianapolis high school history teacher from New Harmony, the Indiana director of the Federal Writers' Project, the president of the Indiana Federation of Clubs, and the president of the Indiana State Federation of Labor. The stated objective of the group was to memorialize the utopian, millennialist Harmonists who occupied the site from 1814 to 1824, the utopian Owenites who took possession

Figure 2. Rappite Community House 4 with its 1850s Opera House façade and 1913 alterations to accommodate its use as a garage. 1940. Lester Jones, photographer, HABS IND 65-NEHAR, 5-2.

Figure 3. Rappite Community House 2. The gabled roof was altered in the last half of the nineteenth century. In addition, entrances were moved to the long street façade from the gable end and the porch added. 1934. Homer Fauntleroy, photographer, HABS IND 65-NEHAR, 2-2.

in 1825 and failed by 1828, and the Afterglow (the period that followed the failure of the Owen experiment but saw the flowering of some of its scientific and educational goals). Memorializing these particular elements of New Harmony's past would create a specific identity for the town, an identity that they intended to reinforce by reviving what they called "the idealistic principles and spiritual conceptions that distinguish these three periods."[15] To do that, they would purchase and preserve several key properties that remained standing from that period, reconstruct significant elements that had been lost, and present public programming. They hoped by doing so to realize their goal of creating "a world shrine to pure idealism."[16]

Here, then, was a key moment in the history of historic preservation in New Harmony. The mostly ad hoc preservation of the town's historic infrastructure was to be formalized, its perceived values not only permanently enshrined but resurrected and enacted through participatory programming set in an inspiring landscape to serve, and perhaps save, a troubled world. They acted within the disciplinary context of a field of preservation that had been professionalizing in the United States since the 1910s, a global context of economic and political upheaval, and the much more localized context of individual personalities and experiences. Between 1939, when the proto-commission was recognized by the Indiana legislature as the official New Harmony Memorial Commission, and 1942, when the state required the Commission to cease operations for the duration of the war, the members of the Commission struggled to achieve their vision. That struggle arose, in part and somewhat surprisingly, from various members working to achieve those ends by drawing on their own strengths and experiences. With so many successful state and local leaders involved in the cause, they no doubt felt confident as a group in tackling a very large project. That confidence, as well as their perceptions of what had been accomplished in this small town by their predecessors, may have blinded them to the overly ambitious nature of their undertaking and to their own lack of consensus on a single vision and method for preserving New Harmony's history.

Appointed director of the Memorial Commission, Ross Lockridge, local historian and director of the Indiana Federal Writers Project, wasted no time in putting into action the proposed plans of the proto-commission. He evidently attempted to get information about how to go about professionally restoring a complex site, writing in early 1940 to V.M. Geddy at Colonial Williamsburg and to E.C. Liebold at the Edison Institute in Dearborn, Michigan, but received only terse replies. The lack of professional guidance did not seem to hinder the group. By the time Lockridge put together his circa January 1940 "Tentative Suggestions for adoption of Master Plan covering four years program of the New Harmony Memorial Commission," the group had already acquired the Old Fauntleroy Home and the Tavern, and an option on Community House No. 2, all of which dated to the Rappite era; they had completed reconstruction of the Rappite Labyrinth and made arrangements with the Recreation Department at Indiana University to promulgate "rhythmical dances and games in and before the Labyrinth in harmony with the mythological tradition of Ceranos or 'Crane Dance' fabricated by Theseus and his companions on the island of Delos"; and they had convinced the state to create June Barrett Park on the shores of the Wabash River, where "historic or pleasure crafts ... may be launched." In that Master Plan, Director Lockridge also highlighted several successful programs that had already taken place, including the Say-Sistaire Shell Hunt and the Thomas Say Entomological Day, named for Owen-era natural scientists Lucy Sistaire and Thomas Say. Befitting the restoration of a utopia, he concluded that all work undertaken by the Commission should result in "exalting imperishable ideals for the benefit of the living present and inspiring hope for the amelioration of mankind by illuminating a pathway of human progress toward universal peace and happiness."[17]

Such lofty goals were no longer in general favor among the growing class of professional preservationists but clearly reflect the romantic local historical tradition that Lockridge embraced and practiced. That romanticism was evident in his 1939 publication, *The Old Fauntleroy Home*. Celebrating the "world-famed example of the economic success of pure communal living" of the Rappites, and positing that their "sterling character lives in their well-built structures," such as the Fauntleroy Home, he still concluded that although the Owenites had failed where the Rappites succeeded, the religious commune had left no lasting influence, while "the intrepid principles of Robert Owen have gained strength from that day to this."[18] After reviewing the numerous recent changes and "improvements" made to the Fauntleroy Home—including a second-floor remodel, modern utilities, porches, and addition of a dining room, kitchen, and sun parlor—Lockridge concluded that "the Old Fauntleroy Home and all it symbolizes remain the same. For one who derives inspiration from reviewing the pageant of bygone days, this home is sacred ground ... Whoever is wearied in the strenuous combats of modern life may escape for a few hours to the precincts of this historic home, there to fill his mind with these pictures of unfading splendor and his soul with inspirations of the past."[19] Escape, rejuvenation, inspiration—these drove Lockridge's vision for the preservation of New Harmony. That the buildings had changed mattered little, if at all. Sustaining, restoring, or otherwise sharing or emulating the ideals of those who had built the place and who had envisioned a new society mattered a great deal. To that end, Lockridge drew on modern education practices, in the spirit of the education reformers who had gathered in New Harmony during the Owen era.[20]

Tasked with instituting "programs and projects of an educational, recreational, patriotic and cultural nature," the director of the Commission partnered with various education professionals to create and evaluate appropriate programming for elementary and high school students.[21] The state Superintendent of Public Instruction, Dr. Clement T. Malan, evidently an adherent of John Dewey's education philosophy, extolled what we might call the utilitarian quality of romanticism in a speech given in New Harmony in 1941. Malan noted,

> It may well be believed that these young disciples [students participating in the Shell Hunt and Entomological Field Days] will never forget either the human or historic associations connected with such educational programs. They are thus brought into contact with history and science through their feet, through their hands, through their eyes, and indeed, through their hearts ... There is a proper relation between romance and education.[22]

Malan further noted that the Department of Education at Indiana State Teachers College at Terre Haute was developing "an approved system of guidance ... whereby the best educational methods may be brought to bear upon the instruction given through such [student] pilgrimage and a scientific test is being worked out by which the benefits derived may be accurately evaluated." In a clear statement of support for Dewey's democratic progressivism, Malan concluded,

> I think it peculiarly timely now, in the midst of world wide depression and dissention that public educational agencies should devote attention to these idealistic conceptions of ameliorating the conditions under which we live by every intellectual means. Robert Owen sought to inaugurate in New Harmony a new empire of peace and good will to men. Surely we shall do everything we can to memorialize that inspired motive.[23]

Thus did Lockridge achieve his memorial to the scientific reformers of the Community of Equality.

Mrs. Bertha Crosley Ball, "public-spirited supporter of great memorial movements throughout the United States," State Vice-Regent of the Colonial Dames, Vice President of the Ball Brothers Foundation of Muncie, and philanthropist, along with Mrs. Frederick Balz, President of the Indiana Federation of Clubs,[24] pursued the Commission's objectives in a fashion well-established among women of the middle and upper classes. In February 1939, a month before legislative approval to create the Memorial Commission, the *New Harmony Times* reported,

> The New Harmony Memorial movement received much impetus last week when the wives of the members of the General Assembly were guests of Mrs. Edmond Crosley Ball and Mrs. Frederick G. Balz at a luncheon given at the Claypool [Hotel in Indianapolis]. Mrs. Ball spoke of what women had done to preserve historic shrines throughout the country and said, "Indiana has much of beauty, but little of history and tradition. We need the latter, and such shrines are the means of bringing people of culture to the state."

To this group of women, Mrs. Balz made the particular argument that "New Harmony is the seat of the oldest women's club, the first infant school, kindergarten, trade school and other educational features, and also the place where were heard the first talks in favor of 'women's rights.'" She and Mrs. Ball concluded by urging support of the bill then pending before the state legislature "for an appropriation to preserve the place as a shrine."[25]

This method of employing influential women to achieve preservation ends had, of course, been inaugurated in the mid-nineteenth century by Ann Pamela Cunningham in her crusade to save Mt. Vernon. Taking a page from Cunningham's play book, the Tavern Committee of the Commission, composed of the missuses Ball and Balz, along with Indiana University President Herman B. Wells, followed up the successful legislative action by organizing "a very strong voluntary committee of leading women from all parts of the state," who as of November 1940 were "enthusiastically working with [the committee] on the general project of furnishing the Tavern, room by room, with rare and selective antique furnishings, without expense to the state." (See Figure 4.) Unfortunately, the bids for restoring the Old Tavern were twice what they had anticipated. Turning to the State Budget Committee, the Tavern Committee argued for additional appropriations in the next two fiscal years to be used for the "restoration" of the Tavern, noting, "We take pride in the conviction that we have both the duty and opportunity of making our old Tavern a great American exhibit of a typical hostelry of the first quarter of the 19th century."[26] No doubt the statement represented the thinking and experience of the women on the committee, but Dr. Wells appended a statement to the memo that reflects a different understanding of the term. Noting that "restoration" was a misnomer, Wells argued that the building could be turned into a museum for a fraction of what they were requesting. While some of the money would be used for restoration, most would actually be used for

> installing plumbing and kitchen facilities and making other alterations necessary to render the Tavern usable as a modern hotel. If the Tavern is made into a hotel, it should yield considerable income; whereas, if it is restored simply as a museum, it will not only fail to yield income but will have to be maintained by an appropriation.[27]

Figure 4. Rappite Community House 3, "The Old Tavern," with late nineteenth-century roofline, porch, and window alterations. Historic Photo. 1958 copy by J. Waring Donne, photographer, HABS IND 65-NEHAR, 10-1.

Dr. Wells was not alone in believing that the town's history could and should be capitalized. Segments of the business community certainly saw rich historical associations as New Harmony and the surrounding Posey County experienced an oil boom in the fall of 1938. The Evansville *Courier* commented that New Harmony "fairly bubbles with comment about the New Harmony Memorial project, designed to give the little village on the banks of the Wabash historical permanency in the world's eye and mind." They opined that because the town's old properties "once housed the nation's first hunters of mineral wealth" and because Dr. David Dale Owen, the chief geologist of Indiana in the mid-nineteenth century, had written about mineral riches contributing to "the civilization and well being of man," it would be appropriate that the "Hoosier romance of oil recovery mark History Row on New Harmony's Church street, and set up its modern towers alongside the still standing pioneer laboratory of Dr. Owen ... with oil derricks heralding the message of riches which [geologists'] studies strove to give one hundred years ago."[28]

Eschewing the romantic language of Lockridge and the historical aesthetic of the Tavern committee women, the author of the regular "Commercial Club Notes" in the *New Harmony Times* noted at the end of 1938,

> New Harmony has a chance to become both famous and prosperous during 1939. Should the state decide to take over our old buildings it will mean much to the future of the town. It will mean that these buildings will all be put back in their original shape even to the Labyrinth. This will attract thousands here each year when the plan is completed. Then comes the oil boom and when better weather comes in the Spring we predict that it will be a boom.[29]

The business community's support for the Memorial enterprise rested on the obvious economic advantages for the town. It was taken for granted that the historic resources could survive an onslaught of thousands of tourists and the pressures of an oil boom, and that all of those things could co-exist. The "universal peace and happiness" that Lockridge envisioned had no place in this pragmatic view of what it meant to preserve the town's past. The Commercial Club evidently saw the restored buildings as the key to capitalizing on New Harmony's illustrious past. People would come to see what the founders had built—those concrete manifestations of pioneer grit, determination, and success they themselves had inherited—not to be inculcated with the old-fashioned principles of the old New Harmonists.

The view from the perspective of New Harmony's business interests nicely encapsulates an ever-present conundrum of historic preservation—what is being preserved, and what does it mean to preserve it? While Lockridge, Balz, Ball, Wells, and the Commercial Club each believed that the physical remnants of New Harmony's early history mattered, they mattered for different reasons. The members of New Harmony's Memorial Commission saw the town's historic structures as inspirational settings for re-enactments and resuscitation of the quite site-specific brilliant scientific and cultural explorations and experiments of the Owen and Afterglow eras, and as a pilgrimage site where tourists might immerse themselves comfortably in the amorphous Indiana pioneer past. To members of the Commercial Club, those same buildings served more as a sort of stage set, a necessary but unanalyzed backdrop to the town's economic development, evidence of New Harmony as a cultured place with a prosperous future.

The 1942 "Preliminary General Plan for the Development of the New Harmony Memorial," prepared in anticipation of the cessation of the Memorial Commission's operations during the Second World War, indicates that the Indiana Department of Conservation intended to move the New Harmony Memorial forward on the basis of a rational, scientific planning process. While perhaps recognizing that the success of the venture ultimately depended on the public's fascination with, and nostalgia for, a rural golden era, the "party of technical planners" used none of the romantic language of Lockridge nor the aesthetic language of the Tavern Committee women to describe how to accomplish the development of New Harmony's memorial. Composed of the director of state parks, the state engineer, a landscape architect, and the supervising architect, this panel of experts concluded that the administration of the Memorial Commission to that point, not having been conducted on a rational basis, had been inefficient and wasteful. They noted that the "scope and complex nature [of the Memorial] makes a waste of effort and funds probable unless every step is planned to satisfy the requirements of the agencies having jurisdiction now or in the future ... [I]f good judgment and good taste can be combined with sound economy and judicious administration" New Harmony might become one of the state's "most interesting and valuable properties."[30]

The party of technical planners repeatedly justified their recommendations, whether for acquisition and restoration of certain buildings or purchase of land along the Wabash, as logical, practical, and efficient. Putting an emphasis on gardens and horticulture, they argued, would not only beautify the Memorial properties but also offer the opportunity for "some degree of self-support" through the sale of "flowers, plants, fruits, etc." In addition, such beautification would rival "the well known Virginia gardens and the cherry trees in Washington, D.C.," thus drawing on an already well-established tourist cohort. Industries carried on in the early days of New Harmony could be resurrected, not as models of industriousness or reminders of Indiana's pioneer past, but as activities that might pay their own way. Not wishing to profit unfairly from the tourists all of these attractions would bring to the town, they recommended that a small fee be charged to see the "exhibit or museum buildings," but "only enough to insure proper maintenance and operation."[31]

In this way, the proposed method for preserving New Harmony shifted, finally, into something more akin to contemporary best practices in preservation. The experts who inspected New Harmony on March 5 and 6, 1942, proposed to move the project forward, after the adoption of a preliminary plan and the acquisition of certain properties and real estate options, by means of a "complete Administrative Plan," a "complete Master Plan," and "complete Project Plans and Estimates."[32] Their plans revolved around the buildings and landscape. The remnants of the Rappite era clearly showed "their contributions to the historic significance of New Harmony." Harder to grapple with were the largely intangible contributions of Robert Owen and his associates, which these planners recognized as "more significant historically than those of the Rappites" but also more easily lost to time.[33] Unlike Lockridge, the members of the Memorial Commission, and many residents, the preservation experts either did not have or chose to ignore the tools of romanticism and the deep personal knowledge of the local that allowed the instigators of the Memorial to conjure the presence of those scientists, inventors, artists, and educators that had once congregated on the banks of the Wabash.

Although grounded in the best scientific evaluation of its efficacy in educating and instilling the values of democratic citizenship, even the educational programming instituted by Lockridge and the state Superintendent of Public Instruction received no mention by the professionals from the Indiana Department of Conservation. Whatever that programming was, it evidently was not preservation.

The preservation professionals could not see that New Harmony was preserved in stories.[34] What stories did these Midwesterners tell of themselves and this town on the Wabash River? Between the World Wars they told tales of the persistence of impossible dreams and visions, and wondered at the ordinariness of a place born out of such extraordinary expectations. They told tales of spiritual and scientific pursuits that celebrated the backwater place from which they had sprung. Over and over, New Harmony's bards wondered over how such a place had been forgotten.

"It was a failure which did not fail," wrote Caroline Dale Snedeker in 1931.[35] Having recounted New Harmony's multiple foundings, demises, and resurrections, she wondered how it was that David Dale Owen's New Geological Laboratory, designed and built by him in 1859, had been forgotten, when "houses so much less beautiful and less rich in history have been preserved for future generations." Embodied in Owen's laboratory was the legacy of the Owenite Afterglow, David Dale having contributed significantly and materially to the understanding of the Midwest in his roles as both a state and a U.S. geologist. The town in which this house stood, she noted, had been called the Cradle of Western American Science, and, "if Western science was ever so unscientific as to be rocked in a cradle, this was it."[36]

Eight years later, as part of his duties as director of the New Harmony Memorial Commission, historian Ross F. Lockridge, Sr., published a different sort of history of New Harmony, focused on one of the original Rappite dwellings occupied in later years by Owenites and their descendants.[37] He asked his son, Ross F. Lockridge, Jr., to compose a "Salutation" for the book's opening.[38] Lockridge's first stanza evoked the sense of remoteness—physical, historical, moral—that seemed to define New Harmony for many of its observers:

> This little book invites you to pursue
> A tale of eld. Yet do not here expect,
> As in the pompous tomes of history,
> To see the lurid lightnings of the sword,
> Or hear the nervous clamor of the drum.
> Far from the giant din of war and death
> These pages lead, and rather turn the mind
> To contemplation of a nobler strife,
> Whose heroes and whose heroines contended
> For higher guerdon than was ever won
> By sword or bayonet. Their weapons were
> The trenchant thought, invincible ideals,
> The mighty armament of hope and right,

> Justice and truth! The setting for their deeds
> Is laid in scenes of sylvan majesty
> Deep in the forests of America.[39]

The people who sought justice and truth in old New Harmony were not only the "scientists, artists, statesmen, educators," nor the Rappites who "raised the beams that built its walls," but the women who, during the Civil War, founded the first women's club in the United States and held their meetings in the Old Fauntleroy Home:

> And here, while guns of fratricidal war
> Made red the rivers of America,
> A group of sprightly maidens met and formed
> A little sisterhood of noble aims
> Expressly dedicate to truth and art,
> Freedom and poesy. Minerva was
> The name they gave to their society—
> Minerva, goddess excellently armed
> With wisdom and decision! We this book
> Inaugurate in verse after the style
> Of those ambitious girls, who dearly loved
> In grave iambics to invest their thoughts.[40]

In New Harmony and the Fauntleroy Home Lockridge *pere* professed to find the embodiment of nobility, ambition, truth, and art. He closed his chapter on Robert Owen's failed experiment by recounting Frances Wright's July 4, 1828 oration at New Harmony: "She declared that the genuine meaning of our liberty is our intellectual opportunity." In her speech, he claimed, "she explained the promise of this enlightened liberty, in which New Harmony has led all America."[41] Lockridge, like Snedeker and others before them, knew New Harmony as a place of firsts and a place of progressive thinking. They claimed it as the site of "The first infant school in America. The first kindergarten in America. The first trade school. The first free public school system. The first woman's club. The first free public library. The first town dramatic club."[42] They sought to preserve the town and its stories in order to restore its ability to lead.

When Marguerite Young lived in New Harmony for a few years in the late 1930s to early 1940s, she too was entranced or entrapped by this odd town.[43] The result was *Angel in the Forest*, a personal account and interpretation of the town published in 1945. Abandoning the celebratory quality of others' writing, she set her narrative in 1940. After leaving the old ferry that carried her across the Wabash, she ascended "a path that seems to lead nowhere" and came "at last to New Harmony, a disappointment." She struggled to see what others had seen: "The past is an intangible in Indiana, you find, as in other parts of these abstract United States—a filling station where there were two Utopias, Mr. Babbitt where there was an angel." The present seemed too pervasive—people went about their lives as they did anywhere else, buildings were in disrepair, the ten-cent store "cobwebbed and insubstantial."[44] But she found it "impossible, even in 1940, to visit at length in New Harmony without catching some of the 'spirit' of the place—few who came were unappreciative of this rare gem, a frontier between eternity and time."[45] She opined that no one wanted to change New Harmony, "decay having its own remorseless attraction."[46] Her tale, less uplifting than that of the New Harmony Memorial Commission members, nevertheless captured the spirit of the place: "New Harmony persisted—old, unresurrected, unredeemed perhaps, yet curiously, unreasonably wonderful."[47]

Seeking to preserve the same landscape, the local amateurs and the preservation professionals diverged significantly in their ultimate goals. The former had adopted the methods of nineteenth-century preservation practice and adhered to broad progressive goals of transforming society and educating youth. The latter had no intention of transforming society, but only of preserving a site of historical significance to the state of Indiana and creating an interesting tourist destination at as little cost to state taxpayers as possible. New Harmony's past had long ago been remade into something far less radical than the actual historical record suggested, and all players were comfortable with it.[48] It was the future that was at stake in this tug-of-war between the romantic progressives and the scientific modernists.

Notes

1. Denise M. Meringolo, *Museums, Monuments and National Parks: Toward a New Genealogy of Public History* (Amherst and Boston: University of Massachusetts Press, 2012), 118.

2. One has to acknowledge the prodigious foundational work of Charles B. Hosmer, Jr., in *Preservation Comes of Age: From Williamsburg to the National Trust* (Charlottesville: University of Virginia Press, 1981), but much remains to be critically investigated. Max Page and Randall Mason have argued for examination and analysis of regional preservation histories. See their "Rethinking the Roots of the Historic Preservation Movement," in Page and Mason, eds., *Giving Preservation a History: Histories of Historic Preservation in the United States* (New York: Routledge, 2004). Daniel Bluestone has featured some midwestern cities in his case studies, including "Chicago's Mecca Flat Blues," in Page and Mason, eds., *Giving Preservation a History;* and "The Arch and the Neighborhood: Marking Westward Expansion in St. Louis," in his *Buildings, Landscapes and Memory: Case Studies in Historic Preservation* (New York: W.W. Norton, 2011).
3. On the MVHA see Ian Tyrrell, "Public at the Creation: Place, Memory, and Historical Practice in the Mississippi Valley Historical Association, 1907–1950," *The Journal of American History* 94, no. 1 (June 2007): 19–46.
4. Don Blair, "Harmonist Construction," *Indiana Historical Society Publications* 23, no. 2 (1964): 48–49.
5. John H. Holliday, "An Indiana Village, New Harmony," *Indiana Historical Society Publications* v, no. 4 (1914): 227–28. See also Maurice Thompson, *Stories of Indiana* (New York: American Book Company, 1898). The chapter on "The Romance of New Harmony" is a paean to the Owenite years and their aftermath.
6. Holliday, "An Indiana Village," 229.
7. Dr. J. Schnack and Richard Owen, *The History of New Harmony, Ind.* (Evansville, IN: Courier Co. Printers, 1890) pamphlet.
8. *New Harmony Times*, August 17, 1894, 2.
9. George B. Lockwood, *The New Harmony Communities* (Marion, IN: The Chronicle Co., 1902), 11.
10. Robert Owen, "Oration, Containing a Declaration of Mental Independence, Delivered in the Public Hall, at New Harmony, Ind," July 4, 1826, as reprinted in the *New Harmony Gazette*, July 12, 1826, in Donald E. Pitzer and Josephine M. Elliott, eds., *New Harmony's Fourth of July Tradition* (New Harmony: Raintree Books, n.d.), 10.
11. Summary of the centennial celebration in Connie A. Weinzapfel, "A Typical Day in Utopia: Uncovering the New Harmony Centennial," *Traces of Indiana and Midwestern History* 26, no. 2 (Spring 2014): 38–43.
12. Schnack and Owen, *History of New Harmony*, 4.
13. Blair, "Harmonist Construction," 51.
14. Ross F. Lockridge, *The Old Fauntleroy Home* (New Harmony Memorial Commission, 1939), 188, 195–96.
15. New Harmony State Memorial Collection, Box G: New Harmony Memorial Movement, Abstract of remarks at conference dinner at the old Tavern at New Harmony.

16. Ibid.
17. Ross Lockridge, "Tentative Suggestions for Adoption of Master Plan Covering Four Years Program of the New Harmony Memorial Commission," typescript, n.d. (New Harmony State Memorial Collection, Office Files, 1939–1942).
18. Lockridge, *Old Fauntleroy Home*, 26, 33.
19. Ibid., 210.
20. On education in Owen's New Harmony, see Daniel Feller, "'The Spirit of Improvement': The America of William Maclure and Robert Owen," *Indiana Magazine of History* 94, no. 2 (June 1998): 89–98; Arthur Eugene Bestor, Jr., *Backwoods Utopias: The Sectarian and Owenite Phases of Communitarian Socialism in America, 1663–1829* (Philadelphia: University of Pennsylvania Press, 1950).
21. "Some Special Educational Projects of the New Harmony Memorial Commission: Address of Dr. Clement T. Malan, State Superintendent of Public Instruction at the Terpsichorean Institute, New Harmony, Indiana, May 12, 1941." Letters between Ross F. Lockridge, Director of New Harmony Memorial Commission and Dr. Clement T. Malan, State Superintendent of Public Instruction, New Harmony State Memorial Collection, Office Files, 1939–1942.
22. Ibid.
23. Ibid.
24. "Members of the New Harmony Memorial Commission, Selected by Governor Townsend, to be publicly announced first in a special feature page of the Indianapolis Star, Sunday, April 18, '37," typescript (New Harmony State Memorial Collection).
25. *New Harmony Times*, February 10, 1939, 2.
26. November 27, 1940 Memo, New Harmony State Memorial Collection, Office Files, 1939–1942, Box A.
27. Dr. Herman B. Wells, appended statement to November 27, 1940 Memo, New Harmony State Memorial Collection, unmarked box, file "Dr. Herman B. Wells, Pres. Indiana University."
28. "Oil Men Watch Wildcat Test Near Hebbardsville," *Evansville Courier*, Nov. 27, 1938, New Harmony Memorial Collection, unmarked box, materials alphabetized T–V.
29. "Commercial Club Notes," *New Harmony Times*, December 30, 1938, 1.
30. "A Preliminary General Plan for the Development of the New Harmony Memorial Prepared by the Indiana Department of Conservation for the New Harmony Memorial Commission," March 25, 1942, New Harmony State Memorial Collection. On the use of modernist principles by preservation professionals, see Barbara Burlison Mooney, "Lincoln's New Salem: Or, the Trigonometric Theorem of Vernacular Restoration," *Perspectives in Vernacular Architecture* 11 (2004): 19–39.
31. Ibid., 6–7.

32. Ibid.
33. Ibid., 2.
34. For a broader context of the midwestern narrative see Andrew Cayton and Susan Gray, "The Story of the American Midwest, An Introduction," in Cayton and Gray, eds., *The Identity of the American Midwest: Essays on Regional History* (Bloomington, IN: Indiana University Press, 2007); and Jon Lauck, "The Prairie Historians and the Foundations of Midwestern History" in *The Lost Region: Toward a Revival of Midwestern History* (Iowa City: University of Iowa Press, 2013).
35. Caroline Dale Snedeker, *The Town of the Fearless* (New York: Doubleday, Doran and Company, Inc., 1931), 271. Snedeker, great-granddaughter of Robert Owen, was born in New Harmony in 1871.
36. Ibid., 348–49.
37. Lockridge, *Old Fauntleroy Home*.
38. Lockridge, Jr., a novelist, was the author of *Raintree County*, published in 1948.
39. Lockridge, Jr., "Salutation," *Old Fauntleroy Home*, x.
40. Ibid., xi–xii.
41. Lockridge, *Old Fauntleroy Home*, 71.
42. Snedeker, *Town of the Fearless*, 271.
43. Born in Indianapolis in 1908, Young went on to become a well-known author, critic, and teacher. Her only novel, *Miss MacIntosh, My Darling* (1965), won critical acclaim.
44. Marguerite Young, *Angel in the Forest* (New York: Charles Scribner's Sons, 1945), 2.
45. Ibid., 3.
46. Ibid., 6.
47. Ibid., 7.
48. See my "Erasing Radicalism in the Rural Midwest? Preservation and Authenticity in New Harmony, Indiana, 1937–1942," paper given at International Conference on Cultural Landscape and Heritage Values: Embracing Change in the Management of Place, U Mass., Amherst, 2015; and the Vreeland Collection, "A Sociological Study of New Harmony," notes for unpublished 1930s work on New Harmony, in the Working Men's Institute Museum and Library, New Harmony, IN.

Camden Burd

In the Land of Hiawatha

Conservation and Literary Sociability in Michigan

For Allen Dyer Shaffmaster, a newspaper editor from Bronson, Michigan, the forests of Michigan's Upper Peninsula held particular importance each autumn from 1898 to 1904. Annual hunting trips to the eastern part of the peninsula gave Shaffmaster access to what he called "the Wild." Out there, amid the balsam, pine, cedar, and birch trees, he felt closer to the natural world. That feeling strengthened when he caught glimpses of the Tahquamenon River's rushing waters through the dense, mixed-coniferous forests. "The river always had a certain mystic charm," he wrote in his recollections. "I cannot look upon its swift rushing waters and darkly fringed forests' shores, without feeling a transcendent happiness, tinged with a sense of awe and supreme nature love for this famous river." He concluded, "There is no doubt in my mind but what Longfellow had the Tah-qua-me-non river in his mind when he drew this beautiful pen picture of the mystic Hiawatha." Everywhere he looked, Shaffmaster saw Henry Wadsworth Longfellow's *The Song of Hiawatha*. He read Longfellow's words in the hills, forests, and waterways of the Michigan landscape. In Lake Superior, he saw the Gitche Gumee or the Big Sea Water. He was certain that he hunted in the same site where "little Hiawatha killed the red deer." Grafting literature onto nature, Shaffmaster prized the northern Michigan environment because it was "not a whit less wild and solitary than it was in the days of 'Hiawatha.'"[1] Every autumn, Shaffmaster transformed the Upper Peninsula's landscape from a seemingly nameless and sprawling forest into a *place*—into his Land of Hiawatha.

Before Shaffmaster's Land of Hiawatha was a *place*, it was a forest. Whether he knew it, Shaffmaster was responding to a series of ecological events. Roughly 10,000 years before Shaffmaster's annual hunting trips, a glacier carved out what would become the entire Great Lakes watershed—including his beloved Tahquamenon River. The sandy soils deposited by the glacier made for an ideal environment for spruce, tamarack, maple, hemlock, pine, and birch trees. Because of the region's general latitudinal orientation and short growing season, few types of vegetation could thrive in the environment. As a result, Native Americans in the region found little agricultural use for the land. To the unknowing eye, this landscape appeared wild—untouched. However, for Shaffmaster to attach meaning to this seemingly nameless forest he needed cultural prompting. Sorting through a series of values, beliefs, desires, and motivations, Shaffmaster fused literature and landscape to create his Land of Hiawatha. He created a *place*.[2]

Other outdoorsmen, too, saw the words of Longfellow's *The Song of Hiawatha* in the northern Michigan landscape. Like Shaffmaster, outdoorsmen made connections between the poem and landmarks of Michigan's Upper Peninsula environment. Throughout this essay I will argue that in the late nineteenth and early twentieth centuries, conservationists named forests, rivers, lakes, streams, and hunting clubs based on the names of the characters and places found in *The Song of Hiawatha*. The poem provided a language for hunters and outdoor enthusiasts to connect with the landscape on a deeper level. So when industrialization and deforestation threatened the region's forests, rivers, and lakes, outdoorsmen called upon the famous poem to safeguard their revered places. *The Song of Hiawatha* became the language of conservation.

Outdoorsmen harnessed their shared language in the fight for conservation through a process scholars refer to as "literary sociability." One historian defines literary sociability as "the formation of relationships among individuals based on a shared encounter with fiction or poems."[3] Books or poems that resemble an idea, place, or movement can be used as a shared language among different readers. Through literary sociability, readers create bonds among one another in a new community with a shared language. For conservationists in Michigan's Upper Peninsula, *The Song of Hiawatha* embodied the environments the conservationists hoped to protect while providing the language to articulate their ideas to a larger public. Conservationists used the epic poem to defend, and create, natural beauty in northern Michigan. *The Song of Hiawatha* became the language through which conservationists shielded Michigan's northern landscapes from deforestation and industrialization.

This language of conservation may have been cultivated in a myriad of ways. Countless Americans in the second half of the nineteenth century encountered Longfellow's epic poem. *The Song of Hiawatha* was one of the most printed poems of the nineteenth century. After its initial publication in 1855, the poem was reused and recycled in various settings. Poets celebrated its epic form and even replicated its structure. Playwrights adapted Longfellow's words for the stage. Educators used the poem to teach language and handwriting. Likewise, publishers made the poem more available to eager customers due to the growth of the printing industry in the years following the Civil War. By the end of the nineteenth century it was not uncommon for an American reader to encounter the work in newspapers, on the stage, or in the classroom.[4]

The prevalence of the poem grew alongside an increase of industrial activity in northern Michigan. Logging, mining, and settlement brought about profound transformations in the landscape. The rising logging industry caused rapid depletion of forests in a region blanketed in green. Logging companies extracted 16.9 billion board feet of lumber from Michigan's forests from 1869 to 1909—an unprecedented amount of production for the logging industry. Alongside lumber activity, mining operations increased drastically following the Civil War. Copper mines in the western portion of the Upper Peninsula and iron mines in the central portion of the peninsula increasingly strained the natural resources of northern Michigan. As mining companies dug, burned, and transported minerals to bustling cities, they scarred the landscape. Industrialization and deforestation put a strain on the ecosystem. Many animal populations, once abundant, decreased in large numbers. From this destruction, conservationists responded to a Michigan landscape that appeared to be consistently losing forests, wildlife, and natural beauty.[5]

The push for conservation began in the second half of the nineteenth century. The Michigan government recognized the need to protect the decreasing populations of fish and game as a result of shrinking forests and capitalistic industrialization. The depletion of forests placed a strain on certain species. As a result, outdoor enthusiasts who enjoyed fishing and hunting led the charge to manage the populations of desirable species. Conservationists fought to keep the hunting of deer, turkey, quail and ruffed grouse to certain seasons with the passage of Michigan's first large-scale conservation law in 1881. By 1887, the Michigan government created the position of "game warden" to enforce laws, collect fines, and protect desirable animals identified in earlier legislation. The plea for conservation appears in the recollections of Shaffmaster's annual hunting trips. He saw his Land of Hiawatha in danger of complete destruction from overhunting. "The time is fast approaching when the sight of large game such as moose, elk, caribou, deer, bear, antelope and other big game will be a curiosity to the younger generations." He challenged all hunters to "exercise good principles when ... in the presence of game." Although they took to the woods with rifles and traps, hunters like Shaffmaster believed the creatures of the woods needed protection from over-killing. He believed the overhunt detracted from the "natural beauty" of Michigan's forests. Shaffmaster called for restraint. He called for conservation. And he did so to protect the essence of the landscape as it had been "in the days of 'Hiawatha.'"[6]

Sportsmen like Shaffmaster placed the protection of deer, elk, and other game as the primary concern of conservation efforts. As a result, the appointed game warden became an influential individual in shaping conservation practices and, in turn, Michigan's landscapes. No game warden proved as influential in shaping the Michigan landscape as Chase Osborn. Osborn was appointed game warden in 1895 shortly after relocating to Sault Ste. Marie, Michigan, from Indiana. In Michigan, Osborn cultivated his passion for the outdoors. He regularly hunted in the nearby forest and fished the St. Mary's River. He took in the Michigan landscape through long hikes and camping along the shores of Lake Superior. As an avid outdoorsman, conservation was more than a job—it was necessary to maintain the natural world he had come to love. Osborn enforced the game laws with vigor. One 1895 report noted that Osborn and his staff successfully convicted forty-seven violators of the game laws. Osborn's successes led to new and expansive conservation laws. Michigan legislators soon introduced hunting licenses, new hunting fees, and limits on the deer allowed to be killed in one season.[7]

Osborn was also moved by Michigan's natural beauty: "The grandeurs of the Lake Superior region are unsurpassable. Its shores are majestic in their contours and their colorings. Its water is as emerald and as pure earth water can be. The sunshine is golden and the air is fragrant with balsam and evergreens." And like Shaffmaster, Osborn used the language from *The Song of Hiawatha* to describe his cherished landscape. He often referred to the landscapes of the Lake Superior basin as "the Hiawatha Country." However, it was not just natural beauty that created his connection with this place. His attachments to "Hiawatha Country" strengthened when he concluded that Longfellow drew from Chippewa legends born in the region. "An actual Indian leader named Hiawatha is known to have lived in New York State and to have become the nucleus of some traditions," he conceded. "But the bulk of the supernatural and other legends that have been combined to create the character of Hiawatha as we know it, were born in and of the sublimity of the Lake Superior Country." For Osborn, the Lake Superior region was the physical embodiment of Longfellow's beloved words.[8]

Osborn's claims regarding the poem carried some truth. The name Hiawatha refers to Iroquois legend; however, many of the stories derived from Ojibwa Indian stories collected by Henry Schoolcraft nearly two decades before the publication of Longfellow's epic poem. Schoolcraft served as an Indian Agent in Sault Ste. Marie, where he began collecting oral stories of the local Ojibwa inhabitants. While many of the shared stories appear in Schoolcraft's massive *Algic Researches,* Schoolcraft invented others. Those used as the basis of *The Song of Hiawatha* followed a character referred to as Manabohzo, rather than Hiawatha. However, read together there is little dispute regarding the connection between Schoolcraft and Longfellow. Despite the discrepancies in nomenclature, many of the landmarks mentioned in Longfellow's poem are pulled from the geography of the Great Lakes region rather than places in New York State. Noting the connections between Tahquamenon Falls, Lake Superior, and Pictured Rocks in Longfellow's poem helped to cultivate a deep connection between outdoor enthusiasts, like Shaffmaster and Osborn, and the landscapes found in Michigan's Upper Peninsula. Due to the prevalence of the poem and the regional significance drawn from its content, *The Song of Hiawatha* added significance to the beauty found in Michigan's natural world.[9]

When Shaffmaster or Osborn claimed to be in the Land of Hiawatha, they attached the Michigan landscape to a poem that

Longfellow intended to write for a mass audience. Longfellow lived in New England, not Michigan. He also based his poem on an amalgamation of other stories. Some were grounded in accurate Ojibwa folklore, and others were not. Schoolcraft believed he was doing serious ethnographic work—work not necessarily intended for public consumption. Those Native Americans who shared their stories with Schoolcraft never imagined that their legends would appear in print or on stage. At each stage of transmission, the stories warped to fit the needs of the author and the desires of the readers. The Ojibwa shared, Schoolcraft collected, Longfellow fictionalized, and conservationists romanticized. When conservationists used the Hiawatha name to describe natural places in northern Michigan they called upon the idea of "Indian-ness" rather than any specific group of Native Americans. As noted, Hiawatha was an Iroquois name, not Ojibwa. When Americans used "Hiawatha," they did so to describe the idea of a primitive past rather than to honor or respect the original owners of the land. Although conservationists and outdoor enthusiasts harnessed Native American language, American conservationists disavowed many of the Native American environmental practices. Conservationists became the principal culprits in restricting the rights of Ojibwa fishing access in the late nineteenth century. Government bodies either overlooked or ignored treaty agreements, resulting in a Michigan environment primarily suited to the environmental concerns of Anglo-American conservationists. Using the language of the stoic Indian, conservationists legally restricted Native Americans' access to the natural world in an effort to create their ideal image of untouched nature—a Land of Hiawatha.[10]

John Munro Longyear, an industrialist and conservationist, embodies the desire to connect a conservation ethic to an idea of "Indian-ness." As an industrialist, he hoped to encourage investors to develop mineral lands or purchase the seemingly unlimited supply of timber. But he also saw beauty in Michigan. While his promotional materials sought to encourage economic development, he also celebrated the pristine beauty of the region. One piece of promotional material titled *Forests, Streams, Lakes, and Resources of Northern Michigan* encouraged hunters and fishermen to visit the Upper Peninsula. The Michigan landscape was described as "rare beauty." The environment boasted a "vast expense of forest, gemmed by countless lakes of incomparable beauty and laced and fringed with brooks and rivers." Longyear appreciated and valued the beauty of the Michigan landscape and hoped to encourage others to visit.[11]

Longyear connected the landscape with an ancestral past. In promotional materials, Longyear repeatedly drew connections between modern hunting and the practices of ancient Indians. In the same pamphlet, Longyear shared a story from an unnamed hunter that explored the beauty found near Lake Gogebic in Michigan's western peninsula. While sitting atop a rocky bluff the hunter stated, "I climbed to a seat overlooking the deep pool at its base, and gave myself over to reveries and unalloyed joy." Here, the hunter romanticized Michigan's beauty. "How many deer have browsed around, or cooled their pliant limbs and parched throats in the crystal water!" For the hunter, Michigan's beauty deepened when he connected his presence with the idea of a romantic and stoic Native American past: "The stealthy hunter has crept to its heights to mark his game, and the wily warrior built here his signal fire." He continued, "This lake was a rallying point when the Ojibeways wrested the country from their hereditary enemies in the Sioux." As the author absorbed the nature of Michigan's Upper Peninsula, he felt compelled to comment on the region's history. His visions of Ojibwa hunting practices only strengthened his reverence for the wooded environment. But regardless of history, the hunter believed this place of "unalloyed joy" was now intended for American use—not Indian: "These almost limitless forests yet hide in their fastnesses great wealth of fur and feather, and a still greater wealth of rare pleasure will sportsmen garner in days to come." Underneath the author's romance and reverence lay bias, concepts of manifest destiny, and the blind spots of nineteenth-century conservation. Conservationists wanted to "play Indian." By harnessing Indian history, legends, and language, conservationists and outdoor enthusiasts found deeper meaning in Michigan's natural world. Like Longyear's unnamed hunter, conservationists used "Indian-ness" to define the landscape as untouched, pristine, native, and romantic.[12]

In 1889, Longyear served as a founding member of the Huron Mountain Shooting and Fishing Club. The original club rested upon a 6000-hectare district established to be a respite from the environmental destruction that seemed to be ongoing in the region. Situated in the Huron Mountains, the property offered to its members vistas of Lake Superior and access to some of the last remaining old-growth forest in the state. The members were determined to preserve the natural world that so quickly seemed to vanish around them. The language of Longyear's promotional pamphlet and the incorporation of the few remaining tracts of old-growth forest into the club property indicate that the founders of the Huron Mountain Shooting and Fishing Club aimed to preserve of the environment and the idea of an unspoiled nature.[13]

Large-scale conservation efforts accompanied the game laws. Because of the massive deforestation associated with the lumber and mining industries, government officials looked to protect and restore desirable lands. Reforesting programs began to restore many of Michigan's barren northern landscapes following the economic depression of 1893. Lumber prices fell, the promise of agricultural production lagged, and government programs encouraged reforestation rather than outright abandonment. Conservationists hoping to restore environments received economic incentive to restore landscapes from cutover lands into replanted forests. This change in direction—from massive industrialization to careful management—represented a changing environmental philosophy. In turn, the very landscape's meaning began to transform. On a map, these places were the same. But in the hearts and minds of outdoors enthusiasts, they meant something more—something romantic.[14]

Conservation continued into the 1920s with the establishment of the Hiawatha Sportsman's Club. Carved out of 35,000 acres of cutover forest, a group of like-minded conservationists established the club in 1927. Members described the landscape as "exceptionally fine" and boasted that the property offered access to Lake Michigan. In the early years of the club, founders hoped to find additional investors to continue to promote their vision of beauty and access to the natural world. "Hiawatha's natural facilities are its greatest asset," one publication noted. "They are so complete and of such magnitude that man-made developments are relatively insignificant. This is a Hiawatha feature that assures members of a source of enjoyment for many years to come." The club promoted access to the beautiful world. It featured "lakes and streams" that "furnish good fishing, bathing, boating, canoeing and other water sports." It was a "better place" to vacation "amidst ideal surroundings and conditions." Coming to the Hiawatha Sportsman's Club was an escape from the built environment and an opportunity to commune with nature.[15]

Members of the Hiawatha Sportsman's Club did more than vacation on the property. Members camped, hunted, and fished. In addition, their membership committed them to the ongoing improvement programs underway throughout the entire property. Massive deforestation caused the depletion of soils and the increase in erosion. As a result, streams and rivers experienced reduced populations of fish. The hunting club instilled a series of conservation and improvement efforts to preserve and protect the property. Members of the club supported water control dams and aqueous replanting as a means to maximize and control fish populations. The club's direction did not necessarily restore a "wild" nature. Instead they hoped to maximize the fishing and hunting opportunities for its members through efficient management. Members worked to create what they believed to be representative of a Land of Hiawatha.[16]

Alongside promotional materials encouraging readers to invest in the club, onlookers encountered the familiar words of Longfellow's poetry. While a reader learned about the ongoing conservation programs at Hiawatha Sportsman's Club, lines from the iconic poem connected literature to landscape:

> Ye whose hearts are fresh and simple;
> Who have faith in God and Nature,
> Who believe, that in all ages
> Every human heart is human,
> That in even savage bosoms
> There are longings, yearnings, strivings
> For the good they comprehend not,
> That the feeble hands and helpless,
> Groping blindly in the darkness,
> Touch God's right hand in that darkness,
> And are lifted up and strengthened;—
> Listen to this simple story,
> To this Song of Hiawatha![17]

The borrowed words may have been familiar to readers. After all, *The Song of Hiawatha* remained a popular poem in the early decades of the twentieth century. The club's pamphlets continued the tradition of attaching Longfellow's poetry with northern Michigan environments. Shortly after Longfellow's lines, the club shared their own take on the iconic poem:

> Ye who love the haunts of nature,
> Love the sunshine of the meadow,
> Love the shadow of the forest,
> Love the wind among the branches
> Full of hope, and yet of heart-break,
> Full of all the tender pathos
> Of the Here and the Hereafter;—
> Come and see this Re-creation,
> Join this Club of Hiawatha![18]

"Come and see this Re-creation," urged the club's leadership. The Hiawatha Sportsman's Club further cemented the perception that Michigan's Upper Peninsula was the Land of Hiawatha. Club leaders encouraged readers to both visit and invest in the efforts to protect and create their Land of Hiawatha.[19]

National conservation efforts continued through the Great Depression. After the purchase of abandoned, burned, and cleared forestland in the central portion of the Upper Peninsula, the federal government created a new National Forest. Harkening on the language of earlier conservationists, President Hoover declared the region the Hiawatha National Forest on January 16, 1931. Whereas previous conservation efforts that harnessed Longfellow's language started with sportsmen and outdoor enthusiasts, the creation of the National Forest meant that the federal government officially recognized this region as the "Land of Hiawatha." After the establishment of the National Forest, employees of the Civilization Conservation Corps transformed the used, abandoned, and ignored lands into a new, forested landscape. Rather than protecting forests from the harmful effects of industrialization as seen with previous conservationists, the young men that reforested Michigan's Upper Peninsula hoped to create the image of Hiawatha's literary world out of the scraps of industrial deforestation.[20]

Due to the work of private and public organizations, Michigan's Upper Peninsula quickly developed into a tourism destination centered on its natural beauty. Following the First World War, large swaths of the American public gained access to cars, held better jobs, and had the opportunity to access the landscapes that had commonly been associated with upper-class conservationists. The Land of Hiawatha soon turned into a tourist destination that could be accessed by steamer, car, and railroad. In the late nineteenth and early twentieth centuries, mostly wealthy individuals saw Hiawatha's storied legends in Michigan's northern environments, but in the years after the First World War, middle-class Americans had access to the Land of Hiawatha.[21]

The democratization of access to the Land of Hiawatha can be seen in the promotional materials surrounding the Hiawatha National Forest. The federal government encouraged all Americans to camp, hike, fish, and enjoy the great outdoors. Promotional materials painted the Hiawatha National Forest more as a recreation site than as an active conservation effort. And they did so by connecting the landscapes to its literary roots. The U.S. Forest Service noted how many "picturesque areas" remained in their natural state despite the previous deforestation: "The famed 'Pictured Rocks' are high bluffs of rain-colored sandstone molded since the recession of the ice cap." Advertisers attached the perception of an untouched and untrammeled environment with a forest that "commemorates the hero of Longfellow's best known poem." Similar to previous conservationists, the federal government used Longfellow's poem to redefine the forest as romantic rather than industrial. However, there is a distinct difference between the conservation efforts of the late nineteenth century and those of the 1920s and 1930s. Whereas conservationists of previous decades had exclusive access to this Land of Hiawatha, large swaths of the American public now had the ability to revel in the beauty of Michigan's natural landscape.[22]

The conservationists' efforts to create a modern Land of Hiawatha soon made their way into tourist booklets. The American Automobile Association championed the conservationist's language in their printed materials. One booklet read, "The Land of Hiawatha! A vast expanse of country so beautiful you find yourself wondering if it can be real." The pamphlet appealed to nature lovers. The Land of Hiawatha was an ideal destination to hunt, hike, and swim. However, one could also connect to the ancient days "when the red man's chant rose in the morning air." The brochure seamlessly blended the idea of pristine nature with Native American imagery. After visiting Crystal Falls, the AAA encouraged travelers to visit a nearby Indian cemetery that "echoes" of "days when red man ruled Michigan's great forests." At the western end of Michigan's Upper Peninsula, near the L'Anse Indian Reservation, tourists could observe a "modern Minnehaha" and "a touch of romance as she weaves baskets in perfection of bygone years." Championing the language of Longfellow's fictional characters, the AAA appropriated Indian-ness to appeal to white Americans. Historical accuracy did not matter. This was about making the Land of Hiawatha, "a perfect playplace," appeal to Americans looking to commune with the natural world they associated with Longfellow's *The Song of Hiawatha*.[23]

The AAA's efforts to commodify the Land of Hiawatha paid off. Tourism boomed in northern Michigan as the twentieth century progressed. Walter Linn and his family embodied this wave of travelers interested in visiting the landscapes they had read about in school, AAA pamphlets, and other advertisements. In a small book of reminiscences titled *Visiting the Land of Hiawatha*, Linn described the family's trip as they left Chicago, traveled up the western shore of Michigan's Lower Peninsula, and ultimately entered the Land of Hiawatha. Linn knew he arrived when he traveled "westward on Route 28, which was the wildest stretch of country on the whole trip." There the family fished for pike and perch, picked berries, and enjoyed boating in the pristine lakes. As they drove through the Hiawatha National Forest, Linn noted "the beautiful winding road through dense woods and over rustic bridges." They felt closer to nature and enjoyed taking in the sights that had been associated with Longfellow's poem. His recollection outlines a family enamored with the forested landscape. Nearly every day of the trip was filled with outdoor activity. Whether fishing, camping, or hiking, the Linn family engrossed themselves with the natural world of Michigan's Upper Peninsula. Linn appreciated the work of past conservationists when he noted the "miles of virgin timber preserved for posterity by the state of Michigan." Linn's Land of Hiawatha was one where natural splendor juxtaposed the industrial cityscape. Past conservationists' work to preserve and restore the natural world became a destination for others.[24]

Today, one can find record of those conservationists' effort while traveling through Michigan. There are three different Hiawatha Streams in Michigan. One can visit the Hiawatha Falls, Hiawatha Village, and Hiawatha Township. Character names from the poem fill out the Michigan map: Manabezho Falls, Winona Village, Winona Lake, Minnehaha Creek, Nokomis Falls, Iagoo Falls, Keewaydin Lake, Nawadaha Falls, Onaway State Park, and Peboan Creek. There are more. As a result of conservationists' efforts *The Song of Hiawatha* grew to be synonymous with Michigan's natural environments. Additionally, Longfellow's epic poem grew to be a language to describe a broad region of the Michigan landscape. Because tourism encouraged more visitors to visit the northern reaches of Michigan, organizations such as the AAA helped to solidify Longfellow's lexicon as a placeholder for an entire region of the state.[25]

Through a process of literary sociability, outdoor enthusiasts shaped many of Michigan's natural environments. *The Song of Hiawatha* served as a shared language that enabled similarly minded individuals to imagine, shape, and use Michigan's forests to fit their literary imaginations over several generations. Beginning in the late nineteenth century, hunters, hikers, fishermen, and tourists harnessed Longfellow's language to protect and create certain landscapes they believed represented a romantic natural world. In turn, the poem's language invoked an environmental expectation among those seeking out the Land of Hiawatha. For the twentieth-century tourist, a trip to the Land of Hiawatha meant grand scenes of rushing waters moving through dense green forests teeming with wildlife. What once were Michigan's nameless or sprawling landscapes soon became romantic destinations that cultivated a sense of place for visitors.

Places and place-names matter. They are historical records of cultural concerns and movements. Often forgotten, and too easily taken for granted, the landscape is a marker of the human experience. Whether named to describe a geographical feature, ownership, association, or commemoration, a place-name shares something to those who encounter that location. When individuals or groups name a river, forest, or settlement, they are sharing their aspirations and assumptions.

Place-names mark origins, embody ideas, and offer insights into the history of Michigan's residents. This is certainly true of late-nineteenth and early-twentieth-century conservationists. In an effort to create meaning out of the environment, conservationists, armed with Longfellow's *The Song of Hiawatha*, took to the woods. From a shared encounter with that poem, conservationists attempted to recreate their imagined Land of Hiawatha on the Michigan landscape. Their labors eventually grew to embody an entire region. Today's maps reflect their labors, and the state's forests embody their vision.

Notes

1. Allen Dyer Shaffmaster, *Hunting in the Land of Hiawatha* (Chicago: M.A. Donohue & Company, 1904), 5, 153–54, 159.
2. For an ecological overview of the region under discussion, see Quanfa Zhang, Kurt S. Pregitzer, and David D. Reed, "Historical Changes in the Forests of the Luce District of the Upper Peninsula of Michigan," *The American Midland Naturalist* 143, no. 1 (2000): 94–98. Landscape scholar John Brinkerhoff Jackson defines a sense of place as a site where an individual or group of persons maintain a "lively awareness of the familiar environment, a ritual repetition," and "a sense of fellowship based on shared experience." Campgrounds, seasonal hunting grounds, and tourism destinations all contribute to a sense of place based on these three elements. See John Brinkerhoff Jackson, "A Sense of Place, a Sense of Time," in *A Sense of Place, a Sense of Time* (New Haven: Yale University Press, 1994), 148–63.
3. Joan Shelley Rubin, "Ideology and Practice in the Career of Robert Shaw," in *Cultural Considerations* (Amherst: University of Massachusetts Press, 2013), 109. For other references on literary sociability, see Robert Dixon and Peter Kirkpatrick, eds., *Republics of Letters* (Sydney: University of Sydney Press, 2012).
4. For a history of the poem as it appeared on stage, see Alan Trachtenberg, *Shades of Hiawatha: Staging Indians, Making Americans, 1880–1930* (New York: Hill and Wang, 2004), 51–97. For an example of how the poem was used as an education tool, see Angela Sorby, *Schoolroom Poets: Childhood, Performance, and the Place of American Poetry, 1865–1917* (Durham: University of New Hampshire Press, 2005), 1–34. For examples of the poem being used in newspapers, see Joan Shelley Rubin, *Songs of Ourselves: The Uses of Poetry in America* (Cambridge: Harvard University Press, 2007), 336–42.
5. Michael Williams, *Americans and Their Forests: A Historical Geography* (Cambridge, UK: Cambridge University Press, 1989), 222–30. For a history of Michigan's copper industry, see Larry Lankton, *Hollowed Ground: Copper Mining and Community Building on Lake Superior, 1840s–1990s* (Detroit: Wayne State University Press, 2010). For a history of Michigan's

iron industry, see Terry S. Reynolds and Virginia P. Dawson, *Iron Will: Cleveland-Cliffs and the Mining of Iron Ore, 1847–2006* (Detroit: Wayne State University Press, 2011).

6. Dave Dempsey, *Ruin & Recovery: Michigan's Rise as a Conservation Leader* (Ann Arbor: University of Michigan Press, 2001), 40–41; Shaffmaster, *Hunting in the Land of Hiawatha*, 181–82, 153–54.
7. Dempsey, *Ruin & Recovery*, 45.
8. Chase S. Osborn and Stellanova Osborn, *Schoolcraft, Longfellow, Hiawatha* (Lancaster, PA: Jaques Cattell Press, 1942), 41–42.
9. Henry R. Schoolcraft, *Algic Researches* (New York: Harper & Brothers, 1839). This is further supported by the fact that Henry Schoolcraft tried to republish the collected stories shortly after the release of Longfellow's poem. In the republished version he noted the change in name from Manabohzo to Hiawatha. Henry R. Schoolcraft, *The Myth of Hiawatha, and Other Oral Legends, Mythologic and Allegoric, of the North American Indians* (Philadelphia: J.B. Lippincott & Co., 1856).
10. Jared Farmer, *On Zion's Mount: Mormons, Indians, and the American Landscape* (Cambridge, MA: Harvard University Press, 2008), 241–81. For a history of the cultural appropriation of Native American culture, see Philip J. Deloria, *Playing Indian* (New Haven: Yale University Press, 1998). For a history of Native American fishing claims on the Great Lakes, see Michael J. Chiarappa and Kristin M. Szylvian, *Fish for All: An Oral History of Multiple Claims and Divided Sentiment on Lake Michigan* (Lansing, Michigan: Michigan State University Press, 2003), 2–11.
11. J.M. Longyear and J.M. Case, *Forests, Streams, Lakes, and Resources of Northern Michigan* (Marquette, MI: J.M. Longyear and J.M. Case, 1884), 5.
12. Ibid., 11–13; "Playing Indian" refers to the appropriation of Native American culture to fit Anglo-American needs, see Deloria, *Playing Indian*.
13. David Flaspohler and Curt Meine, "Planning for Wilderness: Aldo Leopold's Report on Huron Mountain Club," *Journal of Forestry* 104, no. 1 (2006): 32–33.
14. For a history of the economic incentive of conservation in the Great Lakes cutover region, see James Kates, *Planning a Wilderness: Regenerating the Great Lakes Cutover Region* (Minneapolis: University of Minnesota Press, 2001), 15–31.
15. Hiawatha Sportsman's Club, *A Vacation Paradise, Hiawatha's Sportsman's Club* (Lansing, Michigan: The Club, 1943), 7, 9, 32.
16. Ibid., 25.
17. Ibid., 31.
18. Ibid.
19. Rubin, *Songs of Ourselves*, 126, 373.
20. "Our Story: Hiawatha National Forest," *United States Department of Agriculture: Forest Service*, accessed August 11, 2016, http://www.fs.usda.gov/detail/hiawatha/learning/history-culture/?cid=FSEM_033514.

21. For a history of Michigan's growing tourist industry, see Camden Burd, "Imagining a Pure Michigan Landscape: Advertisers, Tourists, and the Making of Michigan's Northern Vacationlands," *Michigan Historical Review* 42, no. 2 (2016): 31–51.
22. *The Upper Michigan National Forest: Jobs, Water, Lumber, Wildlife, Recreation, Pulp & Paper* (Escanaba, Michigan: Forest Supervisor, 1954), 7, 3. For a history of Michigan's expanding tourist industry and the state's role in cultivating the tourism industry, see Aaron Shapiro, *The Lure of the North Woods: Cultivating Tourism in the Upper Midwest* (Minneapolis: University of Minnesota Press, 2013), 43–72.
23. *Upper Peninsula of Michigan as Told by the Old AAA Traveler* (Detroit, Michigan: Automobile Club of Michigan, ca. 1940), 8, 21, 32.
24. By the 1940s some educators considered *The Song of Hiawatha* to be a valuable history of the state of Michigan. See Charles F. Hamilton, *Our Hiawatha Land: By the Boys and Girls of the Upper Peninsula, Dedicated to the Pioneers Who Gave Their Lives to the Development of This Great North Country* (Chicago: Lyons & Carnahan Publishers, 1940). Many other organizations used the poem to encourage tourism. See Henry A. Perry, *Cloverland Tourists' Guide* (Menominee, Michigan: Herald-Leader Co., 1932), 2; Walter Linn, *Visiting the Land of Hiawatha* (Chicago: Walter Linn, 1932), 6, 13.
25. For these and more, see Virgil J. Vogel, *Indian Names in Michigan* (Ann Arbor: University of Michigan Press, 1986), 67–69.

Jim O'Loughlin
Jordan Lea Ludwig

The Midwest Below Me

James Hearst's
Poetry and Prose

By 1981, when poet James Hearst (1900–1983) published his essay collection *Time Like a Furrow*, he proudly asserted his identity as a Midwesterner, writing, "I am glad to have been raised on a farm in the Midwest. To me, the Midwest is a land in its working clothes."[1] However, early in his writing career, Hearst was more ambivalent about his midwestern identity. In the 1924 poem "Voices" he wrote,

> The midland has its voices, but they call to me in vain.
> I care not for the whispering road nor drumming city street.
> My heartbeats do not quicken to the thrush's joyous strain,
> Nor to the sighing music of the wind upon the wheat.
> The bees drone their contented song—but what is this to me?
> For I was born far inland and long to hear the sea.[2]

In "Voices," Hearst celebrates the call of the coast, suggesting that he was better suited to the grandeur of the oceans than to the more mundane pleasures of his birthplace. While Hearst would become known as a farmer-poet, laboring for many years on his family's farm in Cedar Falls, Iowa, and publishing over 600 poems during a prolific writing career, his path to that identity was not straightforward. Counterintuitively, Hearst's development as a midwestern writer went hand in hand with an intellectual struggle with the concept of regionalism. In saying Hearst struggled with regionalism, we are arguing that Hearst's work did *not* suggest that midwestern experience was distinctly different from human experience elsewhere. In his poetry, Hearst crafted a humanistic vision in which the land was a place where meaning was made—meaning that was no less important than that produced by his coastal contemporaries—but meaning that captured something of our shared human experience rather than a distinctly midwestern understanding. Nevertheless, Hearst made that argument in hundreds of poems specifically and intentionally set in the rural Midwest, which rightfully, if counterintuitively, earned him the title of Iowa's unofficial poet laureate.[3]

The path of James Hearst's life and work could have led in many directions. As a teenager he played some semi-pro baseball in Iowa, and though he was called up to serve in World War I, the war ended before he could be sent abroad. He also had several relatives who were doctors, which was one profession he considered, and, of course, there was his family's farm to be worked. But the incident that had the most immediate impact on his life was a diving accident at the age of nineteen that fractured his spine and left him substantially paralyzed for the rest of his life. After a long recovery, Hearst assisted as able on the family farm (often being carried onto a tractor by his brother) and began writing poetry.[4]

Hearst's early poems were traditional in form and content, often inspired by the classic Victorian poets. But, gradually, as his work became more varied in approach, it also began to focus more on the world of his family's farm. Or, to be more precise, his work concentrated on the significance that could be created from his immediate world. In 1937, in the foreword to his first collection, *Country Men*, Ruth Suckow aimed to find a way to explain how Hearst's work drew from the land without suggesting that the poetry's significance was limited to that location. "Not that these are poems of local color; that would be putting them within limits which they do not deserve," she wrote, later adding for emphasis, "I repeat, lest I seem to be over-emphasizing geography, that this verse is not narrowly local, either in form or implication."[5] In accounting for Hearst's work, Suckow's challenge, which her language reflects, was to define the specific midwestern resonance of Hearst's work without limiting its implications.

By 1937, the term "local color," which Suckow was quick to reject in her account of Hearst's work, had become an easy way to dismiss a writer's literary significance. Figure 1, an ngram chart drawn from the Google Book Project, shows the relative usage of terms in printed works. It illustrates the rise in the use of the term "local color" in the late 1800s and its later leveling off, as well as the rise in the use of "regionalism"

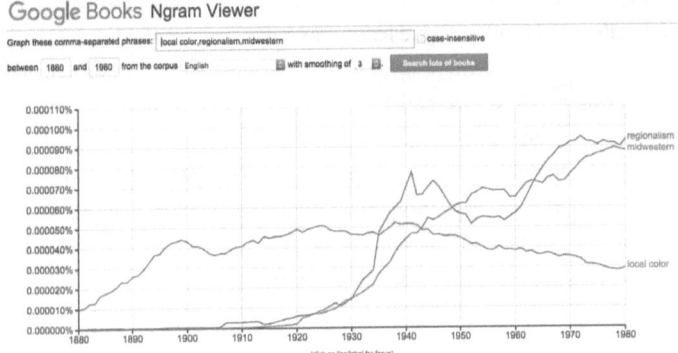

Figure 1. Ngram for the words "local color," "regionalism," and "midwestern."

and "midwestern" in the 1930s, at exactly the time when Hearst was publishing his first collection.

The challenge Suckow found in accounting for Hearst's work is a real one, because while Hearst's poetry so clearly draws inspiration from the farm where he grew up and lived for much of his adult life, it does so at a level of abstraction. There are very few Hearst poems that can be said to be "set" in a particular location. He rarely refers to a specific place or a recognized part of the family's farm. For example, in the poem "Winter Field" from *Country Men*, the speaker gazes at a field and hopes he will be alive in spring to sow it. For while the field itself can be counted on at least to produce weeds, only the farmer's effort will produce a harvest: "I'm ready for work when the spring comes on."[6] The specifics of the field are not noted, because Hearst is not attempting to document a location but to account for an experience.

The power of that metaphor supports Hearst's ambivalence about his midwestern identity in the poem "Voices," quoted in the opening paragraph of this essay. Hearst would have been cautious about being categorized as a writer in a way that would minimize his contribution. Hearst also would have been aware of controversies surrounding midwestern literature, dating back to Carl Van Doren's 1921 article in the *The Nation* that coined the phrase "the revolt from the village." (Hearst himself was an occasional writer for the *The Nation*, focusing on farm-related issues.) The phrase "the revolt from the village" marked a hostility to small-town life in the work of writers such as Sinclair Lewis and Sherwood Anderson. When, following the publication of *Country Men*, Hearst was asked to join the local Rotary Club, he noted with irritation, "It was a time when [H.L.] Mencken was hammering at all service clubs. He accused them of 'boosterism' and ignorance of anything but pious platitudes."[7] Hearst understandably may have been reluctant to be pigeonholed as a midwestern writer if that meant his concerns were thought to extend no further than his farm's property line or beyond his small town, but at the same time, he was a fierce defender of rural life and midwestern institutions.

The need to defend but not be delimited by the Midwest animated much of Hearst's poetry, and it is in his writings that the philosophical nature of Hearst's thinking becomes readily apparent. It goes without saying that, in farming, land productivity is a major preoccupation. For Hearst, who was raised within the farming community, there was a clear distinction between "productive" and "unproductive" land, but this distinction was one that was not restricted to agriculture in his mind. In the poem "Choosing," Hearst meditates on the role of the farmer (at least in a place as fertile as Iowa) in deciding which plants to kill and which to cultivate, why to value fruit over the wild tobacco patch, or as Hearst put it, "how to choose between melon and felon."[8] Such decisions over value, over making land productive, were not arbitrary to Hearst; rather, they were essential: "for he is no farmer who does not choose."[9] This act of choosing is integral for farming, but for Hearst it also has a more fundamental meaning. For Hearst, the act of farming makes land meaningful in that it provides intention and structure, giving the land a productive purpose. Without the role of the farmer, the land does not produce (crops or meaning). Hearst believes this conception applies not only to the farmer but to all human efforts, including those of the poet. Hearst can best be understood as a proto-existentialist, positing that the act of "choosing" illustrates how life itself is given meaning.

It is worth noting that later in his life, long past the time when he was working the family farmstead, and having been influenced by the nascent environmental movement, Hearst would grow wary of the ways in which land could be made productive by industrial agriculture, and he came instead to think of the traditional farm as a place of ecological equilibrium. This can be seen in the appropriately titled introduction to *Time Like a Furrow*, "Balance Sheet." But for much of his career, the farm functioned for Hearst both as workplace and as the space that defined human experience.

This concept carries over into several of Hearst's other poems, including a later poem entitled "Sense of Order."[10] In this poem, Hearst comments on the universality of the human experience through the use of an existential epiphany. He does not write of this epiphany as a chance experience or as some exclusive and elusive phenomenon. Instead he writes, "but I do know that a time comes / when you are transfixed by a special / moment, by a glimpse of your own / promise that tells you who you are" (lines 5–8). These lines imply a certainty, and this implication removes the extraordinary element from the epiphany and makes it a common, everyday sort of occurrence. He then adds that this epiphany could come to you as you "lie / out on the lawn after a hard day's work" (lines 10–11) or "at the end of summer as you listen / to the long corn rows stand / at attention with their full heavy ears" (lines 12–13). Epiphanies are often associated with the poetic, with the amazing, but here he is claiming that they are much more ordinary than that. They do not belong exclusively to anyone or occur only in particular settings but are capable of occurring in fields and farms. In this way, he is rejecting the idea that his poetry is any less profound or any less of a contribution to the literary world because of where it is written, because life's revelations, much like his poetry, are not restricted to place. For Hearst, the Midwest, with its manicured fields and wild expanses, can contain just as many extraordinary revelations as an ancient city or calming coastal province.

In addition to this, he ends the poem with a return to the idea of a deep, encompassing connection with life. He writes,

> You know the spirit within you
> Bears a kinship to all you have seen
> And touched and labored for, and you feel
> An enormous order of things assigned you
> The part you must play. (lines 17–21)

Your purpose, that which is revealed to you in these epiphanies, is an accumulation of experiences, of knowledge, thoughtfully connected, creating a sense of understanding and contentment. They reveal to you the part you must play in the grander scheme of things, the way in which you are connected with everything through experiences, and although experiences vary depending on region, the kinship to the spirit is the same.

From these first poems, we can see how Hearst struggled with accepting his work as regionalist when he saw human experience as universal, that we are all connected by a compulsion—albeit an abstract one—toward a single condition. Despite regional differences, we all communicate the same awarenesses. He adds to this argument in his poem "Where We Live" by commenting on the arbitrariness of physical, regional boundaries.[11] He does this by focusing on the nature of a mailbox. He states,

> The mailbox carries our name
> To show where we live, but holds
> No news why a calf when born
> Staggers to its feet and begins
> To suck its mother's teat, nor why
> A duck sits on her eggs until
> They hatch. (lines 10–16)

He realizes that the mailbox may be a marker for one's physical place in the world, but it does not provide answers for any of life's questions. It is a place with a name, but that name is not that place. One is not defined exclusively by place, and place cannot contain all answers. This is backed up by the next lines that note that a mailbox contains "news of the world, words from friends, / debts we have paid" (lines 17–18). The mailbox is instead full of information from outside his farm, news from loved ones, from the world. This poem is asking us to consider that although mailboxes, like ourselves, are planted in one space, we are not solely defined by them. We are filled with memories and information, filled with multitudes much more worldly and vast than one regional marker can contain. Hearst is using this poem to reject the restrictions and stigmas such divisions put on poets and poetry.

A focus on the making of meaning can also be found in one of Hearst's later poems entitled "Consider a Poem."[12] In this piece,

Hearst examines the act of writing, the act of creating a sort of universal meaning that is capable of producing a greater understanding of why poetry is written in the first place. This poem stands apart from many of the other texts under consideration here because it is not even abstractly placed. Instead we are asked to focus on the lack of place, to view Hearst as something other than a poet of location. It instead concentrates on language and meaning directly. The poem begins,

> If I speak to explain myself
> And you do not understand,
> It is not that I mumble in tongues
> But that my syllables sometimes invest
> The common meaning with a strange humor. (lines 1–5)

With this concentration on language and meaning, there is also a conscious dismissal of strict regionalism. Hearst's overall poetic output is full of allusions and imagery associated with farm life. However, in "Consider the Poem," Hearst drives home the point that there is more to his poetry than the surface. His meaning is common, which is to say that it is universal and it belongs to all of humanity, but it is tinged with his own "strange humor," his own interpretation based on that which he knows. His words are not imbued with complication; they are simply his own distinct vessels, based on his own experience as a farmer in the Midwest, for carrying a much broader meaning.

As the poem progresses, Hearst makes sure to note that the meaning he carries is not meant to answer any of life's deepest questions or to solve any of our basic problems, a consideration he has made before. Instead he comments, "Sounds / I call words are sometimes so deep / in my throat I must wait to hear them" (lines 10–12). In the end, the finding of meaning happens over time with the help of thought and consideration. Hearst is telling the reader to resist the urge to discount something because meaning doesn't reveal itself immediately, to try holding the words within oneself until they reveal themselves.

He then ends the poem with a modest plea, a plea for poets, for readers, for human beings to work toward a better understanding of each other, to open themselves up to possibility. He writes,

> But let us work shoulder to shoulder
> And you listen and you may be able
> To say honestly, I share poetry for the
> Same reason I drink a glass of water. (lines 13–16)

Hearst is asking for the world to work together to create meaning, to listen to each other, and to strive to understand the value in each and every unique voice. Hearst wants us to use poetry as a means to understand each other better, to understand the vitality within poetry and its potential to form a deeper connection.

Although Hearst shows an obvious desire to avoid being labeled a regional writer for the sake of legitimacy, it was not solely that desire that drove him to a conscious struggle with the category. It was also the strong belief that such restrictions do an injustice to the purpose and compulsion of expression and knowledge. In his poem "Each to Its Own Purpose," Hearst comments on the value of expression in the pursuit of knowledge, and how restricting possibility and potential (in both writing and life) is not only unnatural to the human condition but also beside the point.[13]

He begins the poem by saying, "They said don't use words / like epistemology in a poem" (lines 1–2). Instead, he is told to use words that are "short, fat, beetled-browed / Anglo-Saxon words" (lines 3–4), commenting on what was possibly advice he received from those who believed he should stick to what he knows, to use words "that plant, grow, reap, store" (line 7). That is to say, he should use words that are raw and bare, words that he knows and would be seen to belong within his scope. However, Hearst is not willing to accept that his poetry cannot be more, that it is not allowed abstractions or complications. He then writes,

> Epistemology, they said, in a poem
> Is like using a castrated bull
> to settle your cows.
> But I don't buy that, why castrate,
> Let him do what he was born to do. (lines 9–13)

For Hearst, this restriction on language was unnatural and does not allow for growth or expansion, thus hindering what mankind (especially those in academia) has time and time again desired above many things: knowledge. He ends the poem by saying,

> It is the joy of knowing that makes
> The facts shine, or the Wise Men
> Would never have made their long trip,
> Nor any of us found our way
> Out of the dark wood where
> We were lost. (lines 17–22)

The desire to know, to learn, to absorb as much information as possible has driven humanity to transcend boundaries, to explore, to reach for things beyond our imaginations. Putting restrictions around poetry, around language, and categorizing our world, in many ways, defeats the purpose. It limits the possibilities of creating new meanings in new ways. Instead, Hearst believes we should feel free to explore and transcend mankind's unyielding pursuit for expression and knowledge in the ways that can be. If humanity abandoned these pursuits, that which is amazing might be lost to the world, and humanity itself might be lost to the world.

One popular Hearst poem is "Truth." Though its subject matter is similar to other Hearst poems, unlike many Hearst pieces that adopt a contemplative tone, "Truth" begins with a voice that a midwestern reader would immediately recognize as a curmudgeonly farmer:

> How the devil do I know
> if there are rocks in your field,
> plow it and find out. (lines 1–3)

This opening combines impatience with an understanding that realization comes only through experience. One cannot simply theorize as to whether there are rocks in a field. The only way to know for sure is to do the hard, physical work of plowing. Such a line of rebuke could be delivered by any veteran farmer, and it would most likely be directed at the amateur or less-skilled farmer.

The poem goes on to describe, in language that only someone who knows plowing could use, what might happen in the act of plowing if one strikes a rock:

> ... the point
> shatters at a sudden blow,
> and the tractor jerks sidewise
> and dumps you off the seat— (lines 5–9)

Such language is used to draw distinctions between master and novice, drawing on a lifetime of experience to show all that the listener does not know. Yet this is not what happens in the poem. Rather, the speaker goes on to acknowledge that rocks could be found in his field as well as the listener's:

> but the connection with a thing
> is the only truth that I know of,
> so plow it. (lines 16–18)

In simple terms, Hearst lays out here, at a completely unexpected moment, the heart of his poetic philosophy. The statement "The connection with a thing / is the only truth that I know of" insists that experience is the path to understanding. It is arguably the only path. So, if one wishes to understand, to have access to truth, one must have experience. There is no evading that necessity, nor is there any intellectual shortcut to understanding. In making this claim, Hearst both makes a universal claim and targets a stereotype that working with one's hands stands in opposition to working with one's mind.

In one of the essays of *Time Like a Furrow*, Hearst writes of the land in ways that speak of the meaning that can come only from finding knowledge in the space that one inhabits:

> We used to go out on Sunday mornings with my father. We would survey the crops and livestock, the garden and orchard. It was good to see them thriving to prove that we were good husbandmen. A man who works the land is more than a worker. He puts ground, seed, work, and weather together and creates something new, something that did not exist before.[14]

In the simple act of looking over their property, Hearst sees the effects of his efforts. He and his father are not "good husbandmen" because they work hard. Rather, the land and animals they raise are the measure of their worth. Their farm is productive in the literal sense that it produces meaning, it creates "something that did not exist before." To appreciate such a process requires an intimate knowledge of the land, and in this James Hearst's poetry is intensely midwestern.

Figure 2 visually represents the words most frequently used in the poems of James Hearst, and Figure 3 offers an equivalent visualization of his memoir-based essay collection, *Time Like a Furrow*. It is perhaps not surprising at this point to find that the most common language in his writing is, in fact, common language. Many of the most prominent terms are concrete words one would associate with farm life. In *The Complete Poetry of James Hearst* "morning" and "field" are used 190 times, "land" appears 121 times, and "tree" is referenced in 240 instances. *Time Like a Furrow* also contains frequent uses of "work" (315 mentions), "corn" (204), and "farm" (517), as well as "mother" (314) and "father" (558), not surprising in an autobiographical collection.

Yet, other words in the above figures represent terms whose meaning is less immediate and gesture toward multiple resonances, both a "common" definition and one that is more philosophical. Words like "last" (100 uses), "time" (246), "know" (188), and "just" (80) in Hearst's

Figure 2. Word cloud of language in poems in *The Complete Poetry of James Hearst*.

Figure 3. Word cloud of language from James Hearst's *Time Like a Furrow*.

poems, as well as "like" (257), "just" (153), and "made" (153) in his essays, have everyday usage as well as definitions that could be described as more existential. And that, we would argue, is the significance of James Hearst's poetic work. It is not that he is using the world of the Iowa farm as a metaphor by which to explore existential issues. Rather, a careful poetic consideration of the life of the farm *is* an existential issue.

During an interview conducted in 1972, the interviewer attempted to nail down Hearst's conception of midwestern writing and regionalism in general. Hearst was coy, as perhaps most writers would be in resisting categorization. When asked, "How expansive is the Midwest literary culture?" and "Do you feel regional writers have been looked down on and neglected, relegated beneath other writers because of their preoccupation with a certain area or theme?" Hearst sidestepped both questions.[15] Though he said he could "write a book" about the subject, he also claimed he never thought much about the topic: "Iowa is part of the United States and her writers stick to their last without worrying about a midwest tradition."[16] He also refused to allow himself to feel slighted as a regionalist: "Reputations of writers ebb and flow. But I think regionalism has little to do with it. A poem or story or play has to happen somewhere."[17]

In his simultaneous resistance to and embrace of being a midwestern writer, perhaps Hearst was less an outlier than an exemplar.

Throughout the history of midwestern literature, critics have argued over whether it simply serves up a view of a region for cosmopolitan readers or it represents an authentic alternative to the dominant culture. Tom Lutz, in fact, claims that this tension is not to be resolved; rather, it is a defining characteristic: "These opposed readings, which date from the earliest talk about the genre and continue to sprout new oppositions, find ample textual evidence precisely because literary texts are constructed through oscillating attention to both sides of these fundamental cultural divides."[18] James Hearst's struggle over being a midwestern writer, the evidence of which can be found throughout his writing, may have been one of the things that actually defines him as a midwestern writer. Hearst claims that his experience is, in fact, distinctive and important and, yes, midwestern, but that experience is important not for what it tells us about the Midwest, but for what it tells us about life.

Notes

1. James Hearst, *Time Like a Furrow* (Iowa City: Iowa State Historical Department, 1981), 9.
2. James Hearst, *The Complete Poetry of James Hearst*, ed. Scott Cawelti (Iowa City: The University of Iowa Press, 2001), 6.
3. Jack Hovelson and Ken Fuson, "James Hearst Dies; Hailed as Iowa's 'Poet Laureate,'" *Des Moines Register*, July 28, 1983, 1.
4. James Hearst, *My Shadow Below Me* (Ames, IA: The Iowa State University Press, 1981).
5. Ruth Suckow, foreword to James Hearst, *Country Men* (Muscatine, IA: The Prairie Press, 1937), 9.
6. Hearst, *Complete Poetry*, 31.
7. Hearst, *My Shadow*, 130.
8. Hearst, *Complete Poetry*, 48.
9. Ibid.
10. Hearst, *Complete Poetry*, 480.
11. Ibid., 486.
12. Ibid., 401.
13. Ibid., 273.
14. Hearst, *Time Like a Furrow*, 17.
15. Rochelle Holt, "James Hearst: Voice of the Earth We Stand On," *Sunday Clothes: A Magazine of the Fine Arts* 2, no. 2 (Summer 1973): 40–41.
16. Ibid., 41.
17. Ibid.
18. Tom Lutz, "The Cosmopolitan Midland," *American Periodicals: A Journal of History & Criticism* 15, no. 1 (2005): 81.

Owen Cantrell

"Ya Got Trouble"

River City, Main Street, U.S.A., and Nostalgia in the Imagined Midwest

Nostalgia is a powerful force in the white cultural imagination.[1] Conservative politicians since Ronald Reagan have argued that earlier periods in American history were idyllic and innocent for white Americans. For these politicians, the emergence of race as a political issue, which they imagine was not the case in the prelapsarian past, is cause for returning to that past. Because of the desire to return to an innocent era of race relations, the 1950s and early 1960s are an ideal time for conservative nostalgia.[2] While the Civil Rights movement bore the fruits of centuries of slavery and Jim Crow, it was not until the late 1960s that white Americans became overtly aware of racial discord.

If the 1950s and 1960s are the nostalgic time for white Americans, the nostalgic place is the American small town. Both foci of this essay (Main Street, U.S.A., and *The Music Man*) are white, small-town communities. As this essay explains, these imaginary spaces were a way for white Americans to retreat from racial tension at home and promote American exceptionalism abroad while maintaining innocence based in the idealized community of the rural, midwestern small town. Fredric Jameson argues, the "autonomy of the small town . . . functioned as an allegorical expression for the situation of Eisenhower America in the outside world as a whole—contented with itself, secure in the sense of its radical difference from other populations and cultures, insulated from their vicissitudes and from the flaws in human nature so palpably acted out in their violent and alien histories."[3] The idealized American small town is an island barricaded from historical change. Even its own history is removed from representation to retain its innocence. Ryan Poll adds that "the small town is posited as a stable, secure cultural referent that is not itself subject to history, but rather a geographic imaginary outside of history that becomes the ground of possibility for the nation's history."⁴ Since the small town acts as an innocent origin, its moral force remains unquestioned and can be operationalized into the political unit for organizing white American society. Any desire to return to the nostalgic time and place is to reassert innocent American exceptionalism and exempt it from history. Donald E. Pease argues that "throughout the cold war, American exceptionalism supplied a prerequisite horizon of intelligibility for the understanding of American events."⁵ Representations of the small town are immediately incorporated into a Cold War narrative of innocence in the face of the Soviet threat. While the American small town became a symbol of innocence throughout the twentieth century, its status as supremely innocent is assumed rather than defended. While films like *Pleasantville* offer a gentle rebuke to small-town life, the work of David Lynch, especially in *Twin Peaks* and *Blue Velvet*, presents the seedy underbelly to the innocent small town. However, even when the innocent narrative of the small town is called into question, that innocence remains the fundamental cultural narrative to which critiques are responding.

The universality of the American small town is also often assumed. Poll argues that the image of the American small town "transcends any regional, historical, and material specificity."⁶ However, I argue that many conceptions, especially during the 1950s and 1960s, are midwestern. Though Poll is correct in the American small town seeming to lack region and history, that lack is precisely what makes it appear midwestern. The image of the southern small town (or the New England small town) is distinct from images of the Midwest, largely because they have regional markers. The midwestern small town, as Disney's Main Street, U.S.A., suggests, can stand in for the country, not just a specific region. Main Street, U.S.A, which opened in 1955 at Disneyland, and the musical *The Music Man*, which opened on Broadway in 1957, were both representations of the midwestern small town. Main Street, a mixture of Walt Disney's memories of Marceline, Missouri, and art director Harper Goff's memory of Fort Collins, Colorado, becomes midwestern through this amalgamation; its lack of regional signifiers is what makes it midwestern. As I have suggested elsewhere, the Midwest exists in the popular imagination as a representative, rather than a distinctive, region.⁷ The Midwest is not unique due to its specific regional markers, but because it stands in for "General American," much as the midwestern accent became the standard for television broadcasting pronunciation. Historian Andrew R.L. Cayton argues that the conflation of nation and region in midwestern history led Midwesterners themselves to be unable to "take pride in being the particular rather than the universal."[8] The Midwest is a place where regional specificity is in service to the national imaginary: The region is only as important as it speaks to the nation about itself. Consequently, regional details must be subsumed underneath the understanding of the Midwest as *national* rather than *regional* to maintain its representational status. In this sense, the Midwest is the nation; due to that status, it can never be purely midwestern.

In this essay, I argue that Main Street, U.S.A., and *The Music Man* offer examples of the images white Americans created of the ideal community that drove the course of American empire after World War II. While Main Street presented a backward-looking vision of progress, *The Music Man* demonstrated the difficulties that met an insular community unwilling to engage with the outside world. Both representations used the midwestern small town as the springboard toward a vision of American exceptionalism as inherently innocent. Understanding them as neither innocent nor guilty, but instead historically located, allows us to see how representations of the midwestern small town did important cultural work.

In her 2001 book *The Future of Nostalgia*, Svetlana Boym classifies nostalgia into two primary types: restorative and reflective. Restorative nostalgia "stresses nostos and attempts a transhistorical reconstruction of the lost home," whereas reflective nostalgia is based "in algia, the longing itself and delays the homecoming—wistfully, ironically, desperately."[9] For the purposes of this essay, I focus on restorative nostalgia, which Boym states has two "plots: the return to origins and the conspiracy."[10] The images of the midwestern small town in *The Music Man* and Main Street, U.S.A., are instances of restorative nostalgia. Faced with the reckoning of race relations at home and the ideological threat of communism abroad, arbiters of American culture reasserted a comfortable myth to perpetuate American exceptionalism. Stephen Watts argues that during the 1950s, "for Americans, history became an instrument of cultural nationalism in the struggle with an ideology of rootless radicalism."[11] Returning to the recent past became a way for Americans to weaponize that past at home and abroad.

Main Street, U.S.A., is an example of the "return to origins" plot. Walt Disney was a staunch anticommunist and a cultural Cold Warrior. Watts states that during the 1950s, "with communism offering a dramatic rendering of social reform and historical evolution, Americans felt compelled to mount a countervailing crusade to identify a distinct vision of the good society."[12] Disney's version of American exceptionalism could be defined as "libertarian populism," which "stressed the autonomy of citizens in the face of overweaning authority."[13] Disney turns to the small town as the model society in which these values are rooted at the dawn of the American century. *The Music Man*, however, offers the "conspiracy" plot: Harold Hill convinces River City that their town is being invaded by outside influences that will corrupt the youth even though Hill is that influence. While the film ends with a jubilant coming together, the newly reformed community is based in distrust of outsiders and doubling down on the white nostalgia of the town.

Main Street, U.S.A.

While Walt Disney's Main Street, U.S.A., has been one of the most pervasive cultural representations of "Main Street," Main Street has a significantly longer history in its real and mythical forms. Miles Orvell argues, "the idea of the small town lies at the heart of the American ethos, with a strong and continuing appeal for Americans."[14] Main Street has shaped "both the physical and mental space we inhabit" and is "a global symbol of the United States."[15] Richard Francaviglia argues that Main Street "has come to symbolize a place close to the people, people who have few pretenses and honest aspirations; and because it fuses images of place and time, it also symbolizes their past."[16] Main Street is often posed against another region, such as Wall Street or Washington, DC, to argue for the folksy wisdom that Main Street is purported to have. Furthermore, the emergence of small-town imagery during the Cold War was no coincidence. The small town became a synecdoche for the United States; in part, this is because, as Poll argues, "the small town is a form of U.S. exceptionalism that allows the United States to not recognize its own imperialist history and identity."[17] As the nation expanded its global reach during the Cold War era, Americans still wanted to think the United States a supremely innocent nation. Internationally, the small-town form, which was not representative of the American present, gave the nation innocent origins that grounded foreign expeditions. Domestically, the small town worked as a "popular, pervasive imaginary that imagined a white, bourgeois, heteronormative nation."[18] Not only could the small town keep out the dangerous corrupting influence of foreigners, it could also be imagined as racially white; therefore, the nation's fraught racial history could be forgotten. Instead of noting the violence that beset the nation's main streets throughout the 1950s and especially into the 1960s, the imaginary small town could be a place where white Americans could ignore the real, historical issues of slavery, segregation, and racial violence.

Main Street, U.S.A., opened at Disneyland on July 17, 1955. Built to resemble a turn-of-the-century small-town square, Main Street sat as the entry to the park once visitors got off the train from the parking lot. Karal Marling argues that "the act of entry was a rite of passage telling the stranger to shake off the customs of that other place."[19] While Main Street has several historical and imaginative origins, Walt Disney located Main Street's mythological origins in the small Missouri town of Marceline. Marceline became the imaginative location for Disney's unique brand of sentimental Americanism. During a celebration in Marceline held in his honor, Disney wrote, "To tell the truth more things of importance happened to me in Marceline than have happened since—or are likely to in the future. Things I mean, like seeing my first circus parade, attending my first school, seeing my first motion picture."[20] Main Street, U.S.A., attempted to recreate and locate Disney's values into a hybridized midwestern small town.

Walt Disney's childhood was plagued by transience. His father, Elias, worked as a laborer in various capacities, including on the Columbian Exposition in Chicago. In 1906, Walt and his family moved to Marceline, Missouri, where they lived until 1910.[21] Coming from Chicago, Walt was impressed by the quaint small-town life of Marceline. Stephen Watts notes that Disney's animated shorts from the 1920s through the 1940s often "revolved around rural motifs and small-town adventures."[22] Walt suggested that "the cows, pigs, chickens gave me a big thrill, and perhaps that's the reason we use so many barnyard animals in the Mickey Mouse and Silly Symphony pictures today."[23] Though Walt lived in Marceline for only a few years, the small town left an impression on his imagination despite the fact that the rural America Walt found appealing was quickly disappearing. Watts argues, "in the decades from 1880 to 1920 the United States saw a series of sweeping shifts that took it far in the direction of a modern urban industrial society."[24] By 1900, most people lived in urban centers rather than small towns. The small-town life was vanishing by the time Walt left Marceline. By 1955, the dominance of the small town as the model community was a relic from the past. After World War II, the rise of the suburbs created a very different reality than either urban centers or rural farm life. Even if the suburbs attempted to create a planned version of the small community, the communal sensibility that Americans believed motivated small towns was absent.[25]

For Walt Disney, Main Street, U.S.A., was a vantage point to view the past and the future. In 1959, Disney stated that the primary rationale for Main Street was retrospective: "[M]any of us fondly remember our 'small home town' and its friendly way of life at the turn of the century. To me, this era represents an important part of our heritage, and thus we have endeavored to recapture those years on Main Street, U.S.A., at Disneyland."[26] However, as Disney went on to note, the years of "1890–1910," which Main Street, U.S.A., attempted to replicate, were also "the crossroads of an era," when "the discoveries of the late 19th century were beginning to affect our way of life" from the "electric lamp" to the "'horseless carriage.'"[27] Main Street stands at the dawn of the American century, in all its tantalizing (and affirmational) possibilities. Additionally, Main Street also stands at a crossroads into Disneyland. J.P. Telotte argues, "Main Street appropriately occupies a sort of cusp position in the Disney worlds that signals its various technological functions and frames the many 'narratives' that follow."[28] From Main Street, visitors are directed "into both the past (Frontierland) and the technologically driven future (Tomorrowland), into an idealized America, along with its European roots (Fantasyland), and its unspoken imperialist aspirations."[29] As with the larger operation of the small town in the national imaginary, Main Street, U.S.A., symbolizes the progression of the American way of life around the globe. In other words, it's not simply regressive in its idealization of the past; instead, it's progressive by fitting Main Street into a larger national and global narrative of American exceptionalism.

The spatial organization of Main Street, U.S.A., along with Disney's unique aesthetic imagination, is a part of its continued appeal. As critics, and Disney himself, have noted, Main Street is not intended to be realistic. Though Disney used Marceline and Fort Collins, Colorado, as models for Main Street, the park is not a duplication of a real place. Instead, as I discussed in the introduction, Main Street, U.S.A., suggests the idyllic American small town without replicating anything distinctly regional. The imaginary nature of the attraction begins with the size of Main Street: the buildings are made in 5/8 scale. Disney's explanation was that the scale worked to make "the street a toy" since "the imagination can play more freely with a toy."[30] Additionally, visitors to the park who remembered their own Main Streets may "like to think their world is somehow more grown up than Papa's was."[31] This scale made the street a toy by making it "seemingly more approachable or less formidable."[32] Instead of imposing buildings such as Sleeping Beauty's castle, designed to inspire awe, Main Street felt quaint so it could be manipulated by the spectator. Visitors to the park needed to "play" with Main Street so they could move it in their memories and reframe it into different narratives. This is also how visitors could view their world as "more grown up than Papa's was." The small-town past is wonderful in its quaint simplicity; however, even in Disney's narrative, it is but part of a larger story. Instead of the small town being the conclusion of Disney's narrative, it is the beginning. If we view history as a ceaseless progression of building upon the previous generation, it makes sense that Main Street would have to be small enough that you can *literally* build upon its small size into the ever-grander future.

The Music Man

If Main Street, U.S.A., acted to create an origin for the nation to build upon, the town of River City in *The Music Man* showed the small town at odds with the hostile outside world. After four years of success on Broadway, the film version of *The Music Man* came to theaters in 1962. As Leanne Wood notes, the rollout of the film by Warner Brothers was accompanied by a deluge of nostalgic patriotism: marching bands, barbershop quartets, and feelings of "wholesomeness, morality, and robust Americanism."[33] The film was applauded by several critics for its hearty American values, with one critic arguing that *The Music Man* was a "truer picture of our country than is the case with most movies sent abroad."[34]

Regardless of the musical's quality, an important aspect of *The Music Man*'s appeal was its nostalgic look back on the American small town at the turn of the twentieth century, which came at an opportune time in U.S. history. Domestically, the Civil Rights movement questioned the peaceful assumptions that white Americans held of themselves and their past. The country was diverse and those diverse bodies were demanding full representation and citizenship. *West Side Story* premiered the same year as *The Music Man*. Carol Oja notes that "*The Music Man* became an antidote to *West Side Story*—at once a wistful escape from the social and political perils of the present and a comforting reassertion of old-fashioned musical comedy."[35] While *West Side Story* presented the prototypical love story as taking place between a diverse group in an urban setting, *The Music Man* was a retreat back into an all-white rural community, awash with innocent naiveté rather than the streetwise sensibility of *West Side Story*.

Much of the critical work on *The Music Man* oscillates around the question of whether the musical is critical of its central characters in the town of River City, Iowa. Scott Miller argues that, despite the embrace of the musical for its sentimental values, *The Music Man* is actually "the story of a con man in 1912 Iowa who seduces an innocent young woman merely to keep her from mucking up his plan to swindle the honest, hardworking people of a small midwestern town, including the young woman's troubled little brother, who's mourning the premature death of his father."[36] Even the ending of the musical, in which the con man Harold Hill joins with the young woman Marian to march a boy's band down Main Street, is unconvincing as a happy ending. Miller points out that "as in most musicals, Harold Hill, the outsider, must either be assimilated into the community or be removed from it."[37] While he has been assimilated into the town by the musical's conclusion, it seems unlikely that Harold Hill would find conformity in the community of River City exciting or lasting enough for his restless commercial spirit.

Meredith Willson, who wrote and composed *The Music Man*, also seems to have been ambivalent about the people of River City. Wood points out that "the musical's caricatures and satire are so ubiquitous, in fact, that Willson initially hesitated to link the fictional River City with his hometown [Mason City, Iowa] because he worried that real Iowans would take offense."[38] However, the reception of the musical was so positive that "soon Willson was describing *The Music Man* as a 'rosy-colored look over his shoulder at the people and places of his small-town childhood.'"[39] In *"But He Doesn't Know the Territory,"* Willson's telling of the creation and debut of *The Music Man*, he states that despite his criticism of "Iowa stubborn," "Iowa contrary," and "Iowa arrogance," the musical attempts to "pay tribute to his home state."[40] Willson's River City in *The Music Man* depicted a way of life that was also quickly fading. As Miller points out, "*The Music Man* couldn't have happened in any other time frame. Traveling salesmen, as depicted in the musical's first number 'He Doesn't Know the Territory,' were struggling by 1912."[41] Furthermore, marching music, popular in 1912, was "mostly due to Hill's own alleged idol: John Philip Sousa."[42] Traveling salesmen and marching bands create a specific historical framework of the recent past through which to view the musical's American universalism. By 1962, this was a way of life (and included specific cultural references) that existed only in memory.

Despite the patina of nostalgia surrounding *The Music Man*, the film is not without its critique of River City. The townspeople are, as Raymond Knapp writes, "lethargic, dysfunctional, and isolationist."[43] When Harold Hill gets off the train in River City, he is greeted by the townspeople with the song "Iowa Stubborn." In "Iowa Stubborn," the townspeople represent the paradox of their Hawkeye nature: They are both cold to others and friendly beyond compare.[44] Hill himself encounters this when he tries to charm the first few townspeople he meets, all of whom rebuff his attempts at flattery. While "Iowa Stubborn" is Hill listening to the townspeople, Hill's number "Ya Got Trouble" is about the townspeople listening to Hill.[45] The two songs are interesting companion pieces. "Ya Got Trouble" is so effective because Hill tells the townspeople about themselves and their values; he creates them in the image of how they (and he) want them to be. Sitting in the town square and desperate to stir up trouble, Hill asks his friend Washburn for some suggestions of popular topics. He asks him, "What can I use? What's new around here?" and "What do you talk about?"[46] Hill is trying to "create" some trouble to make his boys' band the solution to the town's perceived ailment.

In "Ya Got Trouble," Hill puts on a virtuoso performance that stirs up the townspeople's fears of outside influence corrupting their youth. While Hill pins this influence to the new pool table, the ultimate warning of the song is oriented towards the outsider. His argument that pool will lead to stirring up the "jungle animal instinct" and "ragtime" music cannot help but be racially encoded language about the threats of the racial Other to the all-white River City.[47] The racial Other, in *The Music Man*, is generally signified by its absence and its threat. Oja points out that "in the limited literature about *The Music Man*, race never enters the discussion, as can be the case with art or entertainment coded as white."[48] Race is not directly present in *The Music Man*, since race is not seen to exist when it is white. Orvell adds that, when a small town is represented in popular culture, it is usually pitted against the city. In this dialectic, "the small town is white and the city is nonwhite."[49] The threatening influences Hill points out are coded as distinctly nonwhite since they are not coded as part of the small town—and therefore white.

Shortly after "Ya Got Trouble," we see an additional example of threatening outsiders and their neutralization by the town. Tommy is a teenager courting the mayor's daughter. He is thought of as a troublemaker by the mayor because he belongs to the "Lithuanians south of town" and becomes marked as an outsider by the townspeople. The mayor threatens Tommy with expulsion from the town as well as potential violence. Violence, indirectly or implied, lurks behind all encounters with the racial Other. Hill's genius in "Ya Got Trouble" is that he links the racial Other to the undue influence that may *eventually* impact their young men. Although this subtext is only partially visible, the assumed whiteness of River City is the point; the imagined threat of outside influences becomes coded in racial language to maintain River City's "purity."

Hill uses the associational logic of conspiracy throughout his pitch to the people of River City. His odd collection of American iconography ("Remember the Maine, the Plymouth Rock, and the golden rule") at the end of "Ya Got Trouble" is a prime example.[50] Because of this logic, Hill does not have to be believed by the townspeople to be convincing to them. Indeed, townspeople are suspicious of Hill from the very beginning. His routine is transparent to them as being full of the "gift of blarney" as Mrs. Paroo states.[51] Hill's con is ultimately successful because Marian buys into it. Marian is suspicious and quickly learns Hill is a fraud, but she is convinced by the results of Hill's chicanery. Truth is not the goal for the townspeople, Marian, or even the musical itself; instead, Hill's promise of happiness by keeping out the external Other satisfies their conspiratorial logic of better times ahead.

Conspiratorial logic also applies to the central unsolved mystery of the musical: the relationship between Marian and Mr. Monroe. Monroe was the town's primary benefactor who owned the library. After his death, Monroe left the building to the town, but the books to Marian. Thus, the townspeople cannot kick Marian out of the library, despite their dislike of her "dirty, tasteless" books, since the books belong to her.[52] Hill points out several times in the musical what he thinks Marian's relationship with Monroe might have been. When Hill visits Marian at the library before "Marian the Librarian," he alleges that he understands her relationship with Monroe, especially since she must have been "very young."[53] Later, Hill rebuffs the rumors of his fraudulent nature by comparing rumors about himself to rumors about Marian and Monroe as both based in "jealousy" rather than reality.[54]

Monroe and Marian had a significant relationship; he is one of two characters whose death looms over the musical, along with Mr. Paroo. However, I argue that it makes sense that Marian and Monroe had a romantic relationship, which resulted in little Winthrop. The age discrepancy between Marian and Winthrop (she is twenty-six years old and he is, at most, eight) seems odd, especially given the age of Mrs. Paroo (Marian's mother) and childbearing practices in 1912. Marian's status as the "sadder but wiser girl" is double: she is sadder since she has lost the cultured man she desired (Monroe) and because she has been left as a single, unwed mother who must pretend her child is her brother.[55] While none of this is text in the musical itself, Hill does hit on the "sadder but wiser girl" motif in relation to Marian almost immediately. Furthermore, he immediately begins affiliating himself with Monroe. At the end of "Ya Got Trouble," Hill points his finger to the sky in mimicry of Monroe's statue standing behind him.[56] He becomes a substitute (town) father for Winthrop and a romantic replacement for Marian.

Much as Marian breaks out of her shell to reengage with the world, the townspeople of River City are shaken out of their "summer doldrums" to become less isolationist.[57] Knapp points out that the town's relationship with the outside world in many ways mirrored the state of 1950s America. At the end of World War II, "when America emerged fully as one of two world powers," it was necessary for the country to be "a single nation ready to engage as such with the rest of the outside world."[58] The final image of the film, in which Hill's dim boys' band is transformed by community feeling into a rousing marching band, is one of America on the march. This image, Knapp argues, brings together the "rather terrifying joy of conformity and complete regimentation."[59] The audience joins in the march, in which "the moment of joining, at least, is an exhilarating one."[60] America could march onto the world stage after World War II through denying the reality of racial conflict at home and keeping conspiratorial thinking alive. Since we know the march from *The Music Man* in 1912 leads to two World Wars and the emergence of the United States as a global superpower, the final image poses a triumphant return to American nationalism, if one does not examine too closely the Other(s) kept out of that image.

Conclusion

The midwestern small town holds a unique ideological space in American exceptionalism. Because of the innocence attributed to this imaginary space of the small town, Americans can claim purity when making judgements in policy or politics. In other words, the ahistorical small town permits ahistorical nostalgia directed toward future policies. Main Street, U.S.A., and *The Music Man* teach us that this conception is not unique to our own period. Indeed, the 1950s, which is often viewed as a golden era for conservatives, looked back to the past for its own prelapsarian origin. However, despite the claims of those representing those spaces in the 1950s, they were always rife with nostalgia, as well. For Main Street, U.S.A., the future orientation of the space made it a site of origin, but not a site to which to return in perpetuity. In *The Music Man*, the conspiratorial logic of Harold Hill makes keeping out the racialized Other central to America being "on the march" once again.

Pease argues that American exceptionalism, which "had regulated U.S. citizens' relationship to the political order for the preceding half century," began to break down in the twenty-first century.[61] With rapid transformation in the labor force, global markets, and demographics, the United States found its exceptional status uncertain. Instead of looking toward the future, as perhaps Walt Disney may have suggested, many white Americans began to look toward the past for a sense of importance. In our historical moment, white nostalgia calls to mind the 2016 election of Donald Trump. Ronald Brownstein argued in *The Atlantic* that the "again" part of Trump's campaign slogan of "Make America Great Again" is the key term.[62] The sense of loss that many white Americans feel, including many white Midwesterners, was central to Trump's appeal.

The fact that Trump's campaign was also based on keeping out racial Others and asserting American exceptionalism should be no surprise; it's a story we've seen played out continually in American history, especially in cultural representations of the Midwest. The Midwest has long been a blank slate upon which larger cultural movements are written. Orvell argues that Main Street often functions as "both a *place* and an *idea*."[63] Throughout much of its history, the Midwest has been both, as well. For some critics, the answer to this dilemma is to reassert the historical specificity of the real, live Midwest. However, I argue that investigating these ideological spaces and the uses they are put to can tell us how the Midwest was used, and continues to be used, as an ahistorical paradise designed for national interests. Nostalgia cannot be the only way to represent the Midwest. Making "America great" does not have to imply an "again," but instead can become a prospective goal. On the eve of the 2004 election, Bruce Springsteen wrote that "the country we carry in our hearts is waiting."[64] The country of the Midwest, as scholars of the Midwest know it, is a land often left undiscovered in popular representation. Carrying forward the *idea* and the *place* of the Midwest to combat ahistorical nostalgia is important now more than ever.

Notes

1. This trend has a long academic history. The most comprehensive primer to white nostalgia is Stephanie Koontz, *The Way We Never Were: American Families and the Nostalgia Trap* (New York: Basic Books, 1993).
2. In a 2013 poll published by *The Economist*, Republicans preferred the "morally uncomplicated" period of the 1950s (as well as the Reagan-dominated 1980s) as an ideal time in American history. "We Still Like Ike," *The Economist*, last modified August 20, 2013, http://www.economist.com/blogs/graphicdetail/2013/08/daily-chart-12.

3. Fredric Jameson, *Postmodernism, or, The Cultural Logic of Late Capitalism* (Durham, NC: Duke University Press, 1992), 280.
4. Ryan Poll, *Main Street and Empire: The Fictional Small Town in the Age of Globalization* (New Brunswick, NJ: Rutgers University Press, 2012), 3.
5. Donald E. Pease, *The New American Exceptionalism*, (Minneapolis, MN: University of Minnesota Press, 2009), 7.
6. Poll, *Main Street*, 8.
7. Owen Cantrell, "'It's Not Polite to Talk About Yourself': Regional Identity and Erasure in the Midwest from F. Scott Fitzgerald to *Mad Men*," *MidAmerica* 41 (2014): 39.
8. Andrew R. L. Cayton, "The Anti-region: Place and Identity in the History of the American Middle West," in *The American Midwest: Essays on Regional History*, Andrew R.L. Cayton and Susan E. Gray, eds. (Bloomington, IN: Indiana University Press, 2001), 158.
9. Svetlana Boym, *The Future of Nostalgia* (New York: Basic Books, 2001), xvii.
10. Ibid., xviii.
11. Stephen Watts, *Walt Disney and the American Way of Life* (Columbia, MO: University of Missouri Press, 2001), 289.
12. Ibid., 287.
13. Ibid., 288.
14. Miles Orvell, *The Death and Life of Main Street: Small Towns in American Memory, Space, and Community* (Durham, NC: University of North Carolina Press, 2014), ix.
15. Ibid., 1.
16. Richard Francaviglia, *Main Street Revisited: Time, Space, and Image Building in Small-Town America* (Iowa City, IA: University of Iowa Press, 1996), xviii.
17. Poll, *Main Street*, 23.
18. Ibid., 116–17.
19. Karal Marling, *Designing Disney's Theme Parks: The Architecture of Reassurance* (Paris: Flammarion, 1998), 96.
20. Walt Disney, "The Marceline I Knew," The Walt Disney Hometown Museum, last modified on March 2, 2015, https://www.waltdisneymuseum.org/the-marceline-i-knew-by-walt-disney/.
21. Watts, *Walt Disney*, 5.
22. Ibid.
23. Disney, "The Marceline I Knew."
24. Watts, *Walt Disney*, 6.
25. This understanding of the development of the suburbs is indebted to Kenneth T. Jackson, *Crabgrass Frontier* (Oxford: Oxford University Press, 1985).
26. Watts, *Walt Disney*, 22.
27. Ibid.

28. J.P. Telotte, *The Mouse Machine: Disney and Technology* (Chicago: University of Illinois Press, 2008), 12.
29. Ibid.
30. Quoted in Marling, *Designing Disney's Theme Parks*, 81.
31. Ibid.
32. Francaviglia, *Main Street Revisited*, 146.
33. Leanne Wood, "'Persuasive Americanism'? The Reactionary Promotion and Reception of Warner Bros.' The Music Man (1962)," *American Music* 31, no. 4 (2013): 485.
34. Ibid., 477.
35. Carol J. Oja, "*West Side Story* and *The Music Man*: Whiteness, Immigration, and Race in the US During the Late 1950s," *Studies in Musical Theatre* 3, no. 1 (2009): 16.
36. Scott Miller, *Deconstructing Harold Hill: An Insider's Guide to Musical Theatre* (Portsmouth, NH: Heinemann, 1999), 73.
37. Ibid., 80.
38. Wood, "'Persuasive Americanism,'" 479.
39. Ibid.
40. Meredith Willson, *"But He Doesn't Know the Territory"* (Minneapolis: Minnesota University Press, 1959), 183–84.
41. Miller, *Deconstructing Harold Hill*, 76.
42. Ibid.
43. Raymond Knapp, *The American Musical and the Formation of National Identity* (Princeton, NJ: Princeton University Press, 2006), 147.
44. "Iowa Stubborn," written by Meredith Willson, *The Music Man*, directed by Morton DaCosta (1962; Burbank, CA: Warner Home Video, 2011), *Amazon Prime*.
45. "Ya Got Trouble," written by Meredith Willson, *The Music Man*, directed by Morton DaCosta (1962; Burbank, CA: Warner Home Video, 2011), *Amazon Prime*.
46. *The Music Man*, directed by Morton DaCosta (1962; Burbank, CA: Warner Home Video, 2011), *Amazon Prime*.
47. "Ya Got Trouble."
48. Oja, "*West Side Story*," 19.
49. Orvell, *Death and Life*, 7.
50. "Ya Got Trouble."
51. *The Music Man*.
52. Ibid.
53. Ibid.
54. Ibid.
55. "Sadder but Wiser Girl" is Hill's song detailing his ideal woman. It is contrasted with Marian's "My White Knight," which utilizes a similar melody.
56. Ibid.

57. Knapp, *American Musical*, 146–47.
58. Ibid., 146.
59. Ibid., 151.
60. Ibid.
61. Pease, *New American Exceptionalism*, 1.
62. Ronald Brownstein, "Trump's Rhetoric of White Nostalgia," *The Atlantic*, June 2, 2016.
63. Orvell, *Death and Life*, 3.
64. Bruce Springsteen, "Chords for Change," *New York Times*, August 5, 2004.

Wayne Anderson	"Beautiful Land of Make-Believe"
	Rural Iowa in 1930s Hollywood

The Farmer in the Dell, a 1936 novel by Iowa-born writer Phil Stong, features a scene in which the heads of a fictional film studio hold a meeting to decide how best to develop the career of a promising young actress. The group quickly settles on a plan to order "a script about a poor immigrant girl among the homespuns of Iowa, naturalizing herself, making her place in the community, and so on." With the addition of a "wholesome" leading man and "all the dirt baloney," they recognize the makings of a hit.[1] This scene is fictional, but it provides evidence not only of Hollywood's oftentimes condescending attitude toward rural people, but also of the actual popularity films featuring Iowa settings and characters enjoyed during the Great Depression.

Between 1930 and 1939 no fewer than twelve feature films were either set in Iowa or prominently featured characters from Iowa. The native Iowans in these films typically possess a natural connection to the land, a store of common-sense wisdom, and a healthy skepticism of big-city ways. These traits are abundantly present in the rural characters of the two most successful Iowa films, *State Fair* and *The Stranger's Return*, both released in 1933. These films were based on novels by Phil Stong, and they gained attention just as artist Grant Wood, another native son of Iowa, was making a national name for himself with paintings such as the iconic *American Gothic* (1930). Stong and Wood typically depicted Iowa as a rustic, lush land of plenty populated by hard-working farmers, and that comforting image helped spark a coast-to-coast interest in the rural Midwest. For example, newspaper headlines in 1933 touted a nationwide search by Hollywood producer Irving Thalberg for what was described as a "Corn Fed Iowa Venus" to be his next "It" girl, while New York's high society held a farm-themed charity ball in 1934, complete with live barnyard animals and a corn husking contest.[2] This attention occurred during a distressing period that has been characterized by historians as one in which the "folksy comedy [film genre] ... was the popular favorite," and the "symbols of national community [such as nostalgic cinema] ... offered individual Americans security and a sense of belonging to a greater whole."[3] This sense of order and certainty felt by 1930s movie-goers, however, only placed a temporary veil over the economic difficulties that remained when they returned from the theater. Likewise, many of the executives, directors, writers, and movie stars involved in producing these comforting films were also experiencing tumultuous times in their personal lives or careers, so while the films were celebrating the pastoral myth, they were obscuring the more difficult reality that often existed behind and beyond the screen.

Imaginary Iowa's Fluctuating Reputation

Even though rural Iowa achieved its greatest popularity among film executives and moviegoers during the 1930s, the state had previously been used as a primary setting for at least four silent films: *The Strange Woman* (1918), *Get-Rich-Quick Wallingford* (1921), *Watch Your Step* (1922), and *That French Lady* (remake of *The Strange Woman*, 1924).[4] Each of these films features a plot in which circumstances bring an outsider (whether it is a Frenchwoman, a con-man, or a man running from the law) to Iowa, and in every case the protagonists' troubles are lifted, prompting them to stay and build happier lives. Despite these positive portrayals of rural life on the silent screen, there were also numerous films during the 1920s that called midwestern small-town life into question. Largely inspired by the publication of Sinclair Lewis's Minnesota-set 1920 novel *Main Street*, they expose the lack of cultural, educational, and economic opportunities in rural Iowa. *Stardust* (1921), *Night Life of New York* (1925), *A Slave of Fashion* (1925), and *High Society Blues* (1930) all depict Iowans who journey to New York City either to escape a life of boredom or to pursue dreams that are unattainable in their home state.[5] Even though these films often critique small-town and city dwellers rather than farmers, the broader implication is that the Midwest lags behind other, more vibrant, regions of the United States.[6]

The onset of the Great Depression, however, brought about a reassessment of the Midwest as many Americans wondered whether the nation had moved too quickly away from its agrarian roots. Cultural geographer James Shortridge observes that despite Depression hardships, the Midwest "was once again feeling good about itself" as its farms and small towns were "seen as havens for body and soul."[7] Accordingly, Iowa-set films of the 1930s returned to the positive rural themes of the earliest Iowa silents, particularly in King Vidor's *The Stranger's Return*, in which a struggling young woman from New York City journeys to her grandfather's farm in Iowa and finally finds her true place in the world, remarking, "When I came here I thought ... I was returning to where I belonged."[8] Despite the occasionally violent protests in Iowa over farm foreclosures and plummeting commodity prices that resulted in front-page headlines across the nation, audiences bought into fictional representations that showed the state as being virtually trouble-free. This preference for an imaginary Iowa may be due to the state's rural character and geographical "middleness," as those are two factors that led Dorothy Schwieder, Iowa's premier historian, to describe the state as "the [nation's] heart itself, pulsating quietly, slowly, and evenly."[9]

Smoothing Over Rough Edges

The success of *The Stranger's Return*, however, is negligible when compared to *State Fair*, the 1933 film that sparked Hollywood's renewed interest in Iowa films. An adaptation of Phil Stong's first novel, which was published in May 1932, it follows the Frakes, a farm family of four from southeastern Iowa, as they have a series of adventures during their week at the Iowa State Fair. Abel, the wise patriarch, prepares his prize boar Blue Boy for a run at a blue ribbon, while his wife Melissa hopes that her pickles and mincemeat are looked upon favorably by the judges. Meanwhile their two children, Wayne and Margy, both in their late teens, pursue romantic relationships with more experienced partners from the city. The film owes a great deal of its success to the novel's notoriety, as it was serialized in a number of prominent newspapers, appeared on bestseller lists in many major cities, was a featured selection of the Literary Guild, and was nominated alongside John Dos Passos's *1919* and Willa Cather's *Shadows on the Rock* for the inaugural *Prix Femina Americain* award.[10]

The film version of *State Fair* was directed by the widely admired Henry King, who had already helmed more than sixty films, and starred Will Rogers and Janet Gaynor, two of Hollywood's top five box office draws during the period.[11] Following a successful premiere at New York's Radio City Music Hall on January 26, 1933, *State Fair* went on to garner an Academy Award nomination for Best Picture (and another for Best Adapted Writing), was named one of the Ten Best Films of the Year by the National Board of Review, and for more than a decade after its release was still ranked among the top fifty grossing films of all time.[12] Stong rightfully gave much of the credit for the film's success to King, who initially recommended the novel to the studio and fought for Rogers to be cast in the lead role.[13] The film was far from a sure thing, however, as the Fox studio had suffered from a string of disappointing releases that year, contributing to dangerously low stock prices that had caused the company's shares to lose 83 percent of their value since the 1929 crash.[14] The turmoil within the studio made King's pitch difficult, especially since his previous film, *The Woman in Room 13* (1932), was unsuccessful, as were the recent star vehicles for both Rogers and Gaynor.[15] Fox's chief of production Winfield Sheehan and producer Sol Wurtzel eventually decided the project had a chance to become a much-needed hit, so they gave it a green light with full studio support.[16] Joining Rogers and Gaynor (who played his daughter) were Louise Dresser as Rogers's wife, Norman Foster as Rogers's son, Sally Eilers as Foster's love interest, and Lew Ayres as a Des Moines–based reporter who falls for Gaynor.

The widespread popularity of Rogers and Gaynor had a great deal to do with the film's ultimate success. Rogers, a fifty-four-year-old Oklahoman who was one-quarter Cherokee, was beloved around the world for the folksy charm and political wit he exuded on screen, in his radio show, and in a widely syndicated newspaper column. Stong was among the millions who held Rogers in high esteem, as he once wrote to King, "I don't believe *anything* I read in the newspapers any more, except, occasionally, Will Rogers."[17] Meanwhile, the twenty-seven-year-old Gaynor had already won a Best Actress Academy Award and had successfully made the transition from silents to talkies. Her wholesome on-screen persona, however, belied a complicated personal life that ultimately saw her marry three different men, all of whom were presumed to have been homosexual, while she became involved in separate romantic relationships with two fellow actresses, Margaret Lindsay and Mary Martin.[18] Therefore, the simple small-town girl roles she played, such as Margy Frake in *State Fair*, helped her maintain her image and widespread popularity despite a personal life that could have offended many moviegoers of the time.

While the romantic pursuits of Gaynor and most other stars remained largely unknown to the movie-going public, the Motion Picture Producers and Distributors of America (MPPDA) existed to ensure that the industry's on-screen product adhered to expected moral principles. Colonel Jason Joy, head of the MPPDA's Studio Relations Committee, was among the first to comment on the proposed script of *State Fair* in June 1932. Writing to Fox's Winfield Sheehan, Joy took the opportunity to expound on the recent history of rural literature and film, and of the potential for *State Fair* to shift the paradigm:

> I think you have a magnificent opportunity to tell a new and interesting story of American small-town and farm-life which will be refreshingly different from the usual stories of this character. For years ... novels and pictures of farm life have either poked fun at the farmers for their lack of culture, or they have depicted the latter as repressed creatures choking with Freudian complexes of one sort or another. My guess is that one reason for the great success of this novel is that it puts a new light on the subject and admits that people can be happy and normal in such an atmosphere ... The gusto of farm life, simple pleasures, normal humans—all of these things should be highly acceptable at this time.[19]

Joy is presumably referring to the influence of the Great Depression on audience viewing habits in his qualifier "at this time," which is further indication that studios realized the psychological tonic that "simple" rural films could provide. *State Fair* went on to set a strong example for the rural pictures that followed by doing excellent business and receiving mostly positive reviews from film critics. *New York Times* reviewer Mordaunt Hall praised Will Rogers and called the film "a homey tale, with many an intriguing bit."[20] Eugene Burr, of *The Billboard* magazine, thoroughly enjoyed the tale of "bucolic pleasure and pain ... [which] is so simply and touchingly told, so beautifully played by the name-studded cast, that even a city crowd (unused to hawgs [sic] and pickle tasting and the glories of the midway) should find itself spellbound."[21] Likewise, the film earned plaudits from trade magazine *Variety* for its "charm of naturalness and virtue of sincerity" and from William Randolph Hearst's *New York American*, which hailed it for being as "rich as the soil itself and 'homely' as the heart of the hinterlands."[22]

One notable exception to those who enjoyed the film was Dwight MacDonald, a New York–based social critic, who lambasted the film for ignoring what was really happening in rural Iowa. He complained,

> At a time when the American farmer is faced with ruin, when the whole Midwest is seething with bitterness and economic discontent, a movie like *State Fair* is an insulting 'let them eat cake' gesture ... There was no excuse for the cheerfully trivial tone of the whole thing, the studied avoidance of anything more serious in the life of the farmer than whether his hog will win the state championship ... What a chance for a realistic, documentary film of American farm life in these times! And Hollywood gives us a movie about as earthy as the gingham overalls in a musical comedy number ... The whole fabric was rotten with evasion of reality.[23]

Some observers within Iowa, however, believed the film could gain positive attention for the Iowa farmers suffering through the Depression. One such commentator was *Des Moines Register* columnist Harlan Miller, who gushed over the film, calling it "one of the most magnificent, exquisite, pictures I have ever seen. I think it will seem so to all Iowans and to those who love Iowa. It is the most eloquent argument that the farmer could offer to those eastern critics who think he asks too much."[24] Nevertheless MacDonald's claim has some merit because the novel's ending had been changed to eliminate its one major social critique, which posited that the rural/urban divide is typically too wide for people on either side of it to be truly happy on the other. Instead the film ends with farm girl Margy and Des Moines reporter Pat embracing in a rainstorm after he has desperately driven from the city to reunite with her.

The ending is emblematic of the film industry's tendency to smooth over as many incongruous rough edges as possible. The change came at the behest of the MPPDA's Jason Joy, who described the characters' relationship as a pairing between "farm life at its best which [Margy] represents, and the city life which [Pat] represents."[25] The happy conclusion to *State Fair* suggested to Depression-era audiences that the interests of country and city could come together, given the right circumstances, and that the resolution did not always have to play out on the city characters' terms. Therefore, in this particular case, the happy ending, rather than obscuring the plight of real-life farmers, may have inadvertently offered hopeful encouragement to citizens in the nation's midsection who at the time were wrestling with rural/urban tensions that were being stoked by occasionally violent clashes over government-mandated animal testing, low commodity prices, and farm foreclosures.

Jumping on the Rural Bandwagon

Success in Hollywood often breeds imitators, so almost immediately after *State Fair*'s premiere other movie studios were aiming to follow in its footsteps. In fact, just one week after *State Fair* opened, the *New York Times* reported that Fox had already ordered another "farm yarn" because "the curse seems to be off rural pictures." The article explained, "The acclaim given Phil Stong's novel on the screen convinced [Fox's chief of production] that, whatever prejudices existed in the past, good rural stories will be accepted today."[26] As a result, many members of the cast and crew soon found themselves working on other rural films set in various pastoral locations. Henry King helmed rural films in each of the three following years, including *Carolina* (1934), which is based on a play by *State Fair* co-screenwriter Paul Green and stars Janet Gaynor as a northern farm girl helping to restore the fortunes of a southern plantation family. Will Rogers's career, meanwhile, was reinvigorated by *State Fair*, and his next role was the lead in John Ford's *Doctor Bull* (1933), in which he played a country doctor working to stem a typhoid outbreak in rural Connecticut. Rogers went on to star in nine additional rural films before his untimely death in an airplane crash in 1935.

Phil Stong's Hollywood fortunes were also given a boost by *State Fair*'s success, and he was immediately persuaded to complete his next novel, *Stranger's Return*. Writing to his college roommate Harvey Davis in June 1933, Stong explains that MGM, which had outbid Fox for the rights to the novel, "got anxious to put it out ... They're in a stew about it—I suppose they'll shove it right along."[27] Stong was grateful for the influx of money, but the sale also meant he had to return to southern California to assist with the screenplay, which was a distressing thought for him.[28] He had not enjoyed his first taste of Hollywood while working on *State Fair*, and he expressed his disdain for the place near the end of that experience:

> I've been out in this abhorrent place fighting with the world's choicest collection of subnormal nincompoops for three months ... This is a perfectly beastly little town—all plaster and platinum blondes and trees that look like they had been made in Japan and flowers that seem very improbable indeed. It is just so damned silly and smug and show-offish that by and by you get an irresistible impulse to step on it and squash it.[29]

But the offer of money, along with protective impulses toward his story, lured him back for a second time, and this time he brought along his novelist wife, Virginia Swain. "I like to come out and see that my books get a square shake from the louses," he wrote to Davis.[30]

The "louses" of which Stong spoke were studio executives and middlemen, rather than the respected directors with whom he worked on his first two films. He had complimented Henry King after the completion of *State Fair*, and he similarly characterized King Vidor as "a swell director" after his second Hollywood experience.[31] The Texas-born Vidor was, by that point, a three-time Academy Award nominee for Best Director and, according to a 1933 essay by Dwight MacDonald, he was "once the brightest of Hollywood's bright young directors," but of late he had simply been "grinding out movies with sausage-machine regularity."[32] As one of Hollywood's "resident intellectuals," Vidor often chafed at the constraints of the Hollywood studio system. "It was his hard luck," his biographers explain, "to work the studio system when it was most rigidly an assembly line."[33] They also note that when Vidor was making *The Stranger's Return* in the early- to mid-1930s, it was a "particularly frenzied era in his private life."[34] Just prior to the film's on-location shoot near Chino, the film's leading lady, Miriam Hopkins, had abruptly ended an affair with him. Greatly upset, he commuted to Los Angeles on weekends during filming to undergo psychotherapy, in part because he responded to the breakup by sawing the legs off Hopkins's couch. He remembered, "That's one of the only crazy things I ever did. She didn't think it was funny."[35]

Despite his fragile emotional state at the time, Vidor was a very able director and, like Henry King, felt a kinship with Stong's source material. He told an interviewer in 1971, "The farm has always been my favorite atmosphere. It's proven by the fact that I now live on one. I used to be kidded many times about having a plow in every picture turning over the earth ... It meant a new cycle of life, a new generation going on ... [It] always had a big meaning for me."[36] With this predisposition to the material, it is little surprise that Vidor admired Stong's novel because "[the writer] knew what he was writing about. He had a feeling for the people and atmosphere and characters [of] ... the middle west." Furthermore, Vidor also felt an artistic connection to the setting of Stong's novel. "I was very interested in Grant Wood," he remembered. "I own a couple of Grant Wood paintings and [the novel is set in] Grant Wood country and the people are somewhat Grant Wood types."[37]

Aside from Miriam Hopkins, who plays East Coast–born Louise Storr (the titular "stranger"), the rest of the cast includes believable "Grant Wood types" to fill the Iowan roles. Lionel Barrymore plays Grandpa Storr (even though he was reportedly battling crippling arthritis and a resulting morphine addiction[38]), Beulah Bondi is the conniving in-law Beatrice, Franchot Tone is handsome neighboring farmer Guy, and Stuart Erwin is Simon, a well-meaning, alcoholic hired hand. While shooting *The Stranger's Return*, the entire cast and crew bonded while staying together at an abandoned country club in the Pomona Valley, an area which was "just about as close to farming as you could get" in southern California, remembered Vidor.[39] The rural location was transformed into Storrhaven, the novel and film's family farm setting, and according to noted Hollywood writer and reporter Rosalind Shaffer, it resembled a "typical Iowa farm" and had "all the cast sighing for and talking about 'back home.'"[40]

This careful attention to place is apparent from the first frames of the film, which capture the essence of the midwestern setting. Shots of farmers pitching hay into the barn's hayloft are intermixed with images of grazing cattle, horses, and pigs, as the entire farmyard is brought to life on the screen. These images of agricultural bounty provide the kind of reassurance audiences would have been seeking for their own, and their country's, future. Thus it is notable that in one of the film's relatively few lines of dialogue that does not appear in the novel, Louise Storr turns to Grandpa while they are surveying their family farm of Storrhaven and says, "People in the family always speak of Storrhaven the way other people speak of Iowa or America."[41] Storrhaven, Iowa, and America coalesce here in the minds of the two lead characters as well as for Depression-era audiences who were becoming increasingly accustomed to seeing cornfields, farm houses, and good-hearted, white, working-class farmers presented as symbols of the "real" America.

Upon its release *The Stranger's Return* received reviews that were every bit as positive as those for *State Fair*. The *Des Moines Register* wrote that it belonged in "a class of high class pictures" and praised "the excellence of the performances."[42] Mordaunt Hall of the *New York Times* called it "an excellent example of the successful cooperation of an author and the producers" and declared it to be "gentle and natural and pleasantly free from hokum."[43] *Time*, meanwhile, hailed it as "an even more appealing pastoral [than *State Fair*]." The reviewer also expressed admiration for the emergence of the entire farm picture genre, crediting Stong for writing "novels [which] have supplied the cinema with something it has needed for a long time—true-to-life stories about U.S. farmers."[44]

The Stranger's Return was also more "true-to-life" than *State Fair* in terms of its awareness of contemporary rural problems. Dwight MacDonald did not weigh in on this film, but he likely would have been gratified that it at least acknowledged the existence of the Depression by portraying four Storr relatives who had all been buffeted by economic problems and found themselves seeking refuge in the comforting environs of the ancestral farm. These Depression-era effects are all present in Stong's novel, which stands to reason since the economic situation had worsened in the fourteen months since the publication of *State Fair*. Vidor was also well aware of what was happening in the country. "I had a strong feeling about what was happening in the country," he remembered. "[Farmers] overturning milk trucks and spilling milk on the highway to combat prices ... and farms and ranches being foreclosed, bought up for a few dollars, and all sorts of things going on."[45] His concerns came even further into focus on his next picture, *Our Daily Bread* (1934), in which the unemployed protagonists leave the city (presumably New York) in an attempt to escape from the problems of the Depression. They move to the country when one of them inherits a run-down farm upstate, and it soon becomes a co-operative when they are joined by more individuals facing similarly difficult economic circumstances.

Phil Stong, however, did not go on to explore the effects of the Depression in his later work. Much of his career was spent pursuing the twin goals of literary respect and economic security, and he usually fell short of both expectations, which only fueled his problems with alcohol. His serious problem once led his wife to confide to a friend, "I don't really think he will stop drinking in time to save his life. All I can do is sit tight and wait and see. I'm convinced that he was slated for a drunkard's grave from birth."[46] For multiple reasons he developed a love/hate relationship with the film business, as even though he felt screenwriting work gave him bad habits, he also liked the fast infusion of income a screenwriting job could provide.[47] "My God, how the money rolls in," he wrote to Harvey Davis in the fall of 1933.[48] However, he also worried that his Hollywood jobs amounted to "nothing but a swift and profitable prostitution."[49] Therefore it is not surprising that within two years he would pour his ambivalent feelings about the film business into *The Farmer in the Dell*, a novel about an Iowa farm family and their adventures in Hollywood.

Hollywood's "Genuine" Iowa Folk

Stong's *The Farmer in the Dell* was published in July 1935 and, despite being serialized in the *Saturday Evening Post*, was met with less fanfare than had attended the releases of *State Fair* and *The Stranger's Return*. In a representative review for the *New York Times*, Robert van Gelder gave Stong the most tepid of backhanded-compliments, declaring, "While it is completely unambitious, it has its moments of accuracy and brightness, and Mr. Stong never really achieved much more than that."[50] Great literature it is not, but *The Farmer in the Dell* does provide a fascinating insider's perspective into connections between Iowa and Hollywood during the middle of the Great Depression, when farm pictures were especially prominent. In fact the book is a good example of the "Hollywood novel" literary genre, which had been growing in popularity since the 1910s, and often featured naïve midwestern characters in fish-out-of-water stories.[51] Books in this genre, according to one of its leading chroniclers, typically provide "personal statements of the authors' direct [and often embittered] responses to their Hollywood experiences," while also "defamiliariz[ing] the main ideologies that undergird Hollywood ... [through] protagonists ... who have an ambivalent relation to the film industry."[52] *The Farmer in the Dell* fits squarely within this model because not only are Stong's mostly negative feelings toward Hollywood well-chronicled, but his pragmatic Iowan characters are almost unanimously unimpressed with Hollywood glitz and glamour.

An earlier, and arguably more successful, example of this literary genre was *Headed for Hollywood*, written by Homer Croy in 1932.[53] Croy was a Missourian who grew up approximately twenty miles south of the Iowa border and became well-known for his novels and nonfiction books about the Midwest. He also maintained connections to the film industry, beginning as a film production manager during World War I and continuing as a part-time screenwriter during the 1930s, during which time he developed a close friendship with Will Rogers. Croy's novel follows Pearl Piper, a wholesome beauty contest winner from fictional Bender, Iowa, as she decamps to Hollywood along with her patent medicine salesman father and her star-struck aunt. Hijinks ensue as Pearl ineffectually chases her dream of becoming a movie star and her family blunders its way through attempts to impress the powerful owner of a film studio and his director son. In the end, however, everyone decides they really belong back in Iowa. The book, which received mostly positive reviews, was published concurrently with a twelve-part live radio adaptation of it. Venerable *Los Angeles Times* columnist Lee Shippey points out, "Not only was it the first radio premiere which was handled like a theater premiere, but it was the first time a dramatized version of a popular novel has been put on the air while the book still might be called brand new."[54] The event was significant enough that it was written about in the pages of the *New York Times*, and despite a few technical glitches, Shippey enjoyed the performance, particularly the pastoral sounds and images that were conjured in the minds of the audience.[55]

Three years later Phil Stong published *The Farmer in the Dell* and it became perhaps the most thoughtful depiction of Iowans making their way through Tinseltown. The main characters are Ernie "Pa" Boyer, a retired Iowa farmer who has moved to California to live off the proceeds of his rented Iowa farm along with his wife, Louella, and eighteen-year-old daughter, Adrienne. The family's migration mimicked that of thousands of Iowans who moved to California during the first three decades of the twentieth century, but Stong's primary preoccupation in the novel is the movie business, as the plot revolves around Ernie being accidentally "discovered" and turned into a Hollywood star.[56]

Ultimately Ernie's success sends his diva co-star, Maude Elverill, into a drunken jealous rage at a well-attended Hawaiian-themed party at her home. She calls him a "hayseed," a "rube," a "plow-pushing dumbbell," and a "dirty old muddy-footed pig nurse," but even as she insults his provincial roots, she simultaneously questions his authenticity, asking, "Were you ever in Iowa?" and "Did you ever see a farm?" In his passionate retort he firmly defends his background while displaying pride in his homesteading ancestors and a keen awareness of the economic depression and drought that were afflicting Iowa at that time:

> There's good men workin' out in my country for a dollar a day ... How many [of] your granddaddies cut down trees an' made along with the Indians? What are you? The crops is all burned up, and here you are makin' a [sic] ocean. Where was your folks when mine was talkin' to Black Hawk? You, so mighty proud ... What are you? ... I get along as a rule. I guess we're not goin' to.[57]

This speech, despite its use of a rural dialect, distills the message of Stong's Iowa farm novels and most of the films based on them. Those works present a world populated by honest, hard-working, white middle-class Americans, and anyone who is unable to appreciate those characters' sacred bond with the soil is portrayed as petty, greedy, and duplicitous. All three of those traits are present in Elverill's character, as she embodies Hollywood, which is described in the closing pages of the novel as a "great, foolish city" because of its "mad careers and aspirations," which leave it sorely lacking in the "solid rock, the truth."[58]

This novel about the film adaptations of Iowa novels was itself turned into a film in 1936. Since the release of *State Fair* and *The Stranger's Return* in 1933, four additional Iowa films had appeared during the interim. *As Husbands Go* (1933), *Men of the Night* (1934), and *Times Square Lady* (1935) all tell stories of Iowans mixing with city folks (from Paris, Hollywood, and New York, respectively), while *Village Tale* (1935) was adapted from a Stong novel about the effect of gossip in small-town Iowa. Stong did not go to Hollywood to work on *The Farmer in the Dell* because he and RKO Pictures "couldn't get within $5000 of each other on a price," which caused him to worry, as before the film's release he wrote to a friend, "They've let me know nothing about what they did with the story."[59] He had reason to be concerned, as his criticism of Hollywood artifice, which was a key element of the novel, was largely removed in order to comply with the Production Code's ban against material criticizing the movie industry. Left in its place is a forgettable film with a silly plot that revolves around Ernie's small-minded wife and star-crazed daughter who team up to extravagantly spend every penny he earns as an actor. An unimpressed Stong wrote to his friend Harvey Davis and told him, "I have seen the *Farmer* twice but as yet I haven't been able to find any resemblance to the book except in the first general situation. There isn't a line of my dialogue in it ... I think I did a better job adapting this house with the money they gave me than they did on the novel."[60]

Inexperienced director Ben Holmes was put in charge of the project, which stars Fred Stone as Ernie, Esther Dale as his wife, Jean Parker as his daughter, and Frank Albertson as his daughter's suitor, Davy.[61] Stone, whose performance in the film was described as "ruggedly real" by the *Los Angeles Times*, was a vaudeville actor and close friend of Will Rogers.[62] Review after review singled out his performance as the chief reason to see the film. For example, the *New York Times*'s Frank Nugent declared the picture "quite a bore to the innocent bystander [but] Fred Stone makes it endurable with his warm and believable characterization."[63] *Motion Picture Daily* was the rare publication to offer a positive recommendation, and it went out of its way to praise the film's lead: "Comparisons with Will Rogers here are inevitable, and it cannot be said that Stone suffers particularly by such a comparison."[64] Most reviews, however, were lukewarm at best, such as the one in *Variety* which claims "there is no particular appeal to the outline, and ... probably it will be better suited to the smaller spots, where they react more decisively to homespun sentiment."[65]

Even though the film was not an artistic success, the advance publicity material that RKO sent to movie theater owners and newspapers provides a helpful window into contemporary attitudes toward farm pictures. Most important, the studio uses the packet to emphasize the film's rural virtues rather than its glitzy Hollywood setting, touting what it calls the film's two "capital claims to entertainment." First is Phil Stong, described as "a son of the Iowa farm belt" and "a past master of Middle Western farm folk drama," and second is Fred Stone, labeled "a 'Natural,' one of those rare people to be met once in a lifetime— unpretending, kindly, gentle, and genuine."[66] The terms "natural" and "genuine" are used again and again throughout the packet in an attempt to link this film with the positive feelings many Depression-era audiences had for "simple" rural people and situations. As a case in point the studio proudly asserts, "The characters portrayed in *The Farmer in the Dell* are all real people. The farmer, his wife, their daughter and the girl's Iowa boyfriend are all genuine Midwest rural folk."[67] The publicity materials also provide theaters with ideas for marketing the film, with tag lines such as "An Intriguing Tale of Love, Laughter, and Pathos that Surged in a Hay-Seed Heart" and special events including a contest to determine the "prettiest farmerette." Theaters are also given ballyhoo ideas including staging an auction in the lobby "with various rural household articles," dressing their ushers and usherettes in the costumes of "farmer boys and girls," and partnering with a local dairy to give away milk coupons.[68]

The studio's promotional packet demonstrates that Stong's name still meant something to audiences across America even though his star was no longer shining as brightly as it had just three years earlier. Only one more of his novels, *Career* (1939), would be turned into a film, but he had already made his mark on Hollywood, helping to establish cinematic expectations for the themes and visuals of Iowa films. Two additional late-1930s films with which Stong was not involved, *We Have Our Moments* (1937) and *Keep Smiling* (1938), also feature main characters from Iowa. Those two, along with *The Flying Deuces* (1939), a Laurel and Hardy comedy in which the famed duo play fishmongers from Des Moines, bring to twelve the number of 1930s films in which Iowa or Iowans figure prominently. Only the 1940s witnessed more Iowa-themed films, as World War II, much like the Great Depression, was a traumatic national event that called for a wholesome setting to represent the values for which Americans were fighting.[69]

The Lasting Impact of Depression-Era Iowa Films

The popular notions about Iowa presented in Depression-era films can still be seen on movie screens today even though the state has experienced some notable changes since the 1930s. According to the U.S. census, 60 percent of the state's residents lived in rural areas in 1930, but by 2010 that number had decreased by nearly half, to 36 percent. However, you would not know that by watching movies set in Iowa during the past thirty years. Iowa continues to be portrayed almost exclusively as a location for family-affirming stories set against a backdrop of fields, fairs, and other rural symbols. We have seen this image in *Field of Dreams* (1989), in which a son reconnects with his dead father on a magical baseball diamond in a cornfield; *The Bridges of Madison County* (1995), in which an unfaithful farm wife ultimately chooses the solidity of family over the promise of a romantic life of adventure; and *The Straight Story* (1999), which follows an elderly man as he drives a riding lawnmower across the entire state of Iowa to visit his dying brother. More recently, the 2011 film *Butter* returns viewers to the Iowa State Fair to witness an orphan girl win a butter-sculpting contest and be adopted by a loving family. Even though that orphan girl is African American, film depictions of Iowa usually fail to account for racial, ethnic, sexual, geological, or even occupational diversity. This failure in turn increases the surprise for national commentators when events happen that don't fit neatly into the popular narrative, such as Barack Obama's victory in the 2008 Iowa Democratic caucus or the 2009 judicial decision that made Iowa the third state to legalize same-sex marriage. In 1935, Iowa's governor, Clyde Herring, described southern

California as a "beautiful land of make-believe," but those words equally apply to the way Hollywood filmmakers (and many others) have viewed rural Iowa ever since.⁷⁰

Notes

1. Phil Stong, *The Farmer in the Dell* (New York: Harcourt, Brace, 1935), 148-51.
2. "Wanted—A Corn Fed Iowa Venus," *Des Moines Register*, Dec. 10, 1933, 1X; "Park Av. Cows Moo as Society Dances," *New York Times*, Nov. 29, 1934, 40.
3. Tino Balio, *Grand Design: Hollywood as a Modern Business Enterprise, 1930-1939* (Berkeley: University of California Press, 1993), 258; Gary Gerstle, *Working-Class Americanism: The Politics of Labor in a Textile City, 1914-1960* (New York: Cambridge University Press, 1989), 6.
4. This information comes from a comprehensive study of Iowa films by Marty Knepper and John S. Lawrence, "Iowa Films, 1918-2002," *Annals of Iowa* 62, no. 1 (Winter 2003): 30-100.
5. Knepper and Lawrence, "Iowa Films, 1918-2002"; AFI Catalog of Feature Films. http://afi.com/members/catalog/ . November 17, 2013.
6. Hal Barron, "Rural America on the Silent Screen," *Agricultural History* 80, no. 4 (Autumn 2006): 385.
7. James R. Shortridge, *The Middle West: Its Meaning in American Culture* (Lawrence, KS: University of Kansas Press, 1989), 59.
8. *The Stranger's Return*, directed by King Vidor (1933, Los Angeles: MGM), film. UCLA Film and Television Archive, Los Angeles, California.
9. Dorothy Schwieder, "Iowa: The Middle Land," in *Iowa History Reader*, ed. Marvin Bergman (Iowa City: University of Iowa Press, 1996), 2. The essay was originally published in *Heartland: Comparative Histories of the Midwestern States*, ed. James Madison (Bloomington: Indiana University Press, 1988): 276-95.
10. "Three Books Picked for the Prix Femina," *New York Times*, May 18, 1932, 19.
11. The other top box office draws from 1932 to 1933 were Marie Dressler, Eddie Cantor, and Wallace Beery. Andrew Bergman, *We're in the Money: Depression America and Its Films* (New York: New York University Press, 1971), 71.
12. The film earned $1.8 million in box office receipts. "Gotham Hails First Showing of *State Fair*," *Des Moines Register*, January 27, 1933, 1; Lon Jones, "Which Cinema Films Have Earned the Most Money Since 1914?" *The Argus*, March 4, 1944, supplement, 3.
13. Letter from Phil Stong to Henry King, Nov. 2, 1932, Henry King Papers, File 46, Margaret Herrick Library, Academy of Motion Pictures Arts and Sciences, Los Angeles, California.

14. Fox's shares plunged from $109/share before the 1929 crash to just $19 by 1932. Barrie A. Wigmore, *The Crash and Its Aftermath: A History of Securities Markets in the United States, 1929–1933* (Westport, CT: Greenwood Press, 1985), 63.
15. King, Rogers, and Gaynor were so determined to make *State Fair* their comeback hit that each of them deferred their salaries when the studio found itself unable to meet payroll during filming. Walter Coppedge, *Henry King's America* (Metuchen, NJ.: Scarecrow Press, 1986), 86.
16. Coppedge, *Henry King's America*, 73–74.
17. Letter from Phil Stong to Henry King, November 2, 1932, Henry King Papers, File 46, Margaret Herrick Library, Academy of Motion Pictures Arts and Sciences, Los Angeles, California.
18. William J. Mann, *Behind the Screen: How Gays and Lesbians Shaped Hollywood, 1910–1969* (New York: Viking Penguin, 2001), 83–84.
19. Letter from Jason S. Joy to Winfield Sheehan, June 20, 1932, Production Code Administration Records for *State Fair*, Margaret Herrick Library, Academy of Motion Pictures Arts and Sciences, Los Angeles, California.
20. Mordaunt Hall, "Will Rogers and Janet Gaynor in a Film Conception of Phil Stong's Novel, *State Fair*," *New York Times*, January 27, 1933, 13.
21. Eugene Burr, review of *State Fair*, *The Billboard*, February 4, 1933, 12.
22. *Variety* review quoted in Coppedge, *Henry King's America*, 86; *New York American* review quoted in "Des Moines has *State Fair*, Story of Iowa," *Des Moines Register* Sunday Magazine, February 19, 1933, 5.
23. Dwight MacDonald, "Notes on Hollywood Directors (As of 1933)" in *Dwight MacDonald on Movies* (Englewood Cliffs, NJ: Prentice-Hall, 1969), 88. The essay was originally published in *The Symposium*, April 1933, 159–77; July 1933, 280–300.
24. Harlan Miller, "Over the Coffee," *Des Moines Register*, February 8, 1933, 18.
25. Letter from Jason S. Joy to Winfield Sheehan, June 20, 1932, Production Code Administration Records for *State Fair*, Margaret Herrick Library, Academy of Motion Pictures Arts and Sciences, Los Angeles, California; Barron, "Rural America," 384–85.
26. "Hollywood in Review," *New York Times*, February 5, 1933, X5.
27. Letter from Phil Stong to Harvey Davis, June 19, 1933. Phil Stong Manuscripts, The University of Iowa Libraries, Iowa City, Iowa.
28. Letter from Phil Stong to Harvey Davis, February 14, 1933. Phil Stong Manuscripts, The University of Iowa Libraries, Iowa City, Iowa.
29. Letter from Phil Stong to Harvey Davis, September 19, 1932. Phil Stong Manuscripts, The University of Iowa Libraries, Iowa City, Iowa.
30. Letter from Phil Stong to Harvey Davis, September 5, 1933. Phil Stong Manuscripts, The University of Iowa Libraries, Iowa City, Iowa.
31. Letter from Phil Stong to Harvey Davis, June 19, 1933. Phil Stong Manuscripts, The University of Iowa Libraries, Iowa City, Iowa.
32. MacDonald, "Notes on Hollywood Directors," 78–79.

33. Raymond Durgnat and Scott Simmon, *King Vidor, American* (Berkeley, CA: University of California Press, 1988), 3, 9–10.
34. Ibid., 16.
35. King Vidor, interview, June 19, 1971. MS1778. American Film Institute Oral History Project. UCLA Film and Television Archive, Los Angeles, California. Vidor explains that he took out his anger on the couch because he had always stubbed his toe on it during visits to Hopkins's house. He tipped her butler $5 to let him in to do it.
36. Ibid.
37. Ibid. The two Wood paintings Vidor owned were *Arbor Day* (1932) and *January* (1940).
38. David Thomson, *Lost Hollywood* (New York: St. Martin's Press, 2001), 78.
39. Vidor, interview.
40. Rosalind Shaffer, "Iowa Farm Set Stirs Hearts of Film People," *Chicago Daily Tribune*, May 14, 1963, SC8.
41. *The Stranger's Return*, film.
42. "New Films," *Des Moines Register*, July 30, 1933, Sunday Magazine, 5.
43. Mordaunt Hall, "Phil Stong's Drama of Rural Life," *New York Times*, August 6, 1933, X3.
44. "The New Pictures," *Time*, July 31, 1933, 19.
45. Vidor, interview.
46. Letter from Virginia Swain to Bertha Craver, February 3, 1940. Phil Stong Manuscripts, The University of Iowa Libraries, Iowa City, Iowa. Stong experienced brief periods of sobriety, but he frequently backslid and eventually died of a heart attack at age fifty-eight.
47. Phil Stong, "Writer in Hollywood," *Saturday Review of Literature*, April 10, 1937, 14.
48. Letter from Phil Stong to Harvey Davis, September 5, 1933. Phil Stong Manuscripts, The University of Iowa Libraries, Iowa City, Iowa.
49. Stong, "Writer in Hollywood," 3.
50. Robert van Gelder, "Books of the Times," *New York Times*, July 18, 1935, 17.
51. Nancy Brooker-Bowers, "The Hollywood Novel: An American Literary Genre" (PhD diss., Drake University, 1983), 106.
52. Chip Rhodes, *Politics, Desire, and the Hollywood Novel* (Iowa City: University of Iowa Press, 2008), 2, 6.
53. Homer Croy, *Headed for Hollywood* (New York: Harper and Brothers, 1932).
54. Lee Shippey, "The Lee Side O' L-A," *Los Angeles Times*, March 26, 1932, A4.
55. Ibid.
56. Phil Stong, *The Farmer in the Dell* (New York: Harcourt, Brace and Company, 1935).
57. Ibid., 212–13.

58. Ibid., 217.
59. Letter from Phil Stong to Harvey Davis, April 18, 1935. Phil Stong Manuscripts, The University of Iowa Libraries, Iowa City, Iowa.
60. Letter from Phil Stong to Harvey Davis, June 22, 1936. Phil Stong Manuscripts, The University of Iowa Libraries, Iowa City, Iowa.
61. The cast also included a young Lucille Ball as a sassy script girl.
62. "Best Performances in Current Pictures," *Los Angeles Times*, April 12, 1936, B1.
63. Frank Nugent, "Passing Notes on *The Farmer in the Dell*, at the Palace," *New York Times*, March 7, 1936, 11.
64. "The Farmer in the Dell," *Motion Picture Daily*, February 26, 1936. Farmer in the Dell file, Margaret Herrick Library, Academy of Motion Pictures Arts and Sciences, Los Angeles, California.
65. "The Farmer in the Dell," *Variety*, March 11, 1936, Farmer in the Dell file, Margaret Herrick Library, Academy of Motion Pictures Arts and Sciences, Los Angeles, California.
66. Howard S. Benedict, *The Farmer in the Dell* Publicity Booklet, RKO Pictures, 1936, 1. Margaret Herrick Library, Academy of Motion Pictures Arts and Sciences, Los Angeles, California.
67. Ibid., 4.
68. Ibid., 20–22.
69. 1940s Iowa films are thoroughly discussed in Marty S. Knepper and John S. Lawrence, "World War II and Iowa: Hollywood's Pastoral Myth for the Nation," in *Representing the Rural: Space, Place, and Identity in Films about the Land*, ed. Catherine Fowler and Gillian Helfield (Detroit: Wayne State University Press, 2006), 323–39.
70. "Thousands Crowd Park at Huge Iowa Picnic," *Los Angeles Times*, February 24, 1935, 2.

| Jonathon Josten | Migratory Bodies

Failed Commemoration in Richard Powers's *The Echo Maker* and *Gain*

For the past sixteen years, people of varied political aims have defined September 11, 2001, as a unique event forcing a culture of commemoration. According to Daniel Heischman, "Watching the two planes crash into tall skyscrapers, then seeing those towers of commerce and enterprise collapse, I found myself pulled in two different directions. I could not imagine that such things were happening; it was all like a very bad dream. However, the events felt eerily similar in some small way."[1] Likewise, as Jürgen Habermas claims, "Perhaps September 11 could be called the first world-historical event in a strict sense: the impact, the explosion, the slow collapse—all of which was unfortunately no longer Hollywood but a horrific reality—literally unfolded before the eyes of a global public."[2] As a result, the attacks became linked to one location but were observed by local and non-local viewers; consequently the attacks became described through physical bodies (real) and imagined bodies (a *body* politic).

Along these lines, Richard Powers offers a pre–September 11 world in *Gain* and a post–September 11 world in *The Echo Maker*, each controlled by faceless masters. If we select *The Echo Maker* as an exemplar post–September 11 novel, then *Gain* becomes an exemplar of late capitalism. In effect, the post–September 11 experience becomes not simply a culture of commemoration, as David Simpson suggests, but rather an American culture of loneliness, isolation, and misidentification.[3]

It is unsurprising that authors and critics of the event focus on Manhattan or consider this a necessary place to begin, but for many people, the attacks have always been mediated through camera lenses. At first glance, it would seem true that only those geographically separate from the attacks would have the events mediated through camera lenses; however, as Ingrid Sischy describes in "The Triumph of the Still," those within New York City experienced the attacks similarly to those outside the city:

> Like many others in downtown New York, I saw it with all my own eyes—my office window, 20 blocks north, is like a camera lens pointing toward the World Trade Center site. When the first tower was hit, it seemed unconceivable that such a thing could happen—and impossible that the other tower could be hit. It was. There was no way I could imagine the buildings would come down. They did. I saw the glass and metal fill the sky, and the people jumping ... After all, this was a plot familiar from so many Hollywood movies, which now looked tame compared with what I was witnessing through my windows.[4]

In essence, Sischy's statement operates as a simile; however, the experience—a type of eye-witness—suggests that it was framed in a similar way as the television coverage. That is why the viewer witnesses the attacks and is close enough to see material "fill the sky," but the importance placed on those geographically close to the attacks—twenty blocks away from the attacks—loses its privilege when the experience is similar to those elsewhere in the United States. For instance, Sischy resides in Manhattan, but her view becomes comparable to the television coverage in that no matter where a person viewed the attacks it was impossible to gather a complete account of the event. Sischy's testimony provides a type of eye-witness that aligns itself with Slavoj Žižek, namely the mention of Hollywood and effect of footage. Žižek argues in *Welcome to the Desert of the Real!*, "While the number of victims—3,000—is repeated all the time, it is surprising how little of the carnage we see—no dismembered bodies, no blood, no desperate faces of dying people."[5] Again, we desire physical bodies, yet we achieve imagined bodies. In the weeks and years that followed the attacks, several viewers geographically proximate to the attacks began posting their accounts, and through this mediated lens the body politic began to form.

Sischy and Žižek imply a distinction between those who experienced the attacks directly and those who did not. Comparing experiences in New York City and the Midwest shows a disparity in the body politic and a challenge to forming a singular national identity. While *Gain* was written before September 11, Powers deftly folds late-capitalist paranoia into an example of the failed commemoration explored in *The Echo Maker*, which was written post–September 11. Although Powers presents fragmented events within both narratives, he resists using cosmopolitan cities to critique the American psyche to show failed commemoration in the latter half of the twentieth century leading to September 11, 2001. Instead, he shows the importance of the commemoration occurring in the Midwest, critiquing late-capitalist, pre–September 11 experience and the paranoid, post–September 11 experience through the pieces of the heartland.

A Thinly Veiled Confrontation: Bodies, Chemicals, and *Gain*

Throughout *Gain*, Powers weaves together multiple storylines: one of the Clare soap and candle business beginning in 1803 with Jepthah Clare arriving in the United States, and the story of a single mother in the Midwest dealing with the effect of cancer. As the business transitions from family business to multinational corporation, the reader becomes less certain of its identity. At this moment, Powers offers Laura as an identity for the reader to connect to as Powers signals to the reader through advertising materials for the Clare Corporation. In this way, Powers seems to show late-capitalist identity in the faceless corporation versus the independent person. In effect, Powers yokes these narratives together to offer a choice: Pay attention to the midwestern single mother or the multinational corporation. Given these claims, Ryan Brooks argues, "Laura's story is structured in part by the growing awareness of its main character, a dawning recognition of how much both her mind and body have been shaped by corporations"[6] Powers creates a narrative in which corporations inform the sense of reality within American ideology in the latter half of the twentieth century. Further, Powers writes that "there must have been a time when Lacewood did not mean Clare, Incorporated. But no one remembered it. No one alive was old enough to recall. The two names always came joined in the same breath."[7] In effect, individual citizens' lives became linked to the evolution and success of a corporation, simultaneously eliminating a sense of commemoration or community.

To further explain the unfolding history of both Laura and Clare Incorporated—effectively the corporation's strengthening to Laura's weakening—Powers shows how the characters, though separated by hundreds of years, have similar experiences, particularly moments of managing the emergent sense of capitalism. Given the setting disparity, Powers resists speaking about corporate history in terms of periodization; instead, Powers yokes together societal anxiety from a vast panorama of American experience, ending in the late capital or postmodern era. Frederic Jameson writes, "theories of the post-modern—whether celebratory or couched in the language of moral revulsion and denunciation—bear a strong family resemblance to all these more ambitious social generalizations ... [that] bring us news of the arrival of and inauguration of a whole new type of society."[8] Throughout *Gain*, Powers describes the emergent anxiety of the day while also explaining America's development through the emergent technologies, in order to show the persistence of Clare Incorporated. Despite the presumed community of a corporation, the characters feel a sense of alienation and isolation similar to the experience in *The Echo Maker*.

Powers creates a sense of a body politic—whether a culture of a commemoration or a corporation as a person—versus an individual body. According to literary critic Ralph Clare, Powers becomes interested in the corporation's development until it becomes a body comparable to Laura:

> Powers, after extensively researching corporate history, takes for granted the legal construction of a corporation as a kind of person, and treats it as such with compelling results. In other words, Powers's novel explicitly historicizes the corporation itself as a kind of corrective to the fact that the corporation has become so naturalized that it appears as if it has always existed and, therefore, always will.[9]

Within the narrative, Powers shows both corporation and individual subject historicized and metastasized, though Laura succumbs to cancer. The novel remains undecided about the worth of corporations. However, a possible ruling appears in the last line of the novel where the success of Laura's son is bolstered by the settlement money she received from the lawsuit, allowing her son's firm to incorporate, resulting in the continuation, in a positive manner, of the system Powers had just spent several hundred pages critiquing. The irony underpinning the analysis of Clare and Laura's link becomes that the cancer Laura succumbed to may have been caused by chemicals produced by Clare; however, Clare also produces the drugs that are provided and futilely taken. Thus, Laura ingests Clare chemicals in two ways: first, the chemicals that may have caused the cancer, and second, the antidote.

One productive reading of *Gain* occurs through Jameson's view of corporate history. Jameson writes, "I first want to suggest that if this copiously prepared image is not to sink to the level of sheer decoration, it requires us to reconstruct some initial situation out of which the finished work emerges."[10] It would be tempting to condense the corporation's identity by the present lawsuit and link to widespread cancer in Lacewood. Nevertheless, Powers begins the novel by describing the Clare Corporation from the perspective of the three brothers who founded the company. In other words, Powers does not focus simply on the "finished work" or the "initial situation"; instead, Powers signals how the townspeople of Lacewood are unable to move beyond being linked to the corporation and how Laura is aware of Clare's infiltration into everyday life:

> The firm built her entire town, and then some. She knows where her lunch comes from ... She drives past Clare's Agricultural Division headquarters at least three times a week. The town cannot hold a corn boil without its corporate sponsor. The company cuts every other check, writes the headlines, sings the school fight song. It plays the organ at every wedding and packs the rice that rains down on the departing honeymooners. It staffs the hospital and funds the ultrasound sweep of uterine seas where Lacewood's next of kin lie gray and ghostly, asleep in the deep ... Soap, fertilizers, cosmetics, comestibles: name your life-changing category of substances. But still, she knows Clare no better than she knows Grace or Dow. She does not work for the corporation or for anyone the corporation directly owns.[11]

Power underpins the progress of the town with a slight mention of the ways companies navigate the reoccurring issues, writing "after each national panic or recession—'37, '43, '57, '60, '65—sales always managed to rebound somehow. Business changed to meet the upheavals that business instigated."[12] Within the narrative, Powers describes the destruction of the individual along the creation of the company in order to show late capitalism's responsibility for the failed commemoration and fragmented community.

Jameson explains, "the disappearance of the individual subject, along with its formal consequence, the increasing unavailability of the personal style, engender the well-nigh universal practice today of what might be called pastiche."[13] The collective memory of Clare Incorporated's past engenders its popularity and value in the town despite how it has now become a fragmented, multinational corporation. Powers explicates certain qualities of history, namely that "There is no history. Everything already is. Humanity is a child locked by accident in a library, reading its way through the permanent collection, looking for a way out."[14] In these passages, Powers seems to describe both personal success and corporate success—the corporation gains wealth as the personal subject gains wealth—however, they are different versions of metastasis. While the individual corporation infiltrates the town, garnering power as the individual subject loses power, ultimately the individual subject—its body and its history—is killed by the corporation through fragmentation.

Similarly, the regional economic success of the community—Lacewood—directly displaces a character from joining a regional culture of commemoration. Laura's ex-husband Don turns toward violence in order to reclaim his town. While the corporation inhabits a distanced view of the town, the individual subject witnesses the cracks of the community. Powers writes, "Maybe he's stuck in nostalgia, some image of the Town that Time Forgot. Like, a place where you just *drive*, from start to destination, no complications, no surprises, no fucked-up stoplights, no ... work crews sticking Band-Aids on collapsing infrastructures."[15] Clare Incorporated headquarters is pristine corporate success as Powers writes, "The Stars and Stripes flaps in position one. It strikes Don as a bit of handy nostalgia. How transnationals love to play the citizenship card whenever they're looking for a protective break. But Clare is just like elites everywhere: the company keeps so many residences that it has no fixed place of abode."[16] Powers signals an important difference between the corporation (Clare) and the individual subject (Don)—namely, the importance of a fixed origin. The corporation and the subject maintain similar nationalist ideals; however, Powers shows a late-capitalist anxiety through Don in how to retaliate once displaced by the community:

> One bomb, it occurs to him. One little envelope of plastic explosive slipped into a portfolio while court was in session. The anarchist's dream: fifteen feet away from being able to change things forever. Then the imaginary dust settles, and it dawns on him. The board? The board's not even close to ground zero ... What difference would it make? ... real commerce went on ebbing and flowing, out there, scattered, pressed thin past finding, in the shape that shared life has taken.[17]

Powers describes a midwestern town to show the apparent calm of a late-capitalist society. Within this presumed calm, individual subjects—Don and Laura—are displaced by the exact corporation that built the entire town. Powers writes a narrative within this shared life that follows Jameson's point: "faceless masters continue to infect the economic strategies which constrain our existences, but they no longer need to impose their speech."[18] Clare built the entire town; as such the citizens feel an allegiance toward the company. However, Powers presents a midwestern moment when Clare has infiltrated Lacewood both in building the town and in poisoning the town. To borrow one of Jameson's terms—cultural pathology—it seems that Powers creates *Gain* in order to show the corporation as metastasized or fragmented.

Ultimately, Powers explains Clare's trajectory and Laura's illness in order to show the ways that "history in *Gain* appears as an unfolding conflict between the public interest and the working of the system, expressed as dramas of pattern recognition and misrecognition."[19] In other words, history becomes a pattern of recognition and misrecognition similar to Powers's simile of history being a child locked in a library. Along these lines, Jameson writes, "this shift in the dynamics of cultural pathology can be characterized as one in which the alienation of the subject is displaced by the latter's fragmentation."[20] Within *Gain*, several bodies—companies, humans, towns—become fragmented as dynamics shift from successful commemoration to failed commemoration.

Migratory Feeling: September 11, 2001 and Richard Powers's *The Echo Maker*

Whereas many September 11 narratives focus on a specific place, Powers compels the reader to consider the effect of September 11 outside New York City. In an effort to understand the political and emotional effect of September 11, Powers takes up the way Americans commemorate the attacks as well as the continuation of life after the attacks. According to James Gibbons's review of the novel, "Powers views *The Echo Maker* as a post-9/11 book and [the] interweaving of public events with the fictional narrative ... the political climate of the first Bush term is quietly insistent and impossible to ignore."[21] With subtle references to post–September 11 life, *The Echo Maker* becomes not nostalgic for a pre–September 11 world or a containment of emotions, but an offering of how people survive day to day, in effect, as Powers writes, "stories of how even shattered brains might narrate disaster back into a livable sense."[22] In effect, the common notion has been that September 11 irrevocably damaged the American cultural rhythm and psyche, yet Powers argues for successful recovery. As David Ryan put it, "In the days that followed September 11, Washington and US culture more generally created the framework within which the United States would respond to these monumental crimes committed in New York, Virginia, and Pennsylvania."[23]

If *The Echo Maker* becomes a description of post–September 11, then the following quotation showcases the move from chaos to normal:

> September came and then the attacks ... the endlessly looping, slow-motion, cinematic insanity. From the Central Plains, New York was a black plume on the farthest horizon. Troops were securing the Golden Gate Bridge. Anthrax started turning up in the nation's sugar bowls. Then the bombs began to fall in Afghanistan. A broadcaster in

Omaha declared, *It's payback time*, and all along the river came stony, unanimous assent.[24]

At first glance this passage offers a condensed timeline beginning with the attacks through the beginning of the war in Afghanistan, making the events appear logical and ordered. At the same time, Powers places weight on the phrase "September came and then the attacks," which implies that the force of September 11 needs only to refer to a month and the larger meaning becomes clear. The passage implies that Nebraska, though not directly affected by the attacks, sought redemption for the attacks. The connection of "It's payback time" and "stony, unanimous assent" reflects the need of President Bush and others to evoke the memory of September 11 to build a coalition for the response. As the faceless, disembodied attacks are explored in Kearney rather than Manhattan, Powers deftly shows the local framework being constructed in the Midwest in response to the non-local September 11 attacks.

While President Bush compelled American citizens to unite and remember the attacks on September 11, a central tension occurred between what the citizens remembered and what the Bush administration presented. As Maja Zehfuss argues, "What was it that happened? … we do not really seem to know. And this is not surprising as memory plays tricks on the idea of straightforward knowledge."[25] Within Clare Incorporated of *Gain* and for Mark Schluter in *The Echo Maker*, trouble occurs not because everything is false, but rather because certain qualities remain known but not as straightforward knowledge. In *The Echo Maker*, Mark considers his sister an imposter, yet this recognition depends on a certain memory of his sister. Mark does not feel connection. Along these lines, the famed Dr. Gerald Weber says to Mark's sister Karin, "the loved one's face elicits memory, but no feeling. Lack of emotional ratification overrides the rational assembly of memory. Or put this way: reason invents elaborately unreasonable explanations to explain a deficit in emotion. Logic depends upon feeling."[26] This passage mirrors the connection and estrangement between Mark and Karin, specifically the ways Mark never outright accepts or rejects Karin. Instead, Mark uses a series of names to describe Karin's familiarity and estrangement: "He [Mark] overhears the Special Sister Agent talking to Bonnie,"[27] "He [Mark] looks at Karin's substitute."[28] For every familiar effect, something causes further strain or the attempt at community eventually reduces the individual to loneliness and isolation—failed commemoration. In *Gain*, Lacewood's residents were familiar with the corporation despite the faceless, multinational corporation that results in the destruction of individuals, namely Laura, as a result of cancer. In *The Echo Maker*, the post–September 11 individual is caught between the local commemoration for a non-local terror attack and war effort. In the wake of September 11, many attempted to provide meaning and testimony to the attacks and, as a result, the event became difficult to fully comprehend, which led to a feeling of failed commemoration. Powers illuminates the ways that similar ordering devices were attempted for personal trauma as for national trauma, yet the attacks occurred on both geographical and ideological territory.

If a character fails to commemorate the attacks, then the character feels alienated from the community, resulting in a feeling that the experience is ultimately false and a return to normal has failed. Similar to Žižek's paranoiac fantasy, several characters claim Nebraska as a fake or a dreamed space; those characters did not flip their truck on a cold Nebraska night. Karen quips, "Kearney, Nebraska: a colossal fake, a life-sized, hollow replica. She'd thought as much herself, all while growing up,"[29] while Dr. Gerald Weber states, "the virgin prairies of Nebraska were a dream, after the minefields of Long Island and Manhattan."[30] Weber's relationship with Kearney and Manhattan provides the foundation for an analysis of the effect of geography on a person, in particular how Weber does not fully recognize himself in the commemoration in Manhattan nor in the lack of commemoration in Kearney.

Whereas many September 11 narratives focus on the attacks or the days shortly after the event, Powers describes a different perspective of the fallen World Trade Center, particularly the ways the towers provided orienting devices and now Lower Manhattan seems false. Powers describes Weber's experience walking through Manhattan:

> The shadows were all wrong: still disorienting, more than eight months on. A patch of sky where there should be none. Weber hadn't been in since early spring, when witnessing the unnerving light show—two massive banks of spotlights pointing into the air, like something out of his

book's chapter on phantom limbs. The images flared up in him again, the ones that had slowly extinguished over three-quarters of a year. That one, unthinkable morning was real; everything since had been a narcoleptic lie. He walked south through the unbearably normal streets, thinking he might get by just fine without ever seeing this city again.[31]

The passage signals Weber's failed commemoration, resulting in his alienation from New York City, which could be read as further comparison between Capgras syndrome, a rare neurological disorder that makes the sufferer believe that loved ones are imposters or doubles, and post–September 11 experience, in particular the ways that an individual may misidentify reality. According to Powers, "I suppose that something vaguely like that loss of recognition has happened to me and many people that I care about, since the attacks and America's subsequent response"[32] and "the familiar seems strange, and the strange becomes familiar. We still live in precisely the same country. But nothing about it will ever feel familiar again, in the way it once did."[33] In effect, Powers uses Mark Schluter's car accident in *The Echo Maker* as a stand-in for the widespread effect of post–September 11. The fallen World Trade Center described as a phantom limb serves as a metaphor for Powers's rendering of September 11. Powers states, "More disconcerting still were the phantom limbs. Nothing worse than excruciating pain in a limb that no longer existed, pain dismissed by the rest of the world as purely imaginary—*all in your head*—as if there were another kind. A person could suffer persistent tenderness in any removed part."[34] For many Americans, as well as Weber, the pain of September 11 persists within experience despite attempts at incorporating the attacks into daily life. Whereas most writers locate the pain within Manhattan, Powers suggests the pain transcends geographical location.

To support this claim, Weber attempts to control his memory of the attacks because the cultural memory of the attacks developed from catastrophe to commemoration. In summary, Weber becomes unsettled by how unbearably normal the streets are because the images of the attacks still occupy his psyche. When Powers details the effect of time—"eight months on" and "three-quarters of a year"—on Weber's imagining of September 11, Weber's sentiment at the one year anniversary is telling: "September came, that bleak first anniversary ... He tried to recall the public dread of the year before, turning on the radio to find the world blown away. The force was intact, though the details were gone."[35] For Weber, the anniversary signaled the move from public dread and unfamiliarity to the current state of the world. Or in other words, as President Bush stated, "None of us will forget this day. Yet, we go forward to defend freedom and all that is good and just in the world."[36] Ultimately, for Weber and Bush, the force of the attacks should be ever present; however, the nation had moved on to retaliation. Therefore, the widespread footage of the attacks had been replaced by short clips of the war in Afghanistan, suggesting that the events associated with September 11 had been moved to the background. Powers details a return to normal in the following passage:

> The arid chain stores along the strip gave way, in a handful of blocks, to gingerbread Victorians with wraparound porches. Just past these lay the core of an old downtown. The ghost of a prairie outpost, circa 1890, still looked out from the high, squared-off brick storefront facades ... He could now read the posters in the shop windows: Celebrate Freedom Rally; Corvette Show; Faith In Bloom Garden Tour ... He [Weber] passed a monument to the local dead of the two world wars. The whole tableau left him uneasy.[37]

Within this tableau, the only character from New York becomes discomforted by the local commemoration in Kearney because of its fragmented commemoration from New York and two world wars. Weber seems to worry that September 11 may fade from view instead of remaining the preeminent event that defies all comparison and understanding, in part because the similarly catastrophic events of the two world wars are condensed to the local monuments to which Weber hardly responds. In other words, the individual people and moments have shifted into faceless bodies until they have become part of a tableau.

In *The Echo Maker*, by focusing on how the character responds to the attacks in the Midwest, Powers shifts a September 11 trope of how a New Yorker responds to the attacks into an atypical narrative. Although the tableau signals a typical day in Kearney, the posters in the windows function in two ways. First, the "Celebrate Freedom Rally" offers one type of reaction to September 11: Show defiance by organizing a rally. As Bush put it, "When we fight terror, we fight tyranny; and so we remember,"[38] and "We will remember the dead and what we owe them."[39] President Bush also asked the American people to live their lives, promising, "I will not forget this wound to our country or those who inflicted it; I will not yield; I will not rest; I will not relent in waging this struggle for freedom and security for the American people."[40] The posters' second function is to suggest that if the residents attend the Corvette Show or the Faith in Bloom Tour, they will balance commemoration with the continuation of their lives. Kearney offered commemoration and normalcy, which became what troubled Weber. Despite President Bush's promise, Weber worries that September 11 may fade from view instead of remaining the unique event, in part because Weber hardly responds to the local monuments commemorating the similarly catastrophic events of two world wars. So then will he forget September 11 with enough time, as well? Powers suggests a peaceful city troubles Weber because the United States is at war; Weber thus fails both to commemorate the attacks and to support the national response to the attacks.

Along these lines, President Bush addressed the nation from the U.S. Capitol and began his speech with, "In the normal course of events, Presidents come to this chamber to report on the state of the Union."[41] The remarks were given as a result of an atypical event. In effect, the substance of Bush's address was to define the events that took place on September 11 as themselves exceedingly rare and atypical, an interruption of the routine course of daily events. Even within the context of previous wars and surprise attacks, September 11 was different:

> Americans have known wars—but for the past 136 years, they have been wars on foreign soil, except for one Sunday in 1941. Americans have known the casualties of war—but not at the center of a great city on a peaceful morning. Americans have known surprise attacks—but never before on thousands of civilians. All of this was brought upon us in a single day—and night fell on a different world, a world where freedom itself is under attack.[42]

Bush provides a description of the attacks that would claim September 11 as a unique event while contextualizing the event against other catastrophic events, suggesting the resiliency of the American psyche. Powers situates the personal Schluter event against the first anniversary of September 11, the escalation of the war in Iraq, footage of Afghanistan, and domestic manifestations of these effects to show that reactionary policy decisions had failed to completely take hold in Nebraska. As Kurt Jacobsen writes, "despite a robust government campaign since September 11 to silence any whisper of dissent, the US shows healthy signs of restoring a semblance of democratic give-and-take."[43] Throughout *The Echo Maker*, Powers underpins the central narrative with mentions of September 11, the war in Afghanistan, and the escalation leading to the war in Iraq. Despite the initial claims about the unnaturalness of September 11, Bush evoked the memory of other catastrophic events, thus navigating a fine line between speaking about the event as anomaly and as one we had seen before. Powers mirrors this feeling when Weber is in a restaurant and a television catches his attention:

> A television suspended above their corner booth breaks the news. Operation Iraqi Freedom has begun. War had been so long in coming Weber feels only mild déjà vu. They watch the cycling, impenetrable footage, the president, looping over and over: *May God bless our country and all who defend her.*[44]

Much like the Bush speech on September 20, Weber feels "mild déjà vu" in this moment because the footage is unique, yet the declaration feels similar to those made in films or in war.

Similar to September 11, the wars in Afghanistan and Iraq repeatedly appear within the narrative, yet the experience is tangential. One moment occurs early in the novel when Karin enters the hospital waiting room. Powers writes, "in the corner, a muted television beamed images of a mountain wasteland scattered with guerrillas. Afghanistan, winter, 2002. After a while, she noticed a thread of blood wicking down her right index finger, where she'd bitten through her cuticle."[45] In line with September 11 experience, Karin experiences the war in Afghanistan through the television. The television placed in the corner implies a peripheral existence for the war. The contrast between the blood on the cuticle and the violence on the screen signals a privileging of the personal trauma instead of the cultural trauma. For Karin, the blood on the cuticle becomes easily identified as a wound against her; while the violence on the screen undoubtedly affects her, those wounds are unknown. Along these lines, the people in the waiting room do not acknowledge the television; they focus on their individual trauma instead of the conflict occurring in Afghanistan. Thus, Powers implies the response to September 11 entered the outskirts of people's vision.

Throughout *Gain* and *The Echo Maker* characters retaliate with violence once they are displaced from the communal commemoration. As the cultural memory of September 11 develops into retaliation for the attacks, Mark's life begins to spiral out of control as he learns information about the accident and begins to distrust those closest to him even more, which could be read as a stand-in for the feeling of isolation some Americans may have felt with regard to the reactionary policies of the Bush administration. Now, in 2003, Mark believes those around him continually lie to him. One such character is Tommy Rupp, who has been deployed to Iraq and arrives at Mark's home to bid farewell. The following dialogue suggests the impending war in Iraq was a "Round Two," that is, a continuation of a prior conflict—the Gulf War of the 1990s—and not a response to September 11:

> Round two, Rupp said. The real thing this time. Going after the bastards who brought down the Towers.
> They're dead, Mark said, more to the dog than to Rupp. Died on impact in a flaming fireball.[46]

By incorporating this plotline, Powers suggests the wars in Iraq and Afghanistan affect life in Nebraska, yet Rupp is the only character deployed. On the one hand, Powers may have believed that the wars were outside his central narrative aims, and as such, he did not need to deploy several characters; however, Powers may have felt the political climate was such that it would seem unlikely for a character not to be affected by the military operations. On the other hand, Powers may have considered the wars in Iraq and Afghanistan to be on the periphery to the characters. Thus, commemoration in the Midwest is relegated to the faceless military personnel deployed in Iraq and Afghanistan, and, as a result, September 11 becomes background to the day-to-day life of the characters. *The Echo Maker* thereby reinforces the non-local body politic rather than the local narratives of New York City.

Despite the attempts at unity, Powers describes failed commemoration, particularly the ways certain characters respond to the policy decisions of the Bush administration, resulting in isolation from a sense of national unity. One moment of connection and estrangement between characters occurs in a scene for the Fourth of July. The scene occurs after Mark's release from the hospital and within tense moments of Mark and Karin's relationship. Mark and his friends talk about where America would strike next while Bonnie, Mark's girlfriend, offers that the Iraq War was predicted in the Bible and Karin suggests that every dropped bomb could be creating more terrorists.[47] The variety of responses provides a useful comparison between those willing to consent to the war (the boys), those believing it was predicted (Bonnie), and those who objected to the war effort early on (Karin). In effect, the series of responses illuminates tensions between the meaning of the attacks from the Bush administration and the individual citizens. More important still, the citizens in *The Echo Maker* do not fully identify with the official commemoration or retaliation.

Ultimately, Powers describes an experience that does not unnecessarily heighten the September 11 experience nor ignore the subsequent effects of the attacks. Rather *The Echo Maker* details the "livable sense" of 2002 and 2003. In line with Powers's comparison of post–September 11 life to Capgras syndrome, Barbara, Mark's nurse's aide, states, "Mark is right, you know. The whole place, a substitute. I mean: Is this country anyplace you recognize?"[48] If *The Echo Maker* became the preeminent post–September 11 novel, then experience would comprise misrecognition, loneliness, and alienation, instead of the common notion of a culture of commemoration. Despite the allure of placing a narrative within the familiar frame of the cosmopolitan, Powers returns to the Midwest to show the importance of their response framework. Through the midwestern setting, he shows the hidden cracks and slipshod repairs of an American culture in an era of failed commemoration.

Notes

1. Daniel Heischman, "The Uncanniness of September 11th," *Journal of Religion and Health* 41, no. 3 (2002): 197.
2. Jürgen Habermas, *The Divided West* (Cambridge: Polity, 2006), 7.
3. David Simpson, *9/11: The Culture of Commemoration* (Chicago: University of Chicago Press, 2006).
4. Ingrid Sischy, "Triumph of the Still," *Vanity Fair* (December 2001): 193.
5. Slavoj Žižek, *Welcome to the Desert of the Real!: Five Essays on 11 September and Related Dates* (London: Verso, 2002), 15.
6. Ryan M. Brooks, "'Clean Hands': Post-Political Form in Richard Powers's *Gain*," *Twentieth Century Literature* 59, no. 3 (2013): 449.
7. Richard Powers, *Gain* (New York: Picador, 1998), 2.
8. Frederick Jameson, "The Cultural Logic of Late Capitalism," in *Postmodernism or the Culture of Late Capitalism* (Durham, NC: Duke University, 1991), 3.
9. Ralph Clare, "Your Loss Is Their Gain: The Corporate Body and the Corporeal Body in Richard Powers's *Gain*," *Critique: Studies in Contemporary Fiction* 54, no. 1 (2013): 28.
10. Jameson, "Cultural Logic," 7.
11. Powers, *Gain*, 4.
12. Ibid., 204.
13. Jameson, "Cultural Logic," 16.
14. Powers, *Gain*, 127.
15. Ibid., 68.
16. Ibid., 288.
17. Ibid., 292.
18. Jameson, "Cultural Logic," 17.
19. Brooks, "'Clean Hands,'" 453.
20. Jameson, "Cultural Logic," 14.
21. James Gibbons, "Beyond Recognition," *Bookforum* (September/October/November 2006).
22. Richard Powers, *The Echo Maker* (New York: Farrar, Straus and Giroux, 2006), 414.
23. David Ryan, "Framing September 11: Rhetorical Device and Photographic Opinion," *European Journal of American Culture* 23, no. 1 (2004): 7.
24. Powers, *The Echo Maker*, 212.
25. Maja Zehfuss, "Forget September 11," *Third World Quarterly* 24, no. 3 (2003): 518.
26. Powers, *The Echo Maker*, 106.
27. Ibid., 202.
28. Ibid., 203.
29. Ibid., 197.
30. Ibid., 159.
31. Ibid., 99.

32. Neda Ulaby, "'Echo Maker' Wins National Book Award for Fiction," *NPR*, November 16, 2006.
33. Ibid.
34. Powers, *The Echo Maker*, 259.
35. Ibid., 271.
36. George W. Bush, "Address to the Nation on the Terrorist Attacks," *Weekly Compilation of Presidential Documents* 37, no. 37 (2001), 1301.
37. Powers, *The Echo Maker*, 166.
38. George W. Bush, "The World Will Always Remember September 11," *Weekly Compilation of Presidential Documents* 37, no. 50 (2001), 1775.
39. Ibid.
40. Ibid.
41. George W. Bush, "Address Before a Joint Session of the Congress on the United States Response to the Terrorist Attacks of September 11," *Weekly Compilation of Presidential Documents* 37, no. 38 (2001), 1347.
42. Ibid.
43. Kurt Jacobsen, "US after September 11: Returning to Normal?" *Economic and Political Weekly* 37, no. 28 (2002): 2881–82.
44. Powers, *The Echo Maker*, 432.
45. Ibid., 8.
46. Ibid., 386.
47. Ibid.
48. Ibid.

Seretha D. Williams
Michelle Story-Stewart
Patrick C. Riley

Gary, Indiana, on the Cusp of Greatness

Richard G. Hatcher and the National Black Political Convention of 1972

Not only has Gary, Indiana, been described as "magic city,"[1] "city of the century,"[2] "miracle city,"[3] but also, in the 1990s, "murder capital."[4] Outsiders tend to recognize the city as the home of the fictional character Harold Hill or as the hometown of megastar Michael Jackson and the Jackson Five. Harold Hill, the fast-talking instrument salesman in Meredith Willson's *The Music Man*, tells the unsuspecting residents of River City, Iowa, that he is a 1905 graduate of the Gary Conservatory. Marian, the town's librarian, points out that Gary was not founded until 1906, a fact that causes her to doubt that Harold is who he says he is. The song "Gary, Indiana" has become one of the most recognizable songs from the 1957 musical and its 1962 film adaptation. Its lighthearted homey lyrics capture a certain midwestern midcentury zeitgeist. However, even this song casts a shadow over Gary. The city, through its association with the corrupt Harold Hill, is depicted as a site of corruption or trickery. Similarly, the Jackson Five's song "Goin' Back to Indiana" is, on its surface, celebratory of small-town, slow-paced values most associate with the Midwest. The song does not mention Gary by name, an omission that is suggestive of the creative license Jackson handlers took in constructing the backstory of the famous brothers. The song references Roosevelt High School, a school created specifically for blacks built after the Emerson school strike in 1927,[5] but the lyrics of the song are bucolic and do not directly address the racial and political climate of 1971 when the song was released. However, the underlying message is one of racial solidarity. The Jacksons had gone Hollywood but not forgotten their roots in Gary, a city whose African American population had grown to more than 50 percent of the residents. More important for the Jackson Five's public relations was the lore that the group had been discovered and rescued by Diana Ross and Motown. According to S. Paul O'Hara, "Promoters and reviewers tended to place the Jacksons into a storyline of black ghettoization, hard streets, and escape."[6] In the public imagination, Gary is both industrial utopia and model of urban decay.

Known for a reputation of gambling, prostitution, government corruption, and race riots dating back to its founding, Gary, before the 1967 election of Mayor Richard Gordon Hatcher, the first African American to hold the office, seemed the least likely place to spark a nationwide political revolution. However, in 1972, Gary and Mayor Hatcher hosted a political convention that would signal a defining moment in American politics. The National Black Political Convention of 1972, the first of its kind, was a catalyst for African American leadership in electoral politics. The assassination of Rev. Dr. Martin Luther King, the rise of the Black Power Movement, and the election of Richard Nixon to the presidency influenced the strategies African American leaders and organizations believed would be the most effective and the most expedient. However, the movement in the 1960s and 1970s had not identified key issues around which interested parties could galvanize.

The challenge of the convention, then, was to bring together leaders of established Civil Rights and Black Power organizations, African Americans who held elected office, grassroots activists, and everyday people with a stake in improving the socioeconomic conditions of African Americans. The convention delegates' primary goal was to create a national black political agenda with specific and measurable goals. As Ronald Waters notes, "The whole notion of black agendas was spawned there in Gary."[7] The Black Power Movement of the late 1960s and '70s shaped the social and cultural landscape of the United States and ushered in new methods for agitating. Gary, a symbol of urban America, was an important site of resistance in this post–Malcolm X and post–Martin Luther King, Jr., environment, and its social and political leaders played an important role in fashioning the political identity of Black America.

Gary's Origins

Along the sandy, marshy shores of Lake Michigan, east of Chicago, grew Gary, Indiana, billed as "the model industrial city of the world."[8] The city was founded in 1906 as a company town for the employees of U.S. Steel. From the beginning, the city was blue-collar and multicultural. Immigrants from Poland, Croatia, Italy, Russia, Greece, Hungary, and other southern and eastern European nations composed the majority of the workforce and the population of the city.[9] African Americans were only 10 percent of the early population of the city.

From the city's inception, ethnic tensions were a problem. Although "black and foreign born working class lived in the same south side neighborhoods,"[10] the school board quickly instituted a segregated school system that remained intact into the second half of the twentieth century. Living conditions for immigrant and African American families were deplorable in the early decades of the city. Overcrowding, disease, and crime were major problems for the workers at home, while the inhumane 84-hour workweek, low wages, and unsafe mill conditions occupied workplace debates.[11] Workers in the region were frustrated with U.S. Steel chair Elbert H. Gary's unwillingness to negotiate, and union leaders called for a strike after failed discussions with management. Gary blamed the strike on external meddling by union leaders. The Great Steel Strike of 1919, which failed to gain union recognition for steel workers in major steel centers in Pittsburgh, Chicago, and Gary, added to the racial and ethnic strife in the Midwest.[12] Companies routinely employed African American workers, who were not welcome in organized labor groups, as strikebreakers. As Paul D. Moreno surmises, "Although they were not the only group to act as strikebreakers, blacks were again singled out as having been the cause of the defeat ... The steel magnates were turning blacks into 'a race of strikebreakers,' using them as the czars used the Cossacks, to keep other minorities under control."[13] On October 4, 1919, an ethnically diverse group of striking workers left a union meeting and encountered a group of black workers on a streetcar. According to Jan Voogd, "The mob of white strikers beat the [40 black] workers, dragging them through the streets, and, then, hysterical, they canvassed out over an eight-block area, leaving a wake of unconscious victims falling behind them on the streets."[14] The violence was indicative of the growing epidemic of so-called race riots that occurred that year. The Red Summer of 1919 refers to the outbreak of racial violence during the summer and fall of 1919 in Chicago, Illinois; Elaine, Arkansas; Washington, DC; and other cities. Despite the multicultural mix of the city from its very founding, Gary did not afford the same opportunities to its African American residents as it did to its other ethnic American groups. This hostility, exclusion, and violence toward African Americans in the early twentieth century foreshadowed and certainly influenced the conditions that would eventually lead to white flight and economic demise.

Muigwithania and the Rise of Richard G. Hatcher

Richard G. Hatcher, who would become the first African American mayor of a major city, was born and raised in nearby Michigan City, Indiana. His family, like many other African American families, moved to the Midwest as a part of the Great Migration, a period in which African Americans living in the South left those states in great numbers to take advantage of the opportunities for factory work World War I created. In the Midwest, Chicago, Cleveland, Detroit, and St. Louis received a massive influx of southern blacks between 1910 and 1970.[15] However, Hatcher's parents, both blue-collar laborers, struggled to provide for their family during the Great Depression and beyond. Hatcher, who excelled in sports, earned a scholarship to Indiana University and eventually earned his law degree from Valparaiso University. He was admitted to the bar in 1959, in the midst of the Civil Rights Movement. While marches were an integral tool and strategy of the early and middle periods of the movement, significant shifts in the courts' attitudes toward marchers' rights in the late 1960s would compel activists to shift their focus to the electoral arena.

According to James Lane, "The vehicle through which Hatcher entered Gary politics was Muigwithania,"[16] a northwest Indiana group dedicated to improving political and economic conditions for black people in the region. Muigwithania is a Kikuyu word that describes "an authoritative elder who gets people to agree"[17] for the common good, a reconciler. *Muigwithania* was the name of Jomo Kenyatta's Kikuyu-language monthly newspaper. Jomo Kenyatta, a leader in East Africa's rebellion against colonial rule and later president of independent Kenya, served as an inspiration for the Indiana group that included Hatcher and other black attorneys and businessmen. Hatcher was elected president of the group in 1962, and soon thereafter ran for council-man-at-large in Gary and won. Dozier Allen, a member of Muigwithania, said of Hatcher, "Hatcher was Muigwithania's first president. He emerged as a leader for a number of reasons."[18] Leadership of Muigwithania was a stepping stone for Hatcher, whose sights were set on local government. Hatcher, a natural leader, had an ability to mobilize blacks through speeches that blended the style of Baptist preachers with the message of the rising Black Nationalism. Moreover, he was willing to challenge the political machine and disrupt the status quo.

Nevertheless, black Garyites were unsure of Hatcher, in part because he was an outsider, having grown up in Michigan City, and started his career in East Chicago, Indiana. John Grigsby recalled, "I wasn't sure Councilman Hatcher was that man [for the job]. The only way I could be sure was to meet him. I went to his office in mid-July, 1966, and we talked. I saw a *Mohammed Speaks* paper behind his desk. That really convinced me."[19] Although Hatcher never labelled himself as a black nationalist or as a radical, he never shied away from aligning himself with progressive groups such as the Nation of Islam. He collaborated with a vast array of African American–led organizations with equal ease, and his willingness to include disparate voices and views earned him public trust and political supporters.

In 1967, Hatcher ran against Gary's Mayor A. Martin Katz, who was a part of the Democratic machine that had a stranglehold on government in the region. During the campaign, Hatcher was threatened, cajoled, and offered bribes to get out of the race. In line with Gary's history of racial terrorism, Barbara Farrar and Charlotte Johnson confirmed the persistent threats on Hatcher's life, the surveillance of Hatcher's whereabouts, and the armed thugs sent to his home.[20] Yet, despite the danger and the improbability of his candidacy, Hatcher unseated Katz to win the Democratic nomination. His run against Republican Joseph Radigan was equally challenging. Behind the scenes, county Democratic leaders expected Hatcher to play ball and agree to appoint their people to key city positions; however, Hatcher refused, and Democratic County Chairman John Krupa launched a political attack on Hatcher that characterized Hatcher as a race-baiting communist radical. More significantly, the Democratic Party tampered with voter registration rolls. Hatcher filed a federal suit charging Krupa and the party with violating the 1965 Voting Rights Act; under investigation by the FBI, Krupa added the names of more than 5000 black voters back to the eligible voters list, and "a panel of judges ordered 1,096 'ghost' names stricken."[21]

Hatcher won the election, becoming the first African American mayor of Gary and the first African American mayor of a city with a population greater than 100,000.[22] The inauguration of Richard Hatcher on January 1, 1968, occurring almost three years after the murder of civil rights leader Malcolm X and the signing of the Voters Rights Act, fourteen years after the Supreme Court decision *Brown v. Board of Education of Topeka, KS*, forty-nine years after the nationwide race riots of 1919, and 103 years after the end of the American Civil War, was the culmination of decades of struggle and resistance. Instantaneously Hatcher rose to stardom as a national spokesperson for civil rights, and the city of Gary was suddenly thrust into the national spotlight. His mayoralty became a symbol of African American progress.

Hatcher, who envisioned himself as a reconciler, believed that he could bring the racially divided city together and implement programs for the common good. He used his national standing and connections to leaders such as Julian Bond and Jesse Jackson, Sr., and celebrities such as Muhammad Ali and Harry Belafonte to garner political and financial support for his administration. He applied for and received federal grants to build a social infrastructure that would uplift the poor and disenfranchised of the city, who were disproportionately African American. Hatcher noted, "One thing you learn the first week in the Mayor's office is how little power you actually have ... While I didn't have a lot of political influence locally, I had influence nationally."[23] Gary and its citizens faced a number of local and national challenges during Hatcher's first term. The murders of civil rights leader Martin Luther King, Jr., and Illinois Black Panther Party Chair Fred Hampton, the arrests and trials of Angela Davis and Bobby Seale, and police attacks on students at South Carolina State and Jackson State were national events that concerned Hatcher's constituents. At home, Hatcher battled with the city council and regional and state officials and attempted to address the social and economic realities of inequity in his adopted hometown. Although Hatcher was successful at garnering financial support from the federal government, he was less successful at implementing the change his supporters expected. Crime, unaffordable housing, and joblessness were major problems facing Hatcher's administration, and his constituents allowed him no honeymoon period.[24] Despite voter impatience at the slow pace of change, Hatcher was elected to a second term. Hatcher's coalition with Muigwithania, the loyalty of African American voters, and the influence of high-profile black leaders and entertainers helped Hatcher stave off political challenges.

"It's Nation Time"
In 1969, Shirley Chisholm and twelve other African American members of Congress formed the Democratic Select Committee, the predecessor to the contemporary Congressional Black Caucus. The aim of the committee was to unite and collaborate on issues common to their constituents. Overlapping the growth in African Americans' political enfranchisement was the development and growth of the Black Studies movement on college campuses. Margaret Walker's Institute for the Study of the History, Life, and Culture of Black People at Jackson State University (formerly Jackson State College) and the first Black Studies program at San Francisco State University (formerly San Francisco State College) were pioneering programs founded in 1968 that were a part of a new strategy of civil rights. Institution building was a focal point of black activism in the late 1960s, and institutes and programs such as these served as think tanks for the burgeoning Black Power and Black Convention movements.

    Imamu Amiri Baraka, a poet and activist, was closely aligned with Black Nationalism in the late 1960s and the 1970s. A leader of the Black Arts Movement and involved in political activism, Baraka was integral in bringing together groups that did not ordinarily agree on the best approach for black liberation. In 1972, Baraka was elected national chairman of the Congress of African People, one of the most powerful nationalist groups; as a result, CAP was an important player in the coordination of the National Black Political Convention in Gary.[25] Baraka's poem "It's Nation Time" gave the movement one of its most famous rally cries. The convention was the product of numerous meetings and brainstorming sessions held throughout the country between 1969 and 1971. According to Komozi Woodard, the Modern Black Convention Movement dates back to the 1966 Black Arts Convention in Detroit and the National Black Power conference in Washington, DC Baraka was integral to each of these groups and rose to leadership of the MBCM. Woodard notes, "the Modern Black Convention Movement produced four critical organizations: the Congress of African People, the African Liberation Support Committees, the National Black Assembly, and the Black Women's United Front."[26]

In his second term as mayor, Hatcher offered to host the first National Black Political Convention in Gary, March 10–12, 1972. Other large cities did not want to host it in fear of protests, violence, or police harassment. Gary, with its citizenry comprising more than 50 percent black people and its black mayor, was the most viable option for the convention. Hatcher, Baraka, and Congressman Charles Diggs would be the primary organizers of the event. Hatcher's City Hall organized a cleanup campaign to prepare for the convention. West Side High School, Indiana's largest high school at the time of its opening in 1968, was decorated with red, black, and green streamers and flags, welcoming visitors to the city. Dozens of vendors were set up on site to sell memorabilia commemorating the historic event. Although accounts vary widely, approximately 8000–12,000 delegates and participants attended the convention. Gary had only one downtown hotel, so convention-goers stayed with local residents in their homes or traveled to hotels in Chicago, thirty miles away. Singer, activist, and Hatcher supporter Harry Belafonte remembered the convention thusly:

> I remember talking with, ah, with Richard Hatcher at the convention and, ah, because he had put a lot into making this thing come about. As a matter of fact, it was setting Gary, Indiana to become a center for ongoing civil rights activity and hope that in the city of Gary, Indiana they would be able to build a, a, an institution that would house, become the major think tank of all people involved in the human rights and in the Civil Rights Movement, in the, ah, ah, as a matter of fact it's now being turned into a museum,

ah, some, some of what has been achieved. But this was the, the beginning of that moment, ah, that we would find this place, we'd come to this convening and I had never seen a collection of greater diversification except for the march on Washington. Ah, at this meeting in Gary, Indiana there was everyone represented, the NAACP, Black Republicans, Black communists, Black Democrats, all the, the, the civil rights organizations and individuals, ah, ah. And there was a spirit of hope but there was also a sense that, ah, somewhere in this complex of bodies, people also looking to see in this squash of people, in, in, this overview, if you could look into, all, which one was going to be the leader? Which one or which group was going to be the force? People were looking for answers. People were looking for all kinds of things. It was, it was a very interesting convention.[27]

From the onset, Hatcher, Baraka, and Diggs recognized that the nationalist factions and the moderate factions would be difficult to unite. Some groups and leaders decided not to participate in the convention at all. In a 2012 lecture, former Mayor Hatcher said, "I wanted to be kind of in between" the mainstream elected officials and the black nationalists.[28]

Most notably absent were Congresswoman Shirley Chisholm, who had just launched a campaign for the U.S. presidency, and the leadership of the NAACP, who, instead, issued a repudiation of the convention and some of its more controversial positions. The NAACP objected to the exclusion of whites and the separatist rhetoric of the preamble of the National Black Political Agenda and flatly rejected the platform committee's anti-Israel and anti-busing proposals. A letter from NAACP Director Roy Wilkins to Charles Diggs explains, "For all these reasons, the National Association for the Advancement of Colored People cannot join in the National Black Assembly or in any continuing activity or program sponsored, led or dominated by the structure which was responsible for the staging of the Black Political Convention."[29]

Hatcher's opening address attempted to strike the right tone for the convention. With a balanced mixture of pathos and logos, Hatcher addressed the NBPC.[30] He opened with a familiar biblical analogy that compared blacks in America to Israelites enslaved in Egypt by the pharaoh. He then reminded the audience of W.E.B. DuBois's early work in pan-Africanism, enjoining the delegates to see that the struggles of black people on the African continent and in the diaspora are interrelated. He rejected the public call to denounce communist Angela Davis and Black Panther Bobby Seale, both of whom had been arrested and labelled as a part of the extremist fringe of the Black Power Movement. Hatcher told the crowd, "In our infinite patience, we have tried year after year, election after election, to work with the two major political parties. We believed the pledges, believed the platforms, believed the promises, each time hoping they would come true ... We are through believing. We are through hoping ... If we are to support any political party, the price will now run high—very high."[31] Although Hatcher issued a scathing indictment of U.S. politics, he did not call definitively for the creation of a black political party. Instead, he suggested, "And when, if they leave us no choice—and if we form a third political movement, we shall take with us Chicanos, Puerto Ricans, Indians, Orientals, a wonderful kaleidoscope of colors."[32] Hatcher even included "the best of white America" in this new party. Jesse Jackson, Sr., another convention headliner, invoked the Black Power phrase "It's Nation Time"[33] during his fiery address at the convention. Jackson, who had been a part of Martin Luther King, Jr.,'s inner circle, was especially adept at moving among different groups and speaking the language of black consciousness. He, too, hinted at the possibility of a third party but stopped short of rejecting the Democratic Party as a viable option for implementing a black agenda.

Black nationalists believed the convention speeches were not progressive enough and, throughout the convention, pressed moderates to back an all-black political party. The compromise was the formation of the National Black Assembly, an organization whose role post-convention would be the "shaping, projecting, and institutionalization of an independent, progressive black politics of social transformation, economic democracy, and self determination."[34] Steven F. Lawson suggests that one of the most important outcomes of the convention was the creation of the National Black Political Assembly.[35] However, one could argue that the simple act of gathering without the gaze or judgment of mainstream America was an even greater accomplishment. Only the black press was invited to cover the event; mainstream presses were told to hire black reporters if they wanted full access to the convention.

Betty Shabazz and Coretta Scott King, social justice activists and the widows of slain icons Malcolm X and Martin Luther King, Jr., shared a stage at the event. The symbolism of their presence together was undeniable. King and X's approaches to remedying racism and oppression had been divergent. Black Power advocates of the 1970s embraced Malcolm X's prescription for working outside the system of American justice, which they deemed corrupt, and creating self-sufficient and sustainable black communities more than they did King's prescription for working within the system and improving socioeconomic conditions though integration. Thus, the meeting of their wives signaled an important moment of unification. Other program participants included Georgia Representative Julian Bond; California Assemblywoman Yvonne Braithwaite; U.S. Representatives Barbara Jordan, Walter Fauntroy, and Ronald Dellums; actor Richard Roundtree; Minister Louis Farrakhan of the Nation of Islam; historian Vincent Harding; soul singer Kim Weston; and a host of other celebrities, activists, and politicians. Chants of "It's Nation Time" permeated the room. All of the delegates and attendees called for immediate change with that chant. In spirit, everyone was of one accord, but, in fact, the agenda-making process was not harmonious.

The domestic components of the platform called for the abolishment of death penalties, the establishment of national health insurance, and guaranteed minimum wages for workers and minimum annual incomes for families. The language and principles of socialism heavily influenced the final agenda, a fact that made many moderates and elected officials uncomfortable. Globally, the agenda addressed the political and economic oppression of black and brown people. Charles Diggs said, "We recognize no difference between the political powerlessness in the Bantustans of South African and the Bantustans of America."[36] While black women played an integral role in the convention, they did not have an equitable role in deciding the platform for the convention. The agenda did not address gender inequities directly. Perhaps one of the most stunning slights of the convention was the decision not to support Shirley Chisholm's candidacy, even though her platform aligned well with the platform of the convention.

By all accounts, the convention, though inspirational, was chaotic. Sessions were disorderly and voices were silenced by the absence of rules of order. "Incident-ridden, experimental and raucous, the convention," according to Alex Poinsett, "nevertheless, produced 1) a National Black Political Agenda to serve as a guide for the national black community and a sort of checklist with which to evaluate politicians and their social programs, 2) a National Black Political Assembly to make political demands on the existing political system, and 3) a challenge not only to the effectiveness of American political institutions but also their very legitimacy."[37] Indeed, for blacks in the 1970s it was Nation Time, and for a brief period, Gary, Indiana, once a city hostile to its black residents, was at the center of the Black Power movement. When the convention closed on its third day, delegates and participants prepared to return to their respective states and begin the hard work of nation building.

The landmark election of Richard Hatcher, coupled with the first and only national black political convention held in Gary, affected black political mobilization, electoral advancement, and economic development. The gathering served as an impetus to a never-before-witnessed black political consciousness. In fact, this level of engagement in the political process had not been seen since the Emancipation Proclamation negated chattel slavery and catapulted African Americans into first-ever political positions of power (only to see institutional racism prevail and turn back every political advancement made).[38] To understand the historic significance of both Hatcher's election and the National Black Political Convention, both must be viewed in the context of the symbol versus substance. And since ultimately politics is about the allocation of resources, the convention opened the door and was a platform for nationally advancing both the political agenda and economic agenda of the black community. Hatcher's mayorship and the NBPC paved the way for African Americans across the country. "Getting the right to vote in '65 was the beginning of a process, but the convention in Gary solidified the sense of focus. This convention was overwhelming. It could not be turned around," Jesse Jackson, Sr., recalled. "It was important to have it in a city where the first black mayor of a northern city was the host. We couldn't have had the same convention if the climate had been hostile. Mayor Richard Hatcher was the driving force. He chaired the concept of a national convention into reality."[39] Jackson and others argue that the 1972 National Black Political Convention was a significant milestone in black politics of the Black Power era. As Michael Puente explains, "Over the next 10 years, the number of elected black politicians grew from 2,200 to more than 5,000."[40] There are currently forty-eight black members of Congress. In 1972, there were only fourteen.

Conclusion

Despite the national and international spotlight shone on Gary in the 1970s because of the NBPC or from the lore of its most famous natives the Jacksons, the city languished under the leadership of Richard Hatcher. High crime, unemployment, abandoned buildings, and illegal drug use plagued the city. One-time supporters began to criticize and to challenge Hatcher politically. His golden status as a civil rights champion tarnished over the twenty years he served as mayor. Some of the criticism is deserved, but much of the collapse of Gary was beyond Hatcher's control. Before Hatcher ever arrived in the city, Gary was a hotbed of racial strife. Gary was racially segregated, and its black citizens lived an existence that was separate and unequal. The Ku Klux Klan maintained a strong presence in the region, and black children grew up knowing there were places in the city they just could not go. Students at Emerson and Froebel high schools started a strike to protest the enrollment of black students. Black steelworkers were attacked by white ethnic minorities during the Great Steel Strike. Black men and women were not allowed to work in downtown shopping stores and black families were not allowed to go to the beach in Miller. That is the environment into which Hatcher moved. That is what life had been for black residents decades before Richard Hatcher came of age.

Once Hatcher was in office, he had to deal with the institutionalized racism that stood in the way of governing the city. The Democratic and Republican county parties posed constant problems because Hatcher would not acquiesce to the political machine. The state itself did little to assist, and eventually, federal funding for socioeconomic programming dried up. Many white residents thought Hatcher was bad for the city, felt he was only mayor for blacks, and feared integration of their neighborhoods and schools. They fled south, creating the town of Merrillville in 1971 to create a defined border between white and black.[41]

Perhaps the death knell for Gary was the failure of the steel industry. Layoffs and mill closings decimated the economy.[42] Workers who had been accustomed to living wage or middle-class salaries were forced into minimum-wage occupations that barely kept food on the table. Hatcher's lack of leadership on the day-to-day needs of his citizens and his inability to garner local support were two shortcomings of his administration. However, the plight of Gary is also the plight of other midwestern cities. The Rust Belt runs straight through Gary. Neither Hatcher's race nor his attempts to liberate black people can be blamed for the demise of the magic steel city.

Gary was always a city on the cusp of greatness but never quite made it. Early citizens believed Gary would rival Chicago, supplanting the city of big shoulders as an industry leader. During World Wars I and II, immigrants and black migrants came to Gary in search of the American dream and found steady employment and greater opportunity. In the late 1960s and '70s, Gary, again, was almost great. The city had the Jacksons and other claims to fame—among them Fred Williamson and Deniece Williams. The city had Richard Hatcher, who was a celebrity in his own right. And in 1972, Gary had center stage in the largest political meeting ever convened by black people. As S. Paul O'Hara observed, "For some, Gary was a space lost to a dangerous otherness (after 1967, this would be racial politics, crime, and white flight). Others saw in Gary a microcosm of all American cities and thus a laboratory of progressive experiments and modern solutions to industrialism and urbanism. Both of these were counterbalanced by a narrative of local pride and autonomy."[43]

What then is the legacy of the NBPC and, by extension, the legacy of Gary and Richard Hatcher? According to James Lane, "Hatcher relished playing a national leadership role on issues related to cities and civil rights, hectoring presidents on affirmative action and inspiring a new generation of black office seekers."[44] Black involvement in electoral politics increased exponentially in the 1970s and 1980s. For Hatcher, his personal legacy can be assessed by the number of his supporters and colleagues who went on to hold local, state, and federal positions. U.S. Representative Katie Hall, City Clerk Barbara Leek Wesson, Mayor Thomas Barnes, and countless others benefitted from Hatcher's administration and from his mentorship. Hatcher served as campaign director for both of Jesse Jackson, Sr.'s presidential campaigns and as chair of TransAfrica, a group that called for an end to apartheid in South Africa. Although Hatcher was a successful Civil Rights and Black Power movement leader, he was never able to create a Gary that lived up to its potential. From this history, we must conclude, "Ascension to high public offices by Black politicians in the cities cannot, as a singular strategy, address the multitudinous problems of the Black community."[45]

Notes

1. Birmingham, Alabama, another city built by steel, is also known as the Magic City.
2. Raymond A. Mohl and Neil Betten, *Steel City: Urban and Ethnic Patterns in Gary, Indiana, 1906–1950* (New York: Holmes and Meier, 1986), 11.
3. James B. Lane, *"City of the Century": A History of Gary, Indiana* (Bloomington: Indiana University Press, 1978), 27.
4. Paul Sloan, "Gary Takes Over as Murder Capital of US," *Chicago Tribune*. January 3, 1994, http://articles.chicagotribune.com/1994-01-03/news/9401030009_1_murder-rate-killings-unemployment-rate.
5. African American students were transferred to Emerson to alleviate overcrowding in other schools, and white students protested the integration by going on strike in 1927. Roosevelt was opened in 1931 as an all-black school. James H. Madison, *Indiana through Tradition and Change: A History of the Hoosier State and Its People 1920–1945* (Indianapolis: Indiana History Society Press, 2016), 280.
6. S. Paul O'Hara, *Gary: The Most American of All American Cities* (Bloomington: Indiana University Press, 2011), 142.
7. Ronald Waters, oral history, *Steel Shavings: Tie-Dyes and Color Lines, Life in the Calumet Region during the 1970s* 29, ed. James B. Lane (Gary: Indiana University Northwest, 1999), 149.
8. Raymond A. Mohl and Neil Betten, *Urban and Ethnic Patterns in Gary, Indiana, 1906–1950* (New York: Holmes and Meier, 1986), 13.
9. Ibid., 28.
10. Ibid., 55.
11. Lane, *"City of the Century,"* 52–53.
12. In his 1920 remarks to U.S. Steel stockholders at the company's annual meeting, Gary described the mill as an open shop, "which permits a man to work when and where he pleases, on terms mutually agreed upon ... Our men generally do not belong to unions because they know by long experience it is to their advantage to be free from dictation by outsiders." Elbert H. Gary, *Remarks by Elbert H. Gary, chairman, at annual meeting of the stockholders of the United States steel corporation, April 19, 1920*. (New York, 1922), 10. Hathi Trust Digital Library, https://catalog.hathitrust.org/Record/100110435.

13. Paul D. Moreno, *Black Americans and Organized Labor: A New History* (Baton Rouge: Louisiana State University Press, 2006), 132.
14. Jan Voogd, *Race Riots and Resistance: The Red Summer of 1919* (New York: Peter Lang, 2008), 70.
15. Alferdteen Harrison, *Black Exodus: The Great Migration from the American South* (Jackson, MS: University of Mississippi, 1991), vii–viii.
16. Lane, *"City of the Century,"* 284.
17. Bruce J. Berman and John M. Lonsdale, "The Labors of Muigwithania: Jomo Kenyatta as Author, 1928–45," *Research in African Literatures* 1 (1998), 16–42.
18. Dozier Allen, oral history, *Steel Shavings: Social Trends and Racial Tensions during the 1960s* 25 (Gary, IN: Indiana University, 1996), 83.
19. John Grigsby, oral history, *Steel Shavings: Social Trends and Racial Tensions during the 1960s* 25 (Gary, IN: Indiana University, 1996), 85.
20. Barbara Farrar, oral history, *Steel Shavings: Social Trends and Racial Tensions during the 1960s* 25 (Gary, IN: Indiana University, 1996), 88. Charlotte Johnson, oral history, *Steel Shavings: Social Trends and Racial Tensions during the 1960s* 25 (Gary, IN: Indiana University, 1996), 88.
21. Lane, *"City of the Century,"* 290.
22. It comes as a surprise to many Midwesterners, but there were three African American mayors in office in 1968, including Carl Stokes (the most notable) of Cleveland. However, the first midwestern African American mayor was Robert C. Henry of Springfield, Ohio. He became mayor in 1966 after being elected to the all-white city council and unanimously *appointed* mayor of this smaller city in southwestern Ohio. Although Mayor Hatcher was elected before Carl Stokes, he was inaugurated second—perhaps the reason many consider Stokes the first black man elected mayor of a larger city (population of 100,000+). There are some interesting comparisons among the three city leaders. Henry was a Republican who founded and ran a funeral home business. He served one term after refusing to run for a second in a town with blacks making up nearly 20 percent of the population. Democrat Stokes also served one term and was an Ohio Congressman before being elected mayor. Cleveland's 37 percent black population at the time was only a portion of his constituency; he also had white supporters in the city and suburbs including very well-off suburban businessmen. Hatcher, also a Democrat, served twenty years and was elected to Gary's city council before his successful mayoral run. At the time, Gary's more than 50 percent black population was Hatcher's only constituency.
23. James Lane, *Steel Shavings: Social Trends and Racial Tensions, during the 1960s* 25 (Gary, IN: Indiana University, 1996), 105.
24. Robert A. Catlin, *Racial Politics and Urban Planning: Gary, Indiana, 1980–1989* (Lexington, KY: University Press of Kentucky), 53.

25. Elizabeth Huston, *The New Black History: Revisiting the Second Reconstruction*, ed. Manning Marable (New York: Palgrave Macmillan, 2011), 139.
26. Komozi Woodard, *A Nation within a Nation: Amiri Baraka (LeRoi Jones) and Black Power Politics* (Chapel Hill: University of North Carolina Press, 1999), 2.
27. Harry Belafonte, interview transcript, Blackside, Inc., May 15, 1989, Washington University Libraries, Film and Media Archive, Henry Hampton Collection. http://digital.wustl.edu/e/eii/eiiweb/bel5427.0417.013harrybelafonte.html.
28. Richard G. Hatcher, "MayorHatcher2012BPC," *Youtube*, posted June 1, 2016. https://youtu.be/iitYzsEoa-Y.
29. "The NAACP and the Black Political Convention: Letter by Executive director Roy Wilkins to Representative Charles C. Diggs, Co-chair of the National Black Political Convention, May 3, 1972," *The Crisis* (August/September 1972): 229–30.
30. Richard G. Hatcher, "MayorHatcher2012BPC."
31. Richard G. Hatcher, "We Must Pave the Way: An Independent Black Political Thrust," *Vital Speeches of the Day* 38, issue 13 (April 15, 1972): 415.
32. Ibid.
33. Woodard, *A Nation within a Nation*.
34. Ron Daniels, "The National Black Political Assembly: Building Independent Black Politics in the 1980s," *The Black Scholar* 5, no. 4 (July/August 1984): 34.
35. Steven F. Lawson, *Running for Freedom: Civil Rights and Black Politics in America since 1941* (New York: McGraw-Hill), 146.
36. Alex Poinsett, "Unity Without Uniformity," *Ebony* (June 1972): 45.
37. Alex Poinsett, "Black Politics: An Unfulfilled Promise," *Ebony* (August 1975): 102.
38. Lucius Jefferson Barker, *Black Electoral Politics* (New Brunswick, NJ: Transaction Publishers, 1999), 194.
39. Rainbow PUSH Coalition, "PUSH Highlights the 40th Anniversary of Gary's National Black Political Convention." http://www.rainbowpush.org/news/single/push_highlights_40th_anniversary_of_garys_national_blk_political_convention.
40. Michael Puente, "Gary's National Black Political Convention, 40 years on," *WBEZ News*, March 9, 2012. https://www.wbez.org/shows/wbez-news/garys-national-black-political-convention-40-years-on/449ae089-207e-4547-b87d-844058c116d7.
41. Robert A. Catlin, *Racial Politics and Urban Planning: Gary, Indiana, 1980–1989* (Lexington, KY: University Press of Kentucky), 114.
42. Ibid., 92.

43. S. Paul O'Hara, *Gary: The Most American of All American Cities* (Bloomington: Indiana University Press, 2011), 149.
44. James Lane, *Steel Shavings: Social Trends and Racial Tensions during the 1960s* 25 (Gary, IN: Indiana University, 1996), 112.
45. William E. Nelson, Jr., *Race, Politics, and Economic Development*, ed. James Jennings (New York: Verso, 1992), xii.

Kimberly Wilmot Voss

Midwest Feminism

Kay Clarenbach and the Origin of the National Organization for Women

When Kathryn "Kay" Clarenbach came to the University of Wisconsin in Madison to study political science in 1937, she was not allowed to sit in the Rathskeller—a popular eatery in the Student Union. Her exclusion was based on her gender—women were excluded. In response, after buying her morning coffee at the Memorial Union, she would walk as slowly as she could through the Rathskeller to the Paul Bunyan Room—an area where women were permitted to study. Years later, she returned as a faculty member while also serving in national positions regarding women's roles in society. In fall 2016, an article about Clarenbach ran in the UW alumni magazine. The author noted that few knew of Clarenbach despite her significance. The writer gave the example of Clarenbach's walk through the Ratherskeller: "This quiet act of protest was a preview of Clarenbach's lifelong work, much of which played out in the background of history."[1] Decades later, the National Organization for Women would challenge numerous restaurant and bar policies across the country that excluded women.

In Clarenbach's later, most visible roles, she was a founder of the National Organization for Women (NOW) and the National Women's Political Caucus, as well as coordinator of the historic 1977 Houston National Women's Conference. The Wisconsin native's strong administrative skills and calm demeanor made her the perfect person to mediate the sometimes strident voices that also championed women's causes in the 1960s and 1970s.

The origins of the Women's Liberation Movement owe much to the women of the Midwest who laid the groundwork in the early and mid-1960s, and Clarenbach was at the center of the movement. Her career demonstrates what a woman in the Midwest could do. After the President's Commission on the Status of Women was established in

1961, each state quickly formed its own commission to explore women's roles in society. Clarenbach headed the Wisconsin Commission for more than a decade. One of the missions of the organization was to help women who had been homemakers gain access to the public sphere—whether it was to join the paid workforce or become volunteers. Much of this was accomplished through continuing education programs at local universities or community colleges that provided classes and training. Clarenbach headed the continuing education program at the University of Wisconsin. It was the states' commissions that later led to the creation of NOW. The initial NOW membership was made up of many midwest women; more than a third of members were from Wisconsin. Clarenbach was the first chairperson of NOW—which she largely ran out of her office at the University of Wisconsin, along with her university duties.

Despite her influence, she has often been overlooked by historians—overshadowed by Betty Friedan, Gloria Steinem, and Bella Abzug. In a *New York Times* article about Clarenbach, Senior Fellow at the Roosevelt Institute Ellen Chesler wrote, "Friedan had moxie, but no practical skills to organize a broadly based political movement. Kay Clarenbach had the establishment credentials and genial manner that made her an ideal partner for the more truculent Friedan. She had the presence of mind to collect 27 contributions of $5 each—NOW's first treasury. She became the organization's most trustworthy doer."[2] In a book about the Women's Movement, Clarenbach was described as "cool-headed Kay Clarenbach" and "the tall, dignified Wisconsin women's leader."[3] (Clarenbach said that *The Feminine Mystique* author Friedan viewed her as a "slow-witted Midwesterner."[4] Friedan was then based in New York City, but she was raised in Peoria, Illinois.) Clarenbach preferred to work behind the scenes. She was incredibly successful, but, since she allowed others to take credit, her story is largely unknown. For example, Chesler wrote, "Clarenbach's death in March went almost unnoticed outside her home state." The noted historian Gerda Lerner said at Clarenbach's memorial service, "Kay was the foremost organizer of the modern women's movement, recognized as such by all who worked with her ... the reliable, sustaining force without which there is no social change."[5]

Clarenbach was one of many women from the Midwest who are sometimes left out of women's political history, often overshadowed by the previously mentioned household names. In addition to NOW's initial membership, many of the initial members of the National Women's Political Caucus came from the Midwest. Lerner created an oral history project in 1992 to celebrate these women. As she wrote in an article about the project,

> Without in any way wanting to diminish the importance of Betty Friedan's book and her organizing energy, nor discounting the burst of initiative and creative energy of young women out of the civil rights movement (disenchanted with that movement's sexism) and the breakthrough of theoretical insights and organizing genius of lesbians and others involved in the sexual revolutions, I would argue that up to now we have insufficiently recognized the contributions to the movement made by other groups of women.[6]

The second wave of the women's movement did not magically appear. Many women coming out of the post–World War II era laid the groundwork for women's changing roles in society prior to the protests of the late 1960s and early 1970s. As scholar Nancy A. Hewitt wrote in the book *No Permanent Waves: Recasting Histories of U.S. Feminism*, a lot happened between the so-called waves of women's suffrage and the Women's Liberation Movement: "in reality, such movements overlapped and intertwined across U.S. history."[7] Further, in *Deans of Women and the Feminist Movement*, Clarenbach is mentioned in the challenge against the "dual waves" theory of women's history.[8]

Clarenbach's Background

Kathryn "Kay" Clarenbach was born in the small town of Sparta, Wisconsin, in 1920. She earned a bachelor's degree in political science in 1941 and a master's degree in the same subject a year later from the University of Wisconsin–Madison. After graduation, she passed the federal Civil Service Exam and became an administrative analyst for the War Production Board in Washington, DC. After World War II, she returned to Madison to earn her doctoral degree in political science.

During that time, she met and married fellow student Henry "Hank" Clarenbach. They remained married until his death in 1987. She said of their relationship, "We had as close to an egalitarian marriage and household as any I know. Both in-the-home and outside activities were never divided along gender lines at all but according to whoever was good at it."[9]

Initially, she taught political science at Purdue University before taking a few years off professionally to raise her three children—born in 1949, 1953, and 1957. During this period, she did volunteer work and became a board member of the League of Women Voters. In 1961, Clarenbach took a teaching position at Edgewood College in Madison, Wisconsin. She was also elected to the Board of Trustees at the all-women's Alverno College. In 1962, the focus of Clarenbach's work became women's issues when she was asked to create a program for continuing education through the Universzity of Wisconsin–Extension. Clarenbach and another woman were hired as an experiment to accommodate working mothers with flexible hours. Clarenbach began by interviewing local women about what potential employable skills the homemakers had. In the early years, she ran into some resistance. She said she "often encountered husbands who did not appreciate her efforts to find jobs for their wives. Some of the wives were looked at as freaks."[10]

Clarenbach initiated courses for women who wanted to complete college degrees and seek employment outside the home. At a 1963 conference in Wisconsin about professional opportunities for women, she met Esther Peterson, the director of the Women's Bureau in the U.S. Department of Labor. Clarenbach then persuaded Governor John Reynolds to approve the Wisconsin Commission on the Status of Women. State commissions were created in different ways. For example, Michigan Governor John Swainson created the Governor's Commission on the Status of Women by executive order in 1962, while in 1968, the Michigan Legislature, under the guidance and leadership of Senator Lorraine N. Beebe, enacted Public Act No. 1, which created the Michigan Women's Commission by statute.

Clarenbach planned the first women's conference in Wisconsin, and she went on to chair the state commission for many years. In her role, she championed changes to her state's laws that were discriminatory toward women—of which there were several. For example, in 1965, she asked the governor to change a law that prevented mothers from signing the form that allowed a minor child to get a driver's license. The request was overruled by the motor vehicles department executive who responded that only fathers were the heads of households. Clarenbach was amazed by the limited control women had in their own homes under state laws. She described it as "an absolute shock for me. We had a nose out for that 'what elses' from then on."[11]

A national *Handbook for Commissions on the Status of Women* was produced in 1968 by Clarenbach and published by the University of Wisconsin–Extension. A third edition was published in 1979. In the intervening decade, the Commissions had grown and gained significant influence. According to the *Handbook*,

> The part Commissions are taking in eliminating sex-based discrimination continues to increase in range and effectiveness. The initial efforts of most state and local Commissions to research and publish reports on women's status are a far cry from the sophisticated and knowledgeable efforts now being exerted by the majority of Commissions to bring about change in the economic and social fabric of the nation.[12]

Continuing Education and "Displaced Homemakers"

One of the key findings of the commissions—both federal and the states'—was the need to get more women into the professional workforce. It was a time when many people questioned the value of a woman earning a college degree. For some people—especially in upper-middle-class families—college was not necessarily training for a career; it was about meeting a spouse. A 1962 *New York Times* article noted, "College girl often sees no future but marriage."[13] A 1963 headline in the newspaper *National Observer* read, "College for Girls? An Old Argument Takes a New Turn." The caption under a photo of a female student featured with the story read, "The girl in the laboratory—are her hours with the books wasted?"[14] Numerous media stories questioned the need for women to be educated beyond high school and recommended instead they should focus on their roles in the home.

Yet, upper middle-class women were increasingly going to college by the 1950s. A special 1956 double issue of the popular magazine *Life* provides some perspective. It was titled "The American Woman: Her Achievements and Troubles" and featured a white woman smiling at a young child under the caption "Working Mother." The magazine also included an article about the women's college Bryn Mawr under the headline: "Tough Training Ground for Women's Minds." The reporter noted, "Today, a third of all American college students are women, and college has become almost as much a part of a woman's life as of a man's."[15] It was noted students took courses in the classics, such as Greek and Latin, rather than domestic science classes, such as home economics. The writer also explored the complicated role women navigated between intellectual aspiration and familial roles.[16]

The question of whether females should go to college took on a new direction when several state commissions addressed continuing education for middle-aged women. A 1962 *New York Times* article noted women were likely to eventually enter the paid workforce although they did not anticipate that path initially. (Part of the challenge of paid employment was a lack of child care.) The reporter cited a study predicting seven million women would enter the workforce and a majority would be in their forties. One expert said, "So many returners are not ready to return."[17] For example, at Washington University in St. Louis, a 1963 program was started to help women go back to school. Its goal was help women bypass the red tape of admission and recommend a flexible schedule. One administrator said, "Often a woman has to take courses whenever she can get a babysitter. And she may be able to take only one or two classes at a time." At the time, about 12,000 packets about the program were about to be sent out.[18]

Creation of National Organization for Women

The Third National Conference of Commissions, made up of state commissions, met in 1966. The Washington, DC, meeting's theme was "Targets for Action," although it was a lack of action that laid the groundwork for creating the National Organization for Women. Unofficially, government employee and feminist Catherine East had invited Friedan to attend the meeting, as a member of the press.[19]

Her fame was helpful in attracting attention to the soon-to-be-created organization.

East played a pivotal role for women's rights behind the scenes. She helped organize commission meetings, and the gathering of the women in Friedan's hotel room was a strong example. According to Friedan, East and others said the advocates needed an organization like the NAACP (National Association for the Advancement of Colored People) for women. Friedan said, "I thought of myself as a writer, not an organizer, but Catherine kept emphasizing that what was needed was outside pressure on the Government."[20] Clarenbach and several of the members of the Wisconsin group attended and were taken aback by the discussion that challenged the federal government. According to Clarenbach, "I hadn't been privy to any of their previous conversations in which they had talked about the importance of what Betty Friedan called an NAACP for women."[21] While she shared the women's concerns, Clarenbach still believed they could work through Peterson and others with the Woman's Bureau based on her previous experiences.[22] Clarenbach was inclined to follow the official governmental path because of her success in Wisconsin. She was used to getting things done and had clout in her home state.

While Clarenbach had wanted to work through official channels, the tide was about to change. There was discontent among the women by the end of the conference. They were frustrated by the lack of action by the Equal Employment Opportunity Commission (EEOC) regarding women's employment, especially the continued practice of discrimination in employment ads in newspapers with separate columns for men and women. Further, the group was concerned Richard Graham would not be re-appointed to the EEOC. Graham and Aileen Hernandez had fought hard to support cases of sex discrimination, only to lose on 3–2 votes. Both people would go on to be leaders in NOW.

Peterson said the commission meeting was intended for information purposes only—a resolution would not have any real power. Ultimately, the resolutions were not brought to the floor—blocked by Peterson and others. Clarenbach said in her oral history, "Each one said this would sound critical of the Federal Government and you are here at the invitation of the Federal Government and therefore it's inappropriate to have any resolutions. I was absolutely appalled."[23] With that message

Clarenbach was ready to change course and join the organization that had been discussed in Friedan's hotel room.

Clarenbach told Friedan, "You were absolutely right! It's a no go with these resolutions." It was a pivotal moment for Clarenbach. She had been successful by working within the system and had not been interested in an advocacy organization. The rejection of the resolutions (which had been non-binding) changed her opinion about how to make change going forward. At the conference's closing event, Clarenbach sat at a table with Friedan, Catherine Conroy, who had come out of the labor movement in the Midwest, and Business and Professional Women member Inka O'Hanrahan. Clarenbach recalled the powerful moment:

> As we sat there, dreaming up a name and an acronym, and a Statement of Purpose for this 'to be' organization, Inka would see somebody she knew on the other side of this huge ballroom and she would run over to tell somebody what we were up to, and run back again.[24]

Conroy said, "Let's put our money where our mouths are," and put $5 on the table. It quickly grew to $40. Clarenbach said, "That looked like a sizable chunk. Here I was, from the Wisconsin Commission, which didn't have a penny of budget for its first ten years."[25] Clarenbach ended up as the temporary chair because she had a desk and a secretary. They also put together a temporary Steering Committee. It was not yet clear exactly what the organization would look like. At one of the early board meetings, Pauli Murray asked, "Are we a leadership organization or are we thinking about a mass membership organization?" Clarenbach said, "That was something that (we) hadn't been talked or thought about."[26]

Marguerite Rawalt was in the room that day. She was a leading club woman leader, active with the Business and Professional Women. She was also an attorney for the Bureau of Internal Revenue from 1933 to 1965. Rawalt's biographer wrote of the moment, "Marguerite watched two round tables in the middle of the room fill up with the most militant women at the conference. They were not to be placated. Clarenbach joined the leaders and now the other women were ready to follow."[27] Rawalt would become a member and a lawyer for the organization. Before long the National Organization for Women was officially established with Clarenbach as the first chairperson and Friedan as the first president.

On November 22, 1966, the *New York Times* covered a NOW meeting that served as a form of press conference. The tone of the article was largely condescending: "Although no one in the dim ruby and sapphire Victorian parlor actually got up and cried: 'Women of the world, unite! You have nothing to lose but your chains,' that was the prevailing sentiment yesterday morning at the crowded press conference held by the newly formed National Organization for Women." The new group was clearly trying to find its footing as it debated being exclusive or seeking a large membership. The reporter wrote, "Mrs. Friedan said last week in her apartment that NOW had 'just begun to think about methods' to implement its goals of enabling women to 'enjoy the equality of opportunity and freedom of choice which is their right.'"[28] She claimed 500 members at that time, according to the article, although it would have been difficult to judge as different chapters were being created across the country. The organization continued to grow and Clarenbach would eventually leave the leadership while still working for women's causes.

Media Coverage of Women's Issues

Much of the media's coverage of NOW and other attempts to address gender discrimination was negative—if the topics were covered at all. It is difficult to overestimate how hostile many journalists were to the messages of feminism in the 1960s. Several studies have looked at the intersection of the media and the women's liberation movement—and found mostly negative coverage in the news pages of newspapers and on television.[29] For example, in a study of the print media's framing of the women's movement from 1966 to 1986, researchers Laura Ashley and Beth Olson found the coverage of feminists often delegitimized their goals. However, anti-feminists were listed as well-organized and attractive.[30] Yet, the newspaper coverage in southeastern Wisconsin was particularly friendly to Clarenbach and the issues she raised.

In part, it may have been because Clarenbach was friendly with the local reporters. Jean Otto was a women's page journalist at the *Milwaukee Journal* who often covered women's issues. In a 1970 story,

Otto, a single mother, interviewed women about equal rights and explained the mission of NOW and the members' fight for equality. Otto quoted Clarenbach: "This represents enormous effort on the part of a great many people who have worked their heads off."[31] Otto was the kind of woman who understood Clarenbach's appeal to help working mothers.

Milwaukee Journal and *Milwaukee Sentinel* reporter Dorothy Witte Austin was another trusted reporter for Clarenbach. When there was a NOW meeting in Washington, DC, that Clarenbach could not attend, she suggested Austin go to the meeting instead and the reporter "could keep her eyes and ears open and report back to me."[32] She went and Clarenbach got several phone calls, including one from Friedan: "Who is this Dorothy Austin? This meeting is closed to journalists. We're not allowing any journalist to be here, even women journalists." Clarenbach explained, "I wasn't suspicious of Dorothy Austin because she has been an ally, and a very important ally to us here in the state, but apparently others there had had negative experiences with journalists making fun of it in their stories."[33] In May 1971, Austin wrote about a Wisconsin NOW meeting where Clarenbach was the speaker: "We haven't begun to use our political clout in this or any other state and this is one of the tasks to which N.O.W. must address itself."[34] Southeastern Wisconsin journalists were open to the work done by the state commission and were quick to call Clarenbach as a source.

Another reason for the positive coverage was likely that the Milwaukee journalists were well aware of discrimination at the newspapers they worked for. The Milwaukee Press Club long excluded women. They had requested membership for years and were denied. By fall 1966, the women were ready to publicly protest the exclusion. The women's picket signs read, "Our Sex Edited Out," "Way Past Deadline," and "Oldest and Most Archaic" as they marched in front of the Club building on September 19, 1966.[35] The women journalists were fighting to get into the oldest continuously running press club in the country.[36]

The women journalists issued a press release about their frustrations: "When the spittoons were thrown out of news offices long ago, you forgot to get rid of another archaic practice. Our picketing today is to remind you that you are not addressing yourself to this problem and that it is time to act."[37] In a comment responding to the protest, Press Club President Bennett Waxse said the chance of the women being allowed to join was slim.³⁸ *Milwaukee Journal* reporter Robert Wells dismissed the 1966 protest in the Club's publication *Once a Year*: "The clamor of that valiant band of suffragettes who tried to batter down the Milwaukee Press Club's rules against women last year was noted with a weary smile by the old timers. They have seen feminist movements before."³⁹ The state's commission backed the women in their bid to become part of the press club. Clarenbach was quoted in a news story: "Our major interest in their cause is that women be encouraged to make a contribution to any profession. When a professional organization excludes women, this opportunity is not completely available to them."⁴⁰

A committee was created to fight against women joining the club: Members to Perpetuate Camaraderie Milwaukee Press Club. They sent a letter to the members, explaining attempts to integrate women "have been consistently defeated by a large majority."⁴¹ Further, the committee wrote,

> The author of the resolution to admit women, claimed at a regular membership meeting that we are one of only two press clubs that do not accept women. We have documented proof, based on a survey of press clubs, showing that there are at least five press clubs in addition to the Milwaukee Press Club, which do not admit women!⁴²

A major step forward for inclusion was reached thanks to the American Civil Liberties Union (ACLU).⁴³ At a March 1971 press club meeting, a letter was read from an attorney on behalf of the ACLU that requested action on the gender discriminatory policy in lieu of litigation based on equal access.⁴⁴ Two male club members from the *Milwaukee Sentinel* agreed to join the potential lawsuit along with the women.⁴⁵ The club considered fighting the potential lawsuit and sought legal advice. An attorney for the club advised there was no valid defense for the exclusion of women if the ACLU did file a lawsuit.⁴⁶ Clarenbach was aware of the discrimination and spoke to the Milwaukee chapter of Theta Sigma Phi in 1967. She addressed the issue of gender segregation in the news media. She said, "'People's news' is almost always by, for and of men."⁴⁷ In 1971, the committee eventually voted to present the proposed change that would include women to the entire voting membership. Otto and Austin were on the invitation list for the Milwaukee Press Club.

Conclusion

Clarenbach made significant changes for women in her home state and across the country—although she has not received enough credit. The ripple effect of her work can still be felt today. In references to Clarenbach, her Midwest manner was mentioned several times by historians, reporters, and central figures in NOW's founding. Her calm communication style allowed her to make a difference without being threatening—yet, her demeanor also likely led to her being forgotten by historians. After time, frustration led to a more public role, as demonstrated when Clarenbach headed the International Women's Year in Houston and took on factions within the women's movement. Likewise, the journalists from the women's page sections also took on a public role when they picketed the press club that had denied them membership based on their gender. These Midwest women contributed to the progress that women were making across the country.

Clarenbach raised awareness about women's issues in official capacities and behind the scenes. She was both powerful in the impact that she made in governmental commissions and her work at the University of Wisconsin yet subtle enough to be forgotten in women's history. The fight for equality became more visible in the 1960s although the foundation had been laid as early as the 1950s, fueled by the post–World War II era. It was a world that Clarenbach was familiar with and one that she worked to change. Her work with the commissions, the continuing education programs, and the creation of NOW impacted the lives of numerous women and continues today.

Notes
1. Jenny Price, "This Woman's Work," *On Wisconsin* (Fall 2016): 46–49.
2. Ellen Chesler, "Lives Well Lived: Kathryn F. Clarenbach," *New York Times*, January 1, 1995.
3. Marcia Cohen, *The Sisterhood* (Santa Fe, NM: Sunstone Press, 2009), 134–35.
4. Ibid., 139.
5. Chesler, "Lives Well Lived."

6. Gerda Lerner, "Midwestern Leaders of the Modern Women's Movement: An Oral History Project," *Wisconsin Academy Review* (Winter 1994–95): 12.
7. Nancy A. Hewitt, introduction to *No Permanent Waves: Recasting Histories of U.S. Feminism*, ed. Nancy A. Hewitt (New Brunswick, NJ: Rutgers University Press), 5.
8. Kelly C. Sartorius, *Deans of Women and the Feminist Movement* (New York: Palgrave MacMillan, 2014), 3.
9. David Callender, "Henry Clarenbach Dies from a Long Illness," *Capital Times*, June 20, 1987.
10. Kathryn Clarenbach, Oral History Project, University of Wisconsin–Madison Archives, 16. http://archives.library.wisc.edu/oral-history/guide/401-500/461-470.html#clarenbach.
11. Clarenbach, Oral History, 177.
12. National Association of Commissions for Women, *Handbook for Commissions on the Status of Women*, 3rd ed. (Washington, DC: U.S. Department of Labor, 1979), 3.
13. Marylin Bender, "College Girl Often Sees No Future but Marriage," *New York Times*, March 26, 1962.
14. "College for Girls," *National Observer*, November 11, 1963.
15. "Tough Training Ground for Women's Minds," *Life*, December 24, 1956, 102–107.
16. Ibid.
17. Marylin Bender, "Rusty Skills Bar Women from a Job," *New York Times*, January 5, 1962.
18. Lucinda Benzel, "Back-to-college Program for Women," *St. Louis Globe-Democrat*, September 2, 1963.
19. Judith Paterson, *Be Somebody: A Biography of Marguerite Rawalt* (Austin, TX: Eakin Press, 1986), 164.
20. Anthony Ramirez, "Catherine East, 80, Inspiration for National Women's Group," *New York Times*, August 20, 1996.
21. Clarenbach, Oral History, 127.
22. Paterson, *Be Somebody*, 165.
23. Clarenbach, Oral History, 128.
24. Ibid.
25. Ibid.
26. Ibid., 129.
27. Paterson, *Be Somebody*, 166.
28. Lisa Hammel, "They Meet in Victorian Parlor to Demand 'True Equality'—NOW," *New York Times*, November 22, 1966.
29. See Patricia Bradley, *Mass Media and the Shaping of American Feminism, 1963–1975* (Jackson, MS: University Press of Mississippi: 2003); Susan Brownmiller, *In Our Time: Memoir of a Revolution* (New York: Random House, 1999), 136–66; Laura Ashley and Beth Olson, "Constructing

Reality: Print Media's Framing of the Women's Movement, 1966–1986," *Journalism and Mass Communications Quarterly* (Summer 1998): 263–77.
30. Ashley and Olson, "Constructing Reality," 263–77.
31. Jean Otto, "Equal Rights: 'Wow!' and 'What's That?'" *Milwaukee Journal*, August 11, 1970.
32. Clarenbach, Oral History, 130–31.
33. Ibid.
34. Dorothy Austin, "New NOW Network," *Milwaukee Sentinel*, May 24, 1971.
35. Gordon Gottlieb, "Newswomen's PRESS-ure Club Batters on Men's Bastion," *Milwaukee Sentinel*, September 20, 1966.
36. Marion Marzolf, *Up from the Footnote: A History of Women Journalists* (New York: Hastings House, 1977), 104.
37. Gottlieb, "Newswomen's PRESS-ure."
38. Ibid.
39. Robert Wells, "Not Before 3 p.m.," *Once a Year*, 1967, Milwaukee Press Club, Box 11, Folder 4. Milwaukee Press Club. Records, 1885-[ongoing]. UWM Manuscript Collection 146. University Manuscript Collection. Archives. UWM Libraries. University of Wisconsin–Milwaukee.
40. "Women Backed in Press Club Bid," *Milwaukee Sentinel*, n.d. Box 3, Folder 2. Milwaukee Press Club Records, 1885-[ongoing]. UWM Manuscript Collection 146. University Manuscript Collection. Archives. UWM Libraries. University of Wisconsin–Milwaukee.
41. Letter to members from "Members to Perpetuate Camaraderie Milwaukee Press Club," Box 1, Folder 16. Milwaukee Press Club. Records, 1885-[ongoing]. UWM Manuscript Collection 146. University Manuscript Collection. Archives. UWM Libraries. University of Wisconsin–Milwaukee.
42. Ibid.
43. Associated Press, "Press Club Bias Faces Challenges," *Manitowoc Herald-Times (Wisconsin)*, December 16, 1969.
44. Official Minutes, Milwaukee Press Club, March 10, 1971. Box 2, Folder 45. Milwaukee Press Club. Records, 1885-[ongoing]. UWM Manuscript Collection 146. University Manuscript Collection. Archives. UWM Libraries. University of Wisconsin--Milwaukee.
45. "Milwaukee TSPs Shun Press Club," *The Matrix* (Fall 1969), 23.
46. Official Minutes, Milwaukee Press Club, May 12, 1971, Box 2, Folder 45. Milwaukee Press Club. Records, 1885-[ongoing]. UWM Manuscript Collection 146. University Manuscript Collection. Archives. UWM Libraries. University of Wisconsin--Milwaukee.
47. Kathryn Clarenbach, "Where We Have Been—Where We Are Going," address to Theta Sigma Phi, Milwaukee, Wisconsin, 1967, 1.

Yi-chin Shih | Speaking from the Middle West

Susan Glaspell's Critique of Nation in *Inheritors*

When the play *Inheritors* (1921)¹ was re-staged by the Metropolitan Playhouse in New York in 2005, Victor Gluck lauded it as a "lost gem."² The playwright, Susan Glaspell (1876–1948), best known for *Trifles* (1916), was commercially popular and critically welcomed by the audiences and reviewers of her time, but she and her works faded from public interest after her death. However, due to feminists' efforts to re-read and re-discover texts by women in the 1960s and 1970s, Glaspell's works have attracted renewed interest by critics and audiences.³ Her status in the history of American drama compares with Eugene O'Neill; as Linda Ben-Zvi comments, "O'Neill was the undisputed father of American drama, Glaspell the mother."⁴ Of her fifteen plays, *Inheritors* reveals the dramatist's ambition to deal with the nature of American society on a national scale. This lost gem is considered by Arthur E. Waterman as "Susan Glaspell's most serious play about the American Dream."⁵ Set in the Midwest, *Inheritors* covers four generations, from 1879 to 1920, and portrays the construction of the American Dream since the pioneering period and the excesses of American patriotism after World War I. The character Madeline Morton, a fourth generation Morton and an "inheritor" of the spirits of freedom and tolerance, stands up for the rights of "the other" in the United States, but she ends up in prison for transgressing the Espionage and Sedition Acts.

Inheritors premiered in 1921 by the Provincetown Players after World War I had officially ended in 1918, but the negative impact of the war still disseminated in American society; the so-called Red Scare, which was the fear of a rise of communism, especially panicked Americans. The Espionage Act of 1917 punished conscientious objectors with a heavy fine and a long term of imprisonment for their refusal to serve in the army and to fight for their country; the Sedition

Act of 1918 prohibited voices that dissented from the government or were considered disloyal to the country. These acts symbolized the suppression of the freedom of speech and the rising of xenophobia and jingoism. To criticize excessive patriotism after World War I, Glaspell created *Inheritors* to express her ideal American Dream; however, she was also at the risk of prosecution because of the play.[6] The play thus examines the fundamental principle of freedom and the intention of nationality; more important, Glaspell scrutinizes the nation from the perspective of the experience of women. Starting with the portrayal of a hill in the Midwest, Glaspell links regional identity with national identity, and then focuses on the role of women in the establishment of the nation. Overall, national discourses and feminist ideas interact in the play to produce Glaspell's feminist critique of the nation.

The Midwest: The Most American Part of America

Born in Davenport, Iowa, Glaspell sourced inspiration and material from the Midwest.[7] Her plays, such as *Trifles* (1916), *Close the Book* (1917), and *Woman's Honor* (1918), are filled with a strong sense of place, and Glaspell is usually labeled as a local colorist or regional writer.[8] However, the Midwest is widely recognized as "the cultural core of the nation,"[9] the "heartland" of the United States,[10] and "the most American part of America."[11] It symbolizes not merely a region but also a nation in *Inheritors*. The sense of place in the Midwest extends to national identity; as Gillian Rose proposes, "the image of the American Midwest is central not only to the identity of that region but also to the identity of the United States of America as a whole; its values of individualism, independence, mobility and property ownership are often cited as the epitome of what the USA expects of, and offers, all its inhabitants."[12] Senses of place are generated from individuals and daily experiences. There is no naturally inherent trait in place, but only the meanings humans give to it.[13] Similarly, while a nation is inevitably defined according to its borders and geography, it is a place on a large national scale. Hence, national identity, like place identity, is also created and constructed by individuals as well as their everyday experiences. Having grown up in Iowa, Glaspell never hesitates to mention her roots in the Midwest, and she even uses "the conceptualization of the Midwest as the idealized heart of the country to her thematic advantage."[14] In *Inheritors*, Glaspell delineates how the American Dream is built, believed, and manipulated by people through portraying the history of the Midwest.

Act I of *Inheritors* focuses on a debate over whether to donate a hill to establish a state university, and the final decision to build Morton College is a symbol of the transcendence of barriers of race and gender. Set "on the rolling prairie just back from the Mississippi" (181), the play begins on Independence Day, 1879. A young banker named Smith comes to visit the Morton family to purchase the hill for a housing development, but Silas claims he will donate the land to build a college.[15] He says, "It's a college in the cornfield—where the Indian maize once grew. And it's for the boys of the cornfields—and the girls" (189). Because of a sense of guilt over taking the hill from Native American Indians, Silas wants to pay his debts by establishing a college for all people who want to study, including the Indians. He explains, "Why I can't forget the Indians. We killed their joy before we killed them. We made them less ... I got to give it back—their hill. I give it back to joy—a better joy—joy o' aspiration" (193). Dreaming of friendship between different races like that between his father and Blackhawk, a Sauk leader, Silas wants to utilize the hill in the public interest. In addition, by saying the college is for boys and girls, Silas shows his ideal college is without gender bias. His dream in 1879 was quite feminist; coeducational institutions were not common at the time.[16] Therefore, Morton College symbolically represents a transcendence of racial and gender biases.

Furthermore, the establishment of Morton College also symbolizes peaceful relations among people with different nationalities and different social classes. Silas's decision is supported by Felix Fejevary, a Hungarian refugee who came to America after 1848 when the Hungarian revolution against Austria failed. He came to America for freedom and quickly befriended Silas. The setting of Act I indicates the reason their friendship goes beyond nationality. Act I occurs on Independence Day, and this special day commemorates the American Revolution, when Americans fought for freedom from British domination. Both Silas and Fejevary cherish freedom, and both consider the college a realization of freedom.[17] While Fejevary expects that his assistance to establish the college may "repay America for giving him freedom,"[18] Silas anticipates that anyone, no matter what gender, race, nationality, or "class," will be able to study there. Morton College on the hill is not for elites or middle-class people only, but it is for all the people, including working-class farmers like Silas. Silas explains, "There's few can go to Harvard College—but more can climb that hill" (189). Because of a lack of education, Silas expects that the hill/college may help people to fulfill themselves and "make themselves out of the wanting to be more" (192). In this way, the hill no longer belongs to anyone; instead, it is the "hill of vision" (190). This midwestern college, Morton College, thus becomes an embodiment of the American Dream, which transcends the boundaries of race, gender, nationality, and class, and maintains the spirit of the American Dream for the next generations.

In *Inheritors*, the Midwest, "the most American part of America," stands for a nation, and the landscape of the Midwest also represents America. As Tim Edensor suggests, "It is difficult to mention a nation without conjuring up a particular rural landscape."[19] The large treeless prairie has been symbolized as the pastoral ideal of America and represents the possibility of achieving success through hard work. The landscape of the Midwest does not merely illustrate America, but it also further inscribes the memory of Americans through the changing of the landscape. "Through the landscape the memory of the nation is given concrete form as a reminder of what 'we' have been through and why 'we' need to remember," John Agnew claims.[20] The changing of a landscape, as a result, records the history of a nation and inscribes several crucial memories. Mike Crang believes that the landscape of a place functions as a "palimpsest," which includes every significant crisis in the culture and society of a nation.[21] More important, the palimpsest-like landscape indicates that there are traces of previous inscriptions that never disappear, so the landscape always inscribes different memories to establish the history of a place.

From this perspective, the transformation of the landscape from a hill to a college in *Inheritors* does not simply mean the changing of the land, but the change further implies the historical changing of America from a pioneering period to a postwar period. However, the changing of the land may not always be natural, as Morton College is to be established by Silas and Fejevary's man-made effort, so changing by artificial power becomes a way to remember a crucial memory of a nation. As Tim Cresswell expresses it, "One of the primary ways in which memories are constituted is through the production of places," such as creating monuments and museums.²² In this light, the setting of *Inheritors*, from a hill to a college, represents a man-made force to remember the spirit of the American Dream and to construct a sense of the place/nation.

From the outset, the building of Morton College has an expectation of freedom and multiculturalism without any barrier, so this college, located in the Midwest, symbolizes the spirit of the American Dream. As Noelia Hernando-Real explains, "Morton College is envisioned as a microcosm of what these pioneers want America to be: the land where everybody is welcome, and where further mixtures of immigrants and Americans go on making this country better and better."²³ In other words, what the pioneers want America to be is performed by them and by the building of Morton College; that is, national identity is performed and practiced by people. Place, such as the hill that Morton College is located on, has no inherent meaning, but people give meaning to it and then identify with the meaning they give. According to Cresswell, "Thinking of place as performed and practiced can help us think of place in radically open and non-essentialized ways where place is constantly struggled over and reimagined in practical ways."²⁴ In the pioneering period, Glaspell in *Inheritors* reveals that the Midwest is an open, new world where people can perform and practice their American Dream, so the sense of place and the sense of nation are created simultaneously.

National Identity: Who Is "One-hundred-percent American"?

While Act I is set in 1879, Act II starts in 1920, when Morton College celebrates its fortieth anniversary. One of the purposes of building the college was to remind the people of the spirit of the American Dream, but, in the atmosphere of the Red Scare after World War I, people's national identification with the American Dream is shaken. Rather than "democracy," the "American Dream," a classical sense of American identity, is more acceptable for the American people.²⁵ Although there are a variety of American Dreams, they are always "closely bound up with freedom."²⁶ However, at the time that fear of communism was spreading in America, "who" has freedom to make their dreams come true is a big issue; in other words, topics such as "Who is an American?" and "What is national identity?" have become uncertain and questionable.

To understand how identity is constructed with the sense of place/nation, boundaries are crucial "because they help to define by making not only what/where it *is*, but also what/where it is *not*."[27] Thus, it is clear that boundaries have a dual function: "to establish insiders" and "to establish outsiders."[28] In *Inheritors*, the Red Scare pushes people to distinguish between the insiders as Americans and the outsiders as foreigners to secure the safety of America. Thus, the Hindu students at Morton College must be deported because outsiders should be expelled from America for the sake of the insiders, who are "one-hundred-percent American" (194).

When it comes to national identity, "essentialism" is easily accepted by people because it suggests an authentic set of characteristics that are shared and belong to the people in one nation or in certain territories. Essentialists propose that national identity could be sought "through appeals either to the fixed truth of a shared past or to biological truths,"[29] so they usually see identity "as fixed and unchanging."[30] In *Inheritors*, Senator Lewis, Felix Fejevary Jr., and Horace Fejevary are three proponents of essentialist national identity. The senator is the chairman of the state appropriations committee. He comes to Morton College to threaten Felix Fejevary's son, Felix Fejevary Jr., that if Morton College wants to get state funding, he must dismiss Professor Holden because Holden defended conscientious objectors during war time. The senator doubts Holden's national identity, and he pronounces, "Holden's the man. I've read things that make me question his Americanism" (194). Senator Lewis believes in loyalty and total devotion to the United States of America, especially when communism is going to apparently take over the world, and his belief in Americanism also illustrates a belief in the superiority of America to other countries. His narrow-minded viewpoint turns his patriotism into jingoism, and he further forces people to become "one-hundred-percent American" with his political and economic power; he firmly tells Fejevary Jr., "But your Americanism must be unimpeachable" (201). To make America safe from the danger of communism, the xenophobia and racist prejudice of some Americans are therefore justified after the war.

Fejevary Jr., another proponent of an essentialist national identity, is the president of the board of trustees of Morton College. Although the college symbolizes the American Dream and was established by his father and Silas Morton, he does not fight for freedom of speech and freedom of study for students and professors. Rather, in support of the senator's jingoism, he expels non-American students from Morton College. Claiming Morton College as "a one-hundred-percent-American college" (194), Fejevary Jr. convinces the senator that his college is not a hotbed of radicalism and revolutionists. The Hindu students call for an end to British imperialism in India by delivering handbills on campus about freedom for India, but their anti-imperialist activity is seen as agitative and provocative behavior. Fejevary Jr. expels them, asserting, "This college is for Americans. I'm not going to have foreign revolutionists come here and block the things I've spent my life working for" (207). After a Hindu student is captured by police officers, Fejevary Jr. refuses to help him because he explains, "It isn't what he did. It's what he is. We don't want him here" (211). Obviously, from Fejevary Jr.'s point of view, the spirit of freedom in the American Dream is for Americans only, particularly for "one-hundred-percent Americans" only.

Like his father Fejevary Jr., Horace Fejevary is also xenophobic and jingoistic. He calls the Hindu students "sissies" (197) and "ignorant people" (199). Nevertheless, in terms of nativism, neither Fejevary Jr. or Horace Fejevary are "one-hundred-percent" Americans. Their ancestor, Felix Fejevary, was a Hungarian refugee who came to America for freedom after his country's revolution against Austrian imperialism failed. While they compel foreigners to leave America, they themselves are foreigners, too. They cannot see the similarity between the Hungarian revolution against Austrian imperialism and the Hindu revolution against the British Empire, so their jingoistic view of national identity is manipulated by the ideology of Americanism in the hope of keeping America safe from the threat of the Red Scare. By the same token, the senator also fails to see that both the American Revolution against British imperialism and the Hindu revolution against the British Empire refer to a search for freedom, so he supports and even encourages Fejevary Jr. to expel the Hindu students to make American democracy safe.

The senator, Fejevary Jr., and Horace Fejevary all intend to keep America united and whole, but their view on national identity from an essentialist perspective remains flawed and shows that their national identity is united by concealing differences (such as the deportation of the foreign Hindu students) and by homogenizing differences (such as the Americanization of the Hungarian Fejevary Jr. and Horace Fejevary). Therefore, national identity is "the consequence of discursive power that covers over difference."[31] Chris Barker explains:

> National identity is a way of unifying cultural diversity so that, rather than thinking of nations and national cultures as a "whole," we should understand unity or identity to be the consequence of discursive power that covers over difference. Nations are marked by deep internal divisions and differences so that a unified national identity has to be constructed through the narrative of the nation by which stories, images, symbols and rituals represent "shared" meanings of nationhood.[32]

In other words, by erasing difference, the nation depends on man-made inventions of symbols and traditions to support a people's continuous national identity and to unify the people of a nation. The building of Morton College is a symbol of the American Dream and the spirit of freedom. To remember this national identity and to practice national discourses, the ritual of the anniversary of the college is necessary to remind people of patriotism. Act II begins on the fortieth anniversary of the founding of Morton College, and celebratory activities include several speeches and the arrival of politicians (210). Through performing and practicing rituals and activities, people are unified, and their American identity is re-confirmed, too.[33]

Nevertheless, in the early twentieth century Glaspell points out one special idea: since the nation and national identity are practiced and exercised by man-made rituals, creations, and traditions, they have no inherent meaning and people may redefine the meaning of the nation and their national identity by themselves. This statement is clarified by different interpretations of Abraham Lincoln's speech in *Inheritors*. Lincoln's speeches on freedom represent the American Dream, but the collection of his speeches in books is a man-made effort to unify the American people in remembering the spirit of freedom. The printed speeches are appropriated by the Hindu students to justify their activity of anti-imperialism instead. Lincoln's first inaugural address to Congress in 1861 states, "This country with its institutions belongs to the people who inhabit it ... Whenever they shall grow weary of the existing government, they can exercise their constitutional right of amending it ... or their *revolutionary* right to dismember or overthrow it" (198). Lincoln's speech fulfills the spirit of freedom, especially when he emphasizes that the people have the right to fight for democracy; therefore, his speech represents a shared meaning of America for the American people and indirectly consolidates the collectives as the nation's people. Notably, Lincoln's speeches are collected in books. According to Benedict Anderson, the mechanical production of newspapers and books allows the vernacular language to become the national language, so that national discourses can be spread.[34] Horace Fejevary goes to the library to find Lincoln's speech; to his surprise, Lincoln's words support the foreigners' revolutionary activity and justify the radicals who disturb the peace in America. It is obvious that, although a printed language may unify a nation's people and create a unified national identity, the instability of the meaning of the language cannot be restricted within a certain discourse, and people may appropriate it to define and re-define themselves and their nations. Hence, the American identity can be adapted by foreigners, and the American Dream can be realized by non-Americans. In *Inheritors*, Glaspell reveals that place, nation, and national identity are constructed by artificial effort and repetitious performances; accordingly, the freedom and the possibility of re-defining place, nation, and identity by individuals are the real American Dream that Glaspell intends to express in the play. More important, this freedom and this possibility open a space for women to involve themselves in the construction of national discourses.

Women: Caretakers and Cultural Bearers of the Nation

Nations are imagined and fabricated constructions but, crucially, nations are imagined as "female." Nations are metaphorically described as "mother," as in the motherland, so women are the symbol of nations. It is men who must save and protect female nations.[35] Therefore, the construction of nations is gendered; women are an icon and a symbol of the nation while men are the performers and executors of national discourses and national identity. As Joan Nagel observes, "Terms like honor, patriotism, cowardice, bravery and duty are hard to distinguish as either nationalistic or masculinist, since they seem so thoroughly tied both to the nation and to manliness."[36] While Glaspell describes the history of the Morton family in the Midwest from 1879 to 1920, she is also symbolically depicting American history from the pioneering period to the period after World War I. In her history-telling, Glaspell emphasizes the matriarchal genealogy of the Morton family, which indicates that the playwright intentionally provides a matriarchal view of American history. By highlighting the significant roles of Madeline, Madeline's mother, and her great-grandmother (Grandmother Morton), Glaspell offers feminist critique of the nation and values the roles of women in the construction of national discourses.

Nira Yuval-Davis explains that the division of the public and the private excludes women from public and political issues, and that is the main reason women are marginalized in national narratives. She comments, "As nationalism and nations have usually been discussed as part of the public political sphere, the exclusion of women from that arena has affected their exclusion from that discourse as well."[37] Since women are excluded from national discourses, they are without doubt ignored in national history. While Glaspell re-narrates the American Dream in *Inheritors*, she creates a fictional character as "the first white woman" in the Middle West in the pioneering period of American history (196), Grandmother Morton, to underline the existence of women in history.[38] As the pioneering history is often exclusively about men, female pioneers and their frontier experiences are seldom mentioned in national narratives of westward expansion.[39] However, when Glaspell re-writes pioneer women in national history, she not only points out the fabrication of national discourses, but also emphasizes the important role of women in the construction of the nation.

By portraying Grandmother Morton and her story in the Midwest, Glaspell underscores the existence of women in national history. Grandmother Morton, participating in the Black Hawk War of 1832, fights Indians when the nation encourages people to explore the western territories. She remarks on the war, "I threw an Indian in the cellar and stood on the door. I was heavier then" (181). She continues,

"We used to fight with anything we could lay hands on—dish water—whatever was handy" (181). Without sufficient weapons, Grandmother Morton bravely joins military activities like the pioneer men, and she manifests the truth that women are participants in creating national history.

Nevertheless, while Glaspell focuses on the experience of pioneer women, she simultaneously distinguishes frontier women from masculine and expansionary nationalists. Grandmother Morton, a female caretaker and the matriarch of the family, prepares food and beds for settlers, and the femininity of this caretaker helps her to understand the essential humanity shared by different races rather than military expansion. She tells Smith that in the period of westward expansion, every house is a tavern: "You think the way to settle a country is to go on ahead and build hotels? That's all you folks know" (183). She always leaves food on the stove for the new settlers, whom she does not even know. She recalls an unknown woman who prepares the best meal for her, narrating, "There was a woman I always wanted to know. She made a kind of bread I never had before—and left aplenty for our supper when we got back with the ducks and berries. And she left the kitchen handier than it had ever been. I often wondered about her" (184). Thus, as caretakers, women on the frontier cannot be underestimated and their feminine experience stands out in the masculine national narratives.

Based on the feminine experience of being caretakers, Grandmother Morton cares more about people than property, and she is surprised to find out that the Indians do as well. Grandmother Morton understands, "We'd have starved to death that first winter hadn't been for the Indians" (182). Through sharing food, she transgresses the racial boundary to build a friendship with the Indians. She observes, "The Indians used to like cookies ... One time I saw an Indian watching me from a bush ... After he'd been there an hour I couldn't seem to put my mind on my work. So I thought, Red or White, a man's a man—I'll take him some cookies" (186). Out of expectation, the Indian boy gives her a fish to trade. Therefore, due to the maternal concern for food and people, Grandmother Morton recognizes the similarity between the "white" and the "red" and fundamental humanity without barriers. Although Grandmother Morton killed Indians in the Black Hawk War, she gradually realizes that the "red" share "something of the same nature in white folks" (182) after some interactions with them.⁴⁰ Glaspell, through portraying Grandmother Morton, includes women in the pioneering period of national history and further points out the unique feminine experience on the frontier.

When mentioning the relation between nations and women, many critics refer to women as the biological and cultural bearers of the nation, such as Yuval-Davis commenting that women "are not just the biological reproducers of the nation, but also its cultural reproducers, often being given the task of guardians of 'culture' who are responsible for transmitting it to the children and constructing the 'home' in a specific cultural style."⁴¹ Women, with the ability of biological reproduction, bear the responsibility for the population of the nation. However, if the statement that women are the cultural reproducers of the nation is affirmative, then a further question is: What kind of culture do women pass to the next generations? Do women transfer national discourses that have been gendered as masculine to their descendants, further securing a masculine national ideology without any feminist concern? Likewise, Andrea G. Radke emphasizes that women played "the role of civilizers" in the pioneering period.⁴² If pioneer women pass American values to the next generation in the Midwest, then what values do they convey to their children? Glaspell in the play problematizes the statement of women as cultural bearers of the nation by depicting Madeline's two mothers: Isabel Fejevary and Madeline Fejevary.

Isabel Fejevary, Madeline's aunt and surrogate mother, participates in the construction of the nation by supporting the men, and she therefore reproduces and confirms the masculine national discourses. Madeline's biological mother dies when she is very little, so Isabel, becoming Madeline's second mother, takes on the responsibility of raising and educating Madeline. Like her husband Felix Fejevary Jr., who demands "one-hundred-percent American" students, Isabel claims that "Morton College is one hundred per cent American" (202). Her standpoint of Americanism and her xenophobic attitude are clear when she tries to persuade Madeline to compromise with the Commissioner to escape the punishment meted out by the Espionage and Sedition Acts, and she expresses, "And these are days when we have to stand together— all of us who are the same kind of people must stand together because the thing that makes us the same kind of people is threatened" (218). By emphasizing "us who are the same kind of people," Isabel symbolically enters the mainstream of excessive patriotism and isolationism at that time. More precisely, Isabel participates in the construction of the national identity by supporting masculine nationalism, and her support is encouraged by men. For example, in response to her Americanism, the senator delightedly comments, "I am glad to find you an American, Mrs. Fejevary" (202).

When Djurdja Knezevic investigates the relation between women and nations, she finds that, as women have been excluded from the public and national narratives, supporting men is a way to participate in the political arena. She notes,

> Instead of an opportunity to raise genuine women's issues as political issues, these women were given only an opportunity to play again the very same roles that have always been allocated to them in the male-dominated political sphere ... Women appear as supporters, as participants in social changes, only within and under strict rules of male ideologies, as an addition to the male society.[43]

That is to say, women are welcome to enter the construction of nations by supporting men; furthermore, women become bearers of national discourses and reproduce masculine nationalism, like Isabel who successfully produces a "one-hundred-percent American" son, Horace Fejevary.

However, that women are reproducers of the mainstream of national discourses is not the thesis in *Inheritors*. When the nation is understood as imagination and fabrication, as discussed above, culture is also a social and ideological construction. If women must take the role of supporting men so that they can enter the political sphere, women still are marginalized in the national discourses. Their demands are still disregarded, and their existence in national history is still forgotten, too. Glaspell not only writes women, Grandmother Morton, for instance, back into history, but she also examines the core of American culture that women bear with a portrayal of Madeline's mother, Madeline Fejevary (who has the same first name as her daughter). Because of the female experience as caretakers, Grandmother Morton recognizes the essentialist humanity shared by Americans and Indians. Similarly, Madeline dies due to maternal love for children. In taking care of an ill Swedish child who has diphtheria, Madeline gets the disease and eventually dies. Unlike Isabel, who believes in the importance of "one-hundred-percent Americans" in America, Madeline helps foreigners and welcomes them to be new Americans. Compared with Isabel's xenophobic and isolationist attitude, Madeline's sacrifice manifests the spirit of the American Dream, which transgresses racial boundaries and welcomes the other. Again, Glaspell highlights the significance of the experience of women through depicting the interaction between Grandmother Morton and Indians, and between Madeline and the Swedish child.

After the younger Madeline realizes the truth of her mother's death for the Swedish boy, she is finally released from the dilemma of either coming to a compromise with the Commissioner or facing the consequences of her attack against the police and spending her future in jail. To assist the Hindu students, Madeline assaults the police on campus twice. Rather than supporting the men's viewpoint of Americanism, she articulates her argument in public and actively takes part in the political arena. Moreover, Madeline rejects Fejevary Jr.'s plan, which is to acknowledge herself as a little ignorant girl, to escape the punishment for her attack on the police. "I did realize what I was saying" (216), Madeline claims. Being regarded as ignorant and immature, women are therefore excluded from political issues and are marginalized in national discourses. They are the "other" in contrast to the "subject" of men in the construction of nations. The feminine experience of being the "other" facilitates Madeline's understanding of the Hindu students who are also seen as the "other," and further pushes Madeline to assist them when they are persecuted by the American police. Madeline justifies her assault on the police by arguing, "They're people from the other side of the world who came here believing in us, drawn from the far side of the world by things we say about ourselves" (212). Therefore, based on the experience of women, Glaspell, once again, emphasizes national discourses from a feminist perspective, and thus she opens a new space to interpret the construction of nations.

Grandmother Morton, Madeline's mother, and Madeline all pay more attention to essentialist humanity rather than the boundaries of race, gender, and nationality, so they do not see foreigners, the other, or difference as a threat to themselves or their country. Dani Cavallaro explains the fear of difference: "Fear of the Other far too often degenerates into blind hatred: fascism, racism, genocide, and a fetishistic attachment to national identities, languages and territories."[44] Thus, the American Dream should be based on freedom and tolerance: the freedom of speech and the tolerance of difference. Madeline recognizes the spirit of the American Dream, and she even puts it into practice by standing up for the rights of the Hindu students. The way that women enter the national discourse is not by supporting men; in fact, they themselves, exercising a critical judgment, can be active participants in political and national movements. As Madeline asserts, "I think I'm an American. And for that reason I think I have something to say about America" (216). Madeline studies in Morton College, which symbolizes the spirit of the American Dream, but now the spirit is lost. Nevertheless, she inherits it; she is the real inheritor, the title heroine of the play. Madeline is the performer of the American Dream and the bearer of the pioneer spirit in the Midwest.

Conclusion

In short, Glaspell in *Inheritors* starts with a midwestern family saga to review the spirit of the American Dream and national identity, and then she offers her feminist judgment on national discourses. *Inheritors* manifests that Glaspell is not merely a regional writer who portrays only the Midwest. She is a writer who speaks from the region of the Midwest but aims at the nation. In addition, her description of some of the women in *Inheritors* distinguishes them from the patriarchal discourse on the nation, so the feminist interpretation of the nation also helps to turn the play into a "lost gem."

Acknowledgment

This paper is a partial fulfillment of Taiwan's Ministry of Science and Technology research project "Place and Gender in Susan Glaspell's Plays" (MOST 100-2410-H-032-087-MY2). The author expresses her thanks to the MOST for its financial support.

Notes

1. Susan Glaspell, *Inheritors*, in *Susan Glaspell: The Complete Plays*, ed. Linda Ben-Zvi and J. Ellen Gainor (Jefferson, NC: McFarland, 2010). Subsequent references will be cited parenthetically in the text.
2. Victor Gluck, "Reviews: *Inheritors*," *Backstage.com*, November 22, 2005, accessed August 30, 2016, www.metropolitanplayhouse.org/InheritorsReview.htm.
3. Linda Ben-Zvi and J. Ellen Gainor, introduction to *Susan Glaspell: The Complete Plays*, 7.
4. Linda Ben-Zvi, introduction to *Susan Glaspell: Essays on Her Theater and Fiction*, ed. Linda Ben-Zvi (Ann Arbor: University of Michigan Press, 1995), 1.
5. Arthur E. Waterman, "Dramatic Achievement," in *Drama Criticism*, vol. 10, ed. Lawrence J. Trudeau (Detroit: Gale, 1999), 148.
6. J. Ellen Gainor, *Susan Glaspell in Context: American Theater, Culture, and Politics, 1915–48* (Ann Arbor: University of Michigan Press, 2001), 112–13.
7. Glaspell's works usually are colored with her personal history, such as the use of her birthplace, her family members, and events that happened to her in her works. See Linda Ben-Zvi and J. Ellen Gainor, "A Brief Biography," in *Susan Glaspell: The Complete Plays*, 1.
8. Karen Alkalay-Gut, "Jury of Her Peers: The Importance of Trifles," *Studies in Short Fiction* 21, no. 1 (1984): 9.
9. James R. Shortridge, "The Emergence of 'Middle West' as an American Regional Label," *Annals of the Association of American Geographers* 74, no. 2 (1984): 209.
10. Ibid., 209.
11. Ibid., 213.
12. Gillian Rose, "Place and Identity: A Sense of Place," in *A Place in the World? Places, Cultures and Globalization*, ed. Doreen Massey and Pat Jess (Oxford: Open University, 1995), 92.
13. Ibid., 98.
14. Gainor, *Susan Glaspell in Context*, 124.
15. Glaspell gives her father's first name to Silas Morton. See Ben-Zvi and Gainor, "A Brief Biography," 1.
16. In 1833, Oberlin College, which was located in the midwestern state of Ohio, was the first coeducational college. In Glaspell's home state, the University of Iowa in 1855 became the first public coeducational institution. Few colleges were established as coeducational in the nineteenth century. It was not until the mid-1970s that coeducation was adopted by most of the educational institutions in the United States. See Myrna W. Merron, "Coeducation," in *Dictionary of American History*, ed. Stanley I. Kutler (New York: Charles Scribner's Sons, 2003), 263.

17. The surnames of Morton and Fejevary (or Fejervary) are two real, historical family names in Iowa. See Gainor, *Susan Glaspell in Context*, 121.
18. Waterman, "Dramatic Achievement," 148.
19. Tim Edensor, *National Identity, Popular Culture and Everyday Life* (New York: Berg, 2002), 39.
20. John Agnew, "Nationalism," in *A Companion to Cultural Geography*, ed. James S. Duncan, Nuala C. Johnson, and Richard H. Schein (Malden, MA: Blackwell, 2004), 233.
21. Mike Crang, *Cultural Geography* (New York: Routledge, 1998), 22.
22. Tim Cresswell, *Place: A Short Introduction* (Oxford: Blackwell, 2004), 85.
23. Noelia Hernando-Real, *Self and Space in the Theater of Susan Glaspell* (Jefferson, NC: McFarland, 2011), 52.
24. Cresswell, *Place*, 39.
25. Jim Cullen, *The American Dream: A Short History of an Idea That Shaped a Nation* (Oxford: Oxford University Press, 2003), 5.
26. Ibid., 9.
27. Rose, "Place and Identity," 103.
28. Ibid., 99.
29. Kathryn Woodward, "Concepts of Identity and Difference," in *Identity and Difference*, ed. Kathryn Woodward (London: SAGE, 1997), 13.
30. Ibid., 12.
31. Chris Barker, *The SAGE Dictionary of Cultural Studies* (London: SAGE, 2004), 132.
32. Ibid., 132.
33. That a nation is fundamentally imagined and fabricated has been much discussed in cultural studies since at least Benedict Anderson's claim that nations function as "imagined communities." See Benedict Anderson, *Imagined Communities: Reflections on the Origin and Spread of Nationalism* (New York: Verso, 1991).
34. Ibid., 44–45.
35. Joanne R. Sharp, "Gendering Nationhood: A Feminist Engagement with National Identity," in *Bodyspace: Destabilizing Geographies of Gender and Sexuality*, ed. Nancy Duncan (New York: Routledge, 2005), 99.
36. Joan Nagel, "Masculinity and Nationalism: Gender and Sexuality in the Making of Nations," *Ethnic and Racial Studies* 21, no. 2 (1998): 251–52.
37. Nira Yuval-Davis, *Gender & Nation* (London: SAGE, 1997), 2.
38. Glaspell's grandmother is the prototype of the fictional character Grandmother Morton. Coming from a pioneer family, Glaspell listened to her grandmother's stories about Native American Indians, pioneer days, and experiences when she was little. See Hernando-Real, *Self and Space*, 32–33.
39. Gainor, *Susan Glaspell in Context*, 118.
40. In fact, historians have found that in the pioneering period, white women and Native Americans had good friendships and offered assistance to each

other. See Sara Brooks Sundberg, "Picturing the Past: Farm Women on the Grasslands Frontier, 1850–1900," *Great Plains Quarterly* 30, no. 3 (2010): 208.
41. Yuval-Davis, *Gender & Nation*, 116.
42. Andrea G. Radke, "Refining Rural Spaces: Women and Vernacular Gentility in the Great Plains, 1880–1920," *Great Plains Quarterly* 24, no. 4 (2004): 229.
43. Djurdja Knezevic, "Affective Nationalism," in *Transitions Environments Translations: Feminism in International Politics*, ed. Joan W. Scott, Cora Kaplan, and Debra Keates (New York: Routledge, 1997), 69.
44. Dani Cavallaro, *Critical and Cultural Theory: Thematic Variations* (London: Athlone, 2007), 130.

Bob Mellin | Moses of the Midwest

Gene Stratton-Porter's Populist, Unsustainable Ecofeminism

Gene Stratton-Porter wrote ten best-selling novels, six natural histories of the Limberlost Swamp, and a popular column for *McCall's*. Although she preferred working as a natural historian rather than as a novelist, Stratton-Porter agreed to a contract with her publisher that permitted the publication of a natural history only after a new novel of hers was first published.[1] Stratton-Porter conceded that the arrangement was beneficial, stating that the novels allowed her "to put in the nature stuff.... I realized that I never could reach the audience I wanted with a book on nature alone."[2] Writing during the first wave of popular environmentalism in the United States (roughly 1880–1930), her decision to "put in the nature stuff" helped to make Stratton-Porter one of the most widely read authors of that period. Between 1900 and 1930, only five novels written by U.S. authors had sold more than a million and a half copies, and she wrote four of those works.[3] Stratton-Porter's first novel, *Freckles* (1904), sold more than 600,000 copies by 1914, while *A Girl of the Limberlost* (1909) sold in excess of 90,000 copies in its first year.[4] In addition, Stratton-Porter herself had become an icon of U.S. environmentalism. As noted in the introduction to the 1916 reprint of *At the Foot of the Rainbow* (1907), she received scores of fan letters every day for years after publishing *Freckles*, and "thousands of people" indicated to Stratton-Porter that her books inspired their "first realization of the beauties of nature."[5] Her public acclaim led William Lyon Phelps to argue that Stratton-Porter had become "an institution, like Yellowstone park."[6]

Phelps's claim is apt, but it is ultimately a problematic one that partially informs and complicates Stratton-Porter's fiction. The same is true when Stratton-Porter, as if to match Phelps's hyperbole, declared that her mission was to "lead women back to the forest" and to serve as their "Moses."[7] Both allusions hint at several concerns regarding literary agency. That is, Phelps's Yellowstone reference calls to mind the gendering of the landscape that Annette Kolodny analyzed in her landmark *The Lay of the Land*. Kolodny writes,

> what is probably America's oldest and most cherished fantasy: a daily reality of harmony between man and nature based on an experience of the land as essentially feminine—that is, not simply the land as mother, but the land as woman, the total female principle of gratification—enclosing the individual in an environment of receptivity, repose, and painless and integral satisfaction.[8]

In this construct, "woman" becomes a passive object that is acted upon by males questing in nature. To suggest that Stratton-Porter's position was similar to Yellowstone is to limit her literary agency—if not to that of a mute object, then to one that exists primarily as a call to males questing in nature.

Moreover, Stratton-Porter created a path to lead women to her promised land by linking her natural histories with what were, essentially, novels that served as primers for adolescent females. Her field observations led Stratton-Porter to conclude that biological sex equals gender, that there are only two sexes, and that in this natural construct women are mothers who care for the domestic space. For example, Stratton-Porter claimed that women have a "natural instinct for love, marriage, and children."[9] In addition, she argued, "No man ever had the patience to remain with a bird until he secured a real character study of it. A human mother is best prepared to understand and deal with a bird mother."[10] By extending domestic space beyond the home, Stratton-Porter positioned herself as an expressive realist who, based on her ideas about gender, was uniquely qualified to convey truths to her readers. She was their Moses, but the intertwining of her somewhat didactic novels with natural history created problems. As Donna Landry and Gerald MacLean warn in *Materialist Feminisms*, "If eco-feminists position themselves in such a way that women ... are naturally more nurturing or closer to nature than men, haven't they fallen prey to gender ideology once again?"[11] Landry and MacLean's question is useful when considering Stratton-Porter. Does Stratton-Porter ultimately sustain a gender ideology that she is at least ostensibly resisting in her work? Does her environmentally informed feminism effectively address the maldevelopment of as ecologically sensitive a place as the Limberlost Swamp?

Stratton-Porter's most enduring and widely read work, *A Girl of the Limberlost*, illustrates many of the concerns inherent in her ecofeminism. In this novel, Elnora Comstock is a sixteen-year-old who struggles between her life at the forlorn rural home she shares with her mother, where she is unhappy, and her life as a newly enrolled student at a city school, where she is shunned by her classmates because she is a country girl. The route from home (rural; domestic space) to school (city; public space) includes at least twice-daily trips in and around a wild place, the Limberlost Swamp, which is located between home and school. The swamp functions as a middle-ground, an oft-invoked "pastoral ideal" in U.S. literature that Leo Marx discusses in his 1964 work, *The Machine in the Garden: Technology and the Pastoral Ideal in America*. The pastoral ideal, according to Marx, is located between the "opposing forces of civilization and nature" but is "transcendent" to the binary.[12] Elnora finds a degree of refuge by exploring the swamp, and she also considers the ways that the swamp can enable her to generate the money she needs to buy books, tuition, and dresses. If, as Leo Marx states, "In the pastoral economy nature supplies most of the herdsman's needs and, even better, nature does virtually all of the work,"[13] in what way can the swamp provide for Elnora, and in what way will she transcend it?

Elnora considers but refuses to take any action that will compromise the integrity of the Limberlost Swamp, even though the novel touches on the ways the swamp was already being drained and destroyed. References to the oil industry abound, with Stratton-Porter's observations of the destruction it has caused catalogued with as much care as she catalogues the moths and birds of the Limberlost Swamp throughout the novel (the "nature stuff" she puts into her novels). Elnora's mother laments how the swamp is being covered with "horrid, greasy oil."[14] She recognizes the "changing natural conditions" in the Limberlost, which causes her to speak out against the destruction. Although Elnora's family owns a large portion of the swamp, she states that she and her mother will never allow "oil wells [to be] drilled that would yield to us the thousands our neighbours are draining from under us."[15] She would seemingly rather remain poor than contribute to the swamp's destruction. The refusal to develop the swamp helps to preserve the pastoral ground, although the refusal conflicts with Marx's argument that the pastoral economy can meet the needs of its inhabitant: Cultural needs will be met, but monetary needs are unmet. As Stratton-Porter already recognized by 1909, though, the actual Limberlost Swamp was inexorably being destroyed—a result of the dredging of the swamp by oil and agricultural interests, and the clearfelling of old-growth trees by the lumber industry.

Elnora and other characters of this novel endeavor to avoid the destruction of the swamp, but their perception of the area has already changed so that it is seen less for its intrinsic value as an ecosystem than for its use-value. Whether the Comstocks' trees are felled, each tree seems already inscribed as being worth "at least one hundred dollars each" or others that would be sold for so much that just one "would put Elnora in heaven for a year."[16] Elnora comments that if she needs money for college she will simply chop down some trees or have some oil wells drilled, although she avoids taking such action for most of the novel. Generally, although Elnora Comstock attempts to preserve the Limberlost Swamp, it is clear that its destruction is inevitable. It is already nothing but capital.

The need to preserve the Limberlost Swamp in the novel was based on two related reasons: first, as an environmental advocate, Stratton-Porter of course could not write a novel whose main character aided in the destruction of this ecologically sensitive place; second, as a writer who rested her views regarding female identity on nature, it would be curious to see Elnora damage the very foundation of her identity. Why would Elnora destroy the "talking trees" that teach her how to be "patient," "unselfish," "true," and "clean"?[17] The trees, according to the novel, also "sang" to Elnora.[18] In her most dramatic scenes, Elnora picks up her dead father's violin, which she plays only once in public (and that is in a school play where she is presented as a sort of mother earth), and seemingly "channels" nature through her violin. It is at these moments that Elnora is described as "a part of the setting all around her."[19] To compromise the integrity of the Limberlost Swamp would be to compromise the "forest" to which Stratton-Porter hopes to lead women.

Stratton-Porter is left struggling to find a way to have the novel locate a pastoral economy that provides for Elnora's needs without destroying the swamp. The struggle is one that has been considered extensively in U.S. literary criticism, albeit with only a limited consideration of gender. Leo Marx has described this persistent dialectic in U.S. culture, which shuttles between perceiving the physical environment of the United States as an actual location for a Georgic pastoral and recognizing that arriving at that environment also destroys it. Lawrence Buell, in *The Environmental Imagination: Thoreau, Nature Writing, and the Formation of American Culture* (1995), takes Marx's criticism in a direction that speaks even more directly to the conflict presented in *A Girl of the Limberlost*. Although Buell questions the ecocultural work done by writing within the pastoral tradition, he accepts the usefulness of pastoralism in the formation of U.S. cultural practices. Flawed though it is, Buell envisions "pastoral ideology functioning as a bridge, crude but serviceable, from anthropocentric to more specifically ecocentric concerns. For the pastoralization of new worlds, in spite of some of its original motives, also created a space for the eventual advancement of nature's claims on human society."[20] Although Buell suggests that U.S. literary pastoralism can support sound environmental practices, he pauses only momentarily to consider how "pastoral ideology" can frustrate those who have been marginalized on the basis of race, class, sexuality, and gender. He does pause to consider Kolodny's work concerning the gendered landscape, briefly pointing out the Eurocentric nation-building and male-privileged characteristics of U.S. pastoralism, but, in a refusal to think through the ways that a male-privileged cultural practice limits a socially just relationship of genders, he finds U.S. literary pastoralism to be "serviceable."

A Girl of the Limberlost offers a possible rethinking of the construct that Buell and others tend not to address, although the "pastoral ideal" represented in the novel by the Limberlost Swamp, while emblematic of a possible space for the transcendence Marx describes, cannot be preserved. Stratton-Porter devises an alternate economy for Elnora in this novel—harvesting moths—that provides Elnora with the fanciful means to generate capital while preserving the forest. Elnora captures and sells the moths of the Limberlost Swamp to generate the money she needs. After having made an arrangement with her benefactor, the Bird Woman (a character meant to represent the author herself) to sell her collections of moths gathered from the Limberlost Swamp, Elnora declares, "Oh, you beautiful stuff! You are going to buy the books, pay the tuition, and take me to high school."[21] Although there was an active market for moth collections during this first wave of popular environmentalism, the value of moths is greatly exaggerated in the novel.[22] What is offered in the novel is obviously not a practical solution. There is also some absurdity in having characters marvel at the beauty of various moths and then, immediately after discovering a prized moth, invoke a line used frequently in the novel: "get the cyanide jar."[23] Elnora justifies the killing by stating that once she learned that moths lived for such a short time, "there seemed to be no wickedness in it."[24] And, late in the novel, after she becomes a natural history teacher at the local school, Elnora claims that killing the "creatures" was "the only way to teach the masses of people how to distinguish the pests they should destroy from the harmless ones of great beauty."[25] The pastoral economy, in the version presented here, is a terribly unsustainable one for moths.

Stratton-Porter was aware of the dangers of development in the Limberlost, since she was partially responsible for its change. Her spouse, Charles Porter, was a banker who financed much of the development of the Limberlost Swamp. As Stratton-Porter's daughter notes in *The Lady of the Limberlost*, her mother and father married "During [the] time the oil boom struck Geneva, and Mr. Porter leased his farm, and some sixty oil wells were drilled. These proved to a good source of income."[26] The oil boom period in this portion of Indiana, according to the Indiana Academy of Science's *Natural Features of Indiana* (1966), began in 1889, peaked in 1904, and then declined "until [oil production] was less than a million gallons" in 1912.[27] *A Girl of the Limberlost* was published in 1909 and was set in the 1904–1908 period, a time after the peak oil production in the Limberlost. In her local natural histories, Stratton-Porter offers few critical comments concerning the oil industry, simply noting, for example, "A few oil-wells had been drilled near the head of the swamp."[28] Indeed, she relied on the oil workers to help her collect specimens for her studies.

For Stratton-Porter to create a character whose identity is based upon the swamp that Stratton-Porter was helping to "develop" complicates her version of ecofeminism, a point lost in some current efforts to present her as an environmentalist. Barbara Morrow, for instance, writes, "In the late 1880s, businessmen saw a chance to profit from the timber, oil, and natural gas within the Limberlost,"[29] without acknowledging that Charles was one of the businessmen profiting from the swamp at the very start of the oil boom in the Geneva area. Sydney Landon Plum also avoids exploring Stratton-Porter's complicity in the maldevelopment of the Limberlost Swamp, contending instead that Stratton-Porter "was vehement about conserving natural resources."[30] In fact, Stratton-Porter chose to leave the Limberlost in 1909, the year that *A Girl of the Limberlost* was published, to build a new estate, "Wildflower Woods," with the money she and Charles had made. Oil industry exploitation of the land and a welcoming literary marketplace enabled Stratton-Porter to move from being a lower-class country girl to an upwardly mobile celebrity writer. The degradation of the Limberlost Swamp, both in Stratton-Porter's life and in the fictional life of Elnora, suggests that Stratton-Porter was much more interested in mythologizing the threatened place of female identity—in this case, the Limberlost Swamp—than in offering resistance to the destruction of it.

A perverse spin on Marx's assertion that the pastoral ideal is "transcendent," in light of the Limberlost's impending demise to development, is that Elnora Comstock is able to escape her social class by investing her identity in the Limberlost—she is "a girl of the Limberlost." Elnora comes to represent a kind of "natural woman." Her classmates, who originally avoided Elnora because she was a country girl, now admire her because she teaches them how beautiful the Limberlost is. She comes to be a model of the ideal woman for all of the other characters in the novel, even for her lone antagonist, Edith Carr, with whom she competes for the attention of the upper-class, city-dwelling Phillip Ammon. Edith eventually breaks off her wedding because Phillip whispers to her at a ball they are giving in Chicago, "Be a moth," adding that she should "be like Elnora, the moth collector and nature woman."[31] Even Edith, though, comes to accept Phillip's eventual engagement to Elnora because she confesses that Elnora is "the superior woman"[32] and she herself forsakes her urban ways for moth collecting. Nature is triumphant in Elnora, even though this place of her identity is on the verge of destruction, in part because of her "collecting" of moths.

She apparently seeks to transcend by investing her identity in moths and the Limberlost itself, both of which are exploited and degraded.

Elnora becomes more and more of an idealized "natural" woman when she increases her distance from the dirty means of production in the country. As she comes to associate herself more with city folks, her rude home and rude mother are perceived in new ways. Stratton-Porter distances Elnora from dirty country life as the novel draws toward its conclusion. In a patronizing voice, Elnora tells her fiancé Phillip Ammon late in the novel that she was "reared among those Limberlost people"[33]— she is a girl of the Limberlost, but not a girl of the actual conditions of living in the Limberlost. She now dwells near the romantic, pastoral recasting of the countryside, the "Limberlost." Elnora moves into a city house,[34] but keeps the Limberlost cabin as a second home, which is no longer the depressing ramshackle cabin in the woods from which she dreamt of escaping. Elnora has fully removed herself from its history as the novel comes to an end, with she and her Chicago friends enjoying it as a restorative retreat from the city: "Honk! Honk! Honk! Hart Henderson set the alarm of the big automobile going as it shot from behind the trees lining the Brush wood road. The picture of a vine-covered cabin, a great drooping tree, a green-clad girl.... Edith Carr caught her breath with a snap. Polly Ammon gave Tom Levering a quick touch."[35] The gang from Chicago has arrived to enjoy the countryside. Elnora asks the visitors, "Won't you lay aside your dust-coats and have a cool drink? Phillip, would you ask mother to come, and bring that pitcher in the spring house."[36] Now with surplus capital, Elnora can afford to have a second home and associate with middle- to upper-class city folks, who enjoy the bucolic setting that has been stripped of any hint of the limited means of production in the countryside. It is a pastoral escape from the city, with Elnora shepherding this Georgic excursion. If this is the promised land that Stratton-Porter imagines for her readers, it is neither a place for effective agency for women nor one that enables ecologically sustainable practices.

A generous reconsideration of Stratton-Porter's work might consider this questionable resolution of Elnora's problems for its deconstructive possibilities. *A Girl of the Limberlost* situates a kind of natural identity for woman within the natural boundaries of the Limberlost Swamp, even as the swamp is on the verge of destruction.

Rather than support a notion of natural identity for women, then, *A Girl of the Limberlost* could be read to suggest a non-foundational critique of gendered identity. In this regard, the novel is not really an "ecological" one in a save-the-planet sense, since it offers little to halt the destruction caused by capitalist development. But by taking up the trope of a "natural place"—presented here as the Limberlost Swamp—Stratton-Porter is able to use nature to contain an identity she perhaps sought to leave in the past. That is, if she has succeeded in leading her readers to the promised land of a just gender identity, she might also be indicating that the foundation of such an identity will soon cease to exist, if it ever truly did exist.

Functioning as a temporary marker, the essentialized identity that Stratton-Porter creates for Elnora leaves "woman" in the past. As Gayatri Spivak writes,

> The claim to deconstructive feminism (and deconstructive anti-sexism—the political claim of deconstructive feminists) cannot be sustained in the name of "woman." Like class consciousness, which justifies its own production so that classes can be destroyed, "woman" as the name of writing must be erased in so far as it is a necessarily historical catachresis.[37]

Stratton-Porter's novels generally engage with "woman" as a necessary historical catachresis, willing to essentialize "woman" for anti-sexist objectives. As an ecofeminist manifesto, *A Girl of the Limberlost* does not offer much promise for the environment or for a progressive feminism; however, as a moment that hints at and then erases the nature of woman as not simply a state of being but as a part of the physical environment, Stratton-Porter clears a space for the continuing search for human and environmental justice. Although the Limberlost Swamp has recently been restored to some semblance of ecological integrity, it is useful to distinguish the physical restoration of this landmark, which was done in part to honor Stratton-Porter's environmental legacy, from nostalgia for the early twentieth century, particularly considering the limited means of many rural midwestern women of the time. In this respect, the Limberlost Swamp is not the promised land; Stratton-Porter simply points us to a horizon, a liminal space that adds nuance to the already complex nature of midwestern pastoral.

Notes

1. Judith Reick Long, *Gene Stratton-Porter: Novelist and Naturalist* (Indianapolis: Indiana Historical Society, 1990), 189–90.
2. Gene Stratton-Porter, *At the Foot of the Rainbow*, Reprint (New York: Grossett and Dunlap, 1916), 34.
3. Peter J. Schmitt, *Back to Nature: The Arcadian Myth in Urban America* (Baltimore: Johns Hopkins University Press, 1990), 125.
4. Long, *Gene Stratton-Porter*, 184, 192.
5. Stratton-Porter, *Foot*, 46.
6. Long, *Gene Stratton-Porter*, 9.
7. Gene Stratton-Porter, "My Life and My Books," *The Ladies Home Journal* (September 1916): 13.
8. Annette Kolodny, *The Lay of the Land: Metaphor As Experience and History in American Life and Letters* (Chapel Hill, NC: University of North Carolina Press, 1975), 3.
9. Long, *Gene Stratton-Porter*, 10.
10. Gene Stratton-Porter, *Friends in Feathers* (New York: Doubleday, 1917), 1–2.
11. Donna Landry and Gerald MacLean, *Materialist Feminisms* (Cambridge: Blackwell, 1993), 231.
12. Leo Marx, *The Machine in the Garden: Technology and the Pastoral Ideal in America* (New York: Oxford University Press, 1964), 23.
13. Ibid.
14. Gene Stratton-Porter, *A Girl of the Limberlost* (New York: Doubleday, 1909), 56.
15. Ibid., 212
16. Ibid., 32.
17. Ibid., 313.
18. Ibid., 186.
19. Ibid., 314.
20. Lawrence Buell, *The Environmental Imagination: Thoreau, Nature Writing, and the Formation of American Culture* (Cambridge, MA: Harvard University Press, 1995), 52.
21. Stratton-Porter, *Girl*, 52.
22. Ralph Lutts, *The Nature Fakers: Wildlife, Science, and Sentiment* (Golden, CO: Fulcrum, 1990), 25.
23. Ibid., 298, 328.
24. Ibid., 46.
25. Ibid., 413.

26. Jeannette Porter Meahan, *The Lady of the Limberlost: The Life and Letters of Gene Stratton Porter* (New York: Doubleday, 1928), 111.
27. Alton A. Lindsey, ed., *Natural Features of Indiana: Indiana Sesquicentennial Volume 1816–1966* (Indianapolis: Indiana Academy of Science, 1966), 137.
28. Stratton-Porter, *Friends*, 127.
29. Barbara Olenyik Morrow, *From Ben-Hur to Sister Carrie: Remembering the Lives and Works of Five Indiana Authors* (Carmel, IN: Guild Press of Indiana, 1995), 122.
30. Sydney Landon Plum, introduction to *Coming through the Swamp: The Nature Writings of Gene Stratton Porter*, ed. Sydney Landon Plum, xi–xxvii. (Salt Lake City: University of Utah Press, 1996), xv.
31. Stratton-Porter, *Girl*, 355.
32. Ibid., 394.
33. Ibid., 374.
34. Ibid., 382.
35. Ibid., 407.
36. Ibid., 411.
37. Gayatri Chakravorty Spivak, "Feminism and Deconstruction, Again: Negotiating with Unacknowledged Masculinism," in *Between Feminism and Psychoanalysis*, ed. Teresa Brennan, 206–24. (New York: Routledge, 1989), 218.

Sally E. Parry

Iron George

Myths of Masculinity in Sinclair Lewis's *Babbitt* and *Mantrap*

> We admire the man who embodies victorious effort; the man who never wrongs his neighbor, who is prompt to help a friend, but who has those virile qualities necessary to win in the stern strife of actual life.
>
> —Theodore Roosevelt[1]

In September 2015 a new hashtag, #MasculinitySoFragile, trended on Twitter. Users around the world "shared their views on how society defines masculinity—and the damaging side effects that come with those stereotypes. Though society has become more aware and critical of the impact of male privilege, ways for men to prove their masculinity with specific labels, products and behaviors persist—often with mental, emotional and physical consequences for men and women alike."[2] This trend echoes the concerns that men in American society have had for well over a hundred and fifty years, a fear that men are losing those attributes that make them men. Sinclair Lewis was among the many authors of the early twentieth century who presented this apparent crisis, but he was also very critical of the posturing connected with the presentation of male identity. In *Babbitt* (1922) and *Mantrap* (1926) he presents men who are undergoing midlife crises and trying to find an essential male identity in nature. In both cases, these men learn rather painfully that being a man has little to do with nature and more to do with an honest awareness of their own place in the world.

Twenty-five years before #MasculinitySoFragile, Robert Bly, in *Iron John*, wrote that modern men did not know how to get in touch with their wild, primitive, pre-Christian selves and therefore had become weak, passive, and unmanly. His solution was for men to tap into this

"Wild Man energy" through connections with fathers and other male mentors and become initiated into the "male spirit."[3] Although the words are different, the essence of Bly's search for the male spirit is part of a continuum that looks ahead to #MasculinitySoFragile and looks back ninety years to Theodore Roosevelt's "The Strenuous Life" in 1899: "A mere life of ease is not in the end a very satisfactory life, and above all, it is a life which ultimately unfits those who follow it for serious work in the world.... The man must be glad to do a man's work, to dare and endure and to labor."[4] In each of these writings, there is an expressed desire to define man in an essentialist way, as a true man with a capital M, and also a fear that whatever constitutes this manliness is fading away and needs to be recovered.[5]

Since the end of the Civil War there have been numerous examples in literature and popular culture of American men fearing the loss of their masculinity because they were unable to demonstrate it in any particular way—such as in battle against the enemy or against the elements. For example, following the South's loss in the Civil War, many southern men joined the Klan as a way of "revitalizing southern masculinity."[6] By joining the Klan, these men thought they could feel more manly, in the sense that although they had lost the war, they could assert control over those they felt to be lesser than themselves, mistakenly assuming that this would restore their pride. The novels of Thomas Dixon, such as *The Leopard's Spots* (1902) and *The Clansman* (1905), demonstrate how popular culture accepted the idea of the Klan as heroic and manly, so much so that D. W. Griffith turned Dixon's novels into the highly successful and controversial film *The Birth of a Nation* in 1915.

This concern about what it means to be a man increased as the United States moved from a primarily rural to a more urban society. In the late nineteenth century, as more men worked in offices rather than on farms or ranches, the masculine fantasy of tramping arose, "free from any domestic obligations."[7] Writers such as Jack London wrote about the hard life of the hobo, which many men read as freedom from spheres of control whether at home or in the office. The new model of manhood, where men were caught up in the demands of the office and the factory, placed less emphasis on the self-reliance of the farmer or artisan, and thus such men became "chronically insecure" because they had no way of proving themselves.[8] Lewis's protagonists, George Babbitt and Ralph Prescott, share in this sense of unease. One might think that, with the wars in which the United States was involved in the late nineteenth and early twentieth century, there would be a return to defining manhood through military service. And indeed, Theodore Roosevelt's speeches following the Spanish-American War praised the virile qualities of the men who participated in "the most absolutely righteous foreign war in which any nation has engaged during the nineteenth century."[9] Roosevelt "routinely preached lessons about manhood and American identity because he believed the men of his era had become complacent, seeking physical ease and moral laxity instead of exhibiting masculine vigor."[10] In World War I, it seemed that soldiers became more machinelike and less heroic because of the rise of military technology. Aaron Shaheen suggests that in John Dos Passos's *Three Soldiers*, as men became homogenized into the technological military, there was "a disappearance of the older martial codes that had helped to govern young males' passage in the ranks of men."[11]

Gender historian Gail Bederman noted that civilization at the beginning of the twentieth century was built on a notion of "manliness" that "dealt with moral achievements which only the most civilized men could attain" so that just "as manliness was the highest form of manhood, so civilization was the highest form of humanity."[12] Manliness became not just a physical superiority but also a moral one. When Roosevelt writes in "The Strenuous Life" of what men should aspire to, he is careful to link what a man is to what he does.

Cultural critics have written about a recurrent American phenomenon where groups of men, feeling their culture's definition of masculinity is excluding them, band together in some sort of intense male bonding that has taken the form of guilds, lodges, sports teams, fraternal organizations, or the military.[13] These male groups are often hierarchical, secretive, and exclusionary, all as a way of providing validation or a rite of passage for the individual man through a group to become part of the brotherhood of man. These groups become especially important in times when there is a perceived masculinity crisis.

Lewis was aware in his own time of middle-class male insecurity, especially among male office workers who wondered whether they fit into the real world of men. What they did had become to some extent genderless, as both men and women worked in business offices, doing more or less the same kind of work.[14] In the America of the 1920s, the "workplace was not masculine in the same sense that it had been."[15] In a number of his novels Lewis portrayed the somewhat pathetic urges of his male characters to be considered he-men and good fellows despite their sedentary occupations. In particular, George Babbitt of *Babbitt* and Ralph Prescott of *Mantrap* seem to feel this need to connect with manliness or develop a sense of masculine identity they feel to be lacking in their urban, business-driven lives.[16] Their search leads them to view the wilderness as a place where they can get down to being real men, in harmony with nature and other men.[17] However, although Lewis feels sympathy for the sterility of their lives, he deconstructs the romantic fantasies that these men participate in and use as a substitute for thinking seriously about their place as men in modern society. Real estate salesman Babbitt and lawyer Prescott feel degendered by their office-bound existences and hope to gain some masculine vigor through nature.

George Babbitt seems to be participating in a masculine culture from the beginning of the novel, with his interest in cars, cigars, alcohol, and men's clubs. He engages in outward displays of manhood, such as a pride in and fascination with his automobile. His automobile is "poetry and tragedy, love and heroism."[18] Parking for him is a "virile adventure" (*Babbitt* 32). Babbitt smokes cigars and finds great satisfaction in a new electric cigar-lighter for his automobile, "the last touch of class to a gentleman's auto" (*Babbitt* 54). He even introduces his son Ted to the "'brotherhood' of the smoking car"[19] when they take a train trip together.[20] For him, drinking, too, is part of being a man, as is his pride in being able to find liquor for his friends despite Prohibition. He becomes the mighty hunter who has to track down the quarry of liquor and endure the scorn of the salesman of the illegal booze rather than the snarl of the wild animal. He finds camaraderie, he thinks, at the Zenith Athletic Club, which provides some of the fraternity he longs for. It is truly a male enclave. When Babbitt bounds into the Athletic Club for lunch he whoops, "How's the boys? How's the boys?" (*Babbitt* 55). Frederick Hoffman notes that being a part of Babbitt's society "requires a tribal solidarity with 'the boys.'"[21]

However, Babbitt may be using these outward poses of masculinity to thwart the control that women have over his life. He received his job with the Babbitt-Thompson Realty Company because his wife Myra's father owned the firm. Myra functions almost as mother as well as wife to Babbitt and firmly controls the domestic sphere. He realizes early on "that his wife was too busy to be impressed by that moral indignation with which males rule the world" (*Babbitt* 109). In the office Miss Magoun, his secretary, is the woman Babbitt relies on to correct his correspondence and by extension control certain aspects of his business life.

The same things that Babbitt thinks define his manliness also can emasculate him. In an effort to stop smoking, he tells Miss Magoun to hide his cigars, and later has to beg her to tell him where they are. When he attempts to cheat on his wife, his car breaks down and he has to hire a taxi to take Ida Putiak, his manicurist and would be amour, out to dinner. While out with Ida, "they were unable to get anything to drink [because] [t]he head-waiter refused to understand who George F. Babbitt was" (*Babbitt* 290). Babbitt is denied two things that he thinks make him a man, a car and alcohol. He also is denied his identity as an important person. As one might guess, the night for him is a dismal failure.

Even the fraternal support that Babbitt has is shown to be superficial, for his friends distance themselves from him whenever he tries to do anything out of the ordinary, such as demonstrate interest in liberal lawyer Seneca Doane's support for striking workers. His friends also frown on his affair with Tanis Judique when his wife is away from home, partly because it is too public and so mocks proper domestic life, and partly because he is socializing with the "The Bunch," a mixed gender group, rather than a fraternal group like the Elks. Wilson Carey McWilliams notes that Babbitt's friends' "boisterous but genuine delight in affection, is only a veneer which conceals their own fear of difference and suspicion of each other."[22]

Ralph Prescott of *Mantrap* does not have any fraternal support like the Athletic Club, nor does he have a domestic sphere from which to flee. He is a forty-year-old lawyer, quiet and conservative, and a confirmed bachelor. He lived with his mother until her death two years before the novel takes place and has not been involved in any romances because he found his mother "so much more serene and fine and instantly understanding than any girl he encountered that he had preferred her dear presence to insinuating romance."[23] His life since her death has been bound up with the office, leading him, at the time the novel begins, to a midlife crisis and the edge of a nervous collapse. His work was "insufficient to lull his jangling nerves, and night by night he awoke to obscure panics, lay rigid with black and anonymous apprehensions" (*Mantrap* 8). His condition was shared by many other white-collar workers of the time who also suffered from "neurasthenia," an illness caused by "excessive brain work and nervous strain."[24] Prescott has no real male friendship to sustain him, which may be why he responds so quickly to an offer from sales manager E. Wesson Woodbury to accompany him on a Canadian fishing trip. Woodbury says they'll have a chance to "Get out among real men and eat real grub and sleep on Mother Earth" (*Mantrap* 18). Prescott sees this as a panacea for his strained nerves and a way to feel like a real man. Although Prescott may have wanted male companionship to validate his masculinity, Wes Woodbury will turn out to be an obnoxious boor, and Prescott will have to be rescued by a more manly person, the guide Joe Easter.

Babbitt is forty-seven years old to Prescott's forty, and he does have male companionship, through his membership in the Elks, the Boosters' Club, the Athletic Club, and especially through his friendship with Paul Riesling of whom he was fonder "than of any one on earth except himself and his daughter Tinka" (*Babbitt* 41). However, it is this friendship that leads to a midlife crisis similar to Ralph Prescott's. Paul is like George's younger brother and his only true friend. Paul sells roofing, but he is also a talented violinist and sensitive soul to whom George feels he can talk in more than a superficial manner. George believes he is at his best with Paul and the finest time he has in the novel is the week he spends in the Maine woods with Paul and a guide, before their families join them.

George's idealization of their relationship sours when he discovers that Paul has been having an affair to compensate for a loveless marriage. Echoing Roosevelt, he scolds Paul, telling him, "a man who doesn't buckle down and do his duty, even if it does bore him sometimes, is nothing but a—well, he's simply a weakling" (*Babbitt* 65). And he is truly frightened when Paul shoots his nagging wife Zilla, is convicted of attempted murder, and is sent to prison for three years. The depth of Paul's despair, which he had not understood, makes Babbitt realize how little he knows about Paul and forces him to reconsider his own life and lack of happiness.²⁵ Babbitt soon embarks on an affair of his own, hoping to find some purpose to his life, or at least to have some fun.

This crisis in his relationship with Paul sends Babbitt back to the woods: "He saw himself returning; finding peace there, and the presence of Paul, in a life primitive and heroic" (*Babbitt* 294). This primitive life is the one that Bly speaks of as defining true masculinity. Babbitt sees the wilderness as a place for purity of spirit and a return to an essential maleness. David G. Pugh notes that "men, historically tied to civilization … have periodically fled to nature to indulge in a self-saving primitivism."²⁶ Babbitt lies to his wife about this need to go back to the woods, just telling her he needs a vacation, "since it was inconceivable to explain that he was going to seek Paul's spirit in the wilderness" (*Babbitt* 295).

Babbitt, Riesling, and Prescott have all developed romantic ideas about the wilderness.²⁷ They belong to a culture where a fantasy world of nature, part Jack London and part Robert Service, provides a simple way for them to think about what it means to be a man. Jonathan Mitchell describes this view of the frontier as a "geomythical space" where nature becomes a sort of theme park.²⁸ Paul describes to George his modest dream before the trip to Maine to "just loaf by ourselves and smoke and cuss and be natural" (*Babbitt* 66). When George returns to Maine to try to re-create the magic of his week with Paul, he pictures something a bit more exciting: "Moccasins—six-gun—frontier town—gamblers—sleep under the stars—be a regular man" (*Babbitt* 295). Prescott thinks of himself as an "exiled Dan'l Boone" (*Mantrap* 22) whose soul will be made right by a visit to the woods. But it is a theme park woods, and Woodbury confirms that it won't be too rugged: "an awful easy trip, the way I make it. The Injuns do all the carrying on the portages; they cook the chow and clean the fish and put up the tents. And when we don't use the outboard motor, they do the paddling, not us" (*Mantrap* 14). Lewis moves between the mystical idea of nature and the reality of camping for this middle-aged lawyer. As he is outfitted for his trip in a flannel shirt and riding breeches, Ralph sees himself as "virile and competent," but he has to remove his "rimless eyeglasses which took away slightly from his appearance as a tough man of action" (*Mantrap* 23).

Of these different expectations of the wilderness, Paul's less romantic expectation comes closest to reality. He and George loaf and fish and do not feel called upon to act the part of substantial men of business or he-men of action. They revert to the comradeship they felt in college and even get close to discussing their feelings. But the "shame of emotion overpowered them; they cursed a little, to prove they were rough good fellows" (*Babbitt* 151). Even in nature, real men don't talk about feelings. Victor J. Seidler notes that in male friendships, there is a fear of rejection, even between close friends, that prevents true intimacy.[29]

In the wilderness George and Ralph think that the guide each has met is the epitome of manhood and the one by whom they seek to redefine themselves as men. The very names of Joe Paradise of *Babbitt* and Joe Easter of *Mantrap* intimate that they are able to bring men to a better place, leaving the stultifying urban world behind. They seem to participate in a controlling discourse "of the Adamic myth and the return to Eden."[30] Both names have religious overtones, as though returning to nature were a transcendent experience. Paradise and Easter are described as Jack London–like natural men, "ruggedly independent yet a remarkably compassionate breed who paid allegiance only to the inexorable laws of nature and to the authority of conscience, and who possessed a capacity for selflessness and comradeship very much like the agape of primitive Christianity."[31] George imagines the Maine guides as "simple and strong and daring, jolly as they played stud-poker in their unceiled shack, wise in woodcraft as they tramped the forest and shot the rapids.... If he could but take up a backwoods claim with a man like Joe [Paradise], work hard with his hands, be free and noisy in a flannel shirt, and never come back to this dull decency" (*Babbitt* 295).

However, although these guides are good men, they aren't perfect, either as male role models or as saviors. Joe Paradise "shatters Babbitt's illusions by displaying insensitivity to the joys of the wilderness, by proving to be in worse physical condition than the pampered Babbitt, and finally, by admitting that, if he were able to do anything in the world, he would move to town and open a 'swell shoe store.'"[32] The wonderful woods that Babbitt wants to be a part of are the ones that Paradise wants to escape. No wonder Babbitt is unable to re-create the sense of happiness he felt when he goes back to the Maine woods without his friend Paul: "Save the snoring guide, there was no other human being within ten miles. He was lonelier than he had ever been in his life" (*Babbitt* 300).

Babbitt needs the companionship of his own kind, other businessmen like himself.

Joe Easter more completely bears out Ralph's faith in him, although he is a complex person, not just a masculine icon. He is also a more developed character than Joe Paradise, because so much more of *Mantrap* is set in the woods than *Babbitt*. Easter is attuned to nature, as a good guide ought to be, but he has a softer, seemingly less masculine, side as well. He is proud of carrying around a pillow and silk pajamas for camping out. He is also more poetic about the wilderness: "Through Joe's halting stories, Ralph saw that great white unknown land. The crackle and shimmer of the Northern Lights in a vast darkness over dark vast forests. The savage stars of the winter night. The joy of a cabin's yellow lights seen far down a frozen and snowy river when a fur-buyer was numb with hunger" (*Mantrap* 169). Easter's stories create the mythos of the frontier that Ralph has dreamed of. It is as though Easter's tales are more representative of what Ralph expects from nature than what he actually experiences.

Alverna, Joe's wife, heard the same sort of stories that Ralph hears and was caught up in the same sort of fantasy of nature. Easter had met her in Minneapolis a year before when she gave him a manicure at the barbershop where she worked. He buys her dinner, is attracted both to her beauty and her preference for a "man-sized steak" (*Mantrap* 109), and marries her the next day. Although she is fascinated by his stories about fur-buying and the "dandy little house" at Mantrap Landing (*Mantrap* 107), she finds the day-to day living there has little in common with the stories Easter told of the romantic north. Most of the men her husband knows spend more time drinking, talking, and playing poker than doing anything adventurous or manly. She is like Carol Kennicott of *Main Street*, who is dazzled by her new husband's description of Gopher Prairie as well as the snapshots he shows her.[33] But when Carol actually arrives in town, she finds the reality of it much less exciting. The town is small, the people ordinary, and the future seems unpromising.

Like Carol, Alverna finds her life doesn't measure up to the romance that has been promised her. She flatters Ralph, appealing to his masculine ego, hoping that he will bring her back to civilization. Ralph has not had much feminine attention and this attention makes him feel like a real man. However, his boasting is not about his manly attributes but about his travels to Europe, his attending the opera and visiting nightclubs, his arguing before the Supreme Court, and his friends, "the classmate who was now a diplomat, the doctor who had performed an operation in an aeroplane, the explorer who had been tortured to death in North China" (*Mantrap* 217). He at least knows men who sound romantic to Alverna, and he exudes a sort of sophistication that she aspires to. Eventually she convinces him they should run away together, even though Ralph realizes he would be betraying the friendship Joe has shown him. Ralph and Alverna's adventure in the wilderness does not last long. They really only know the woods through the mediation of guides and so when they are left on their own, they are unable to cope, quickly becoming cold, tired, and hungry. Their romantic escapade falls flat.

Joe Easter, along with his Indian guide Saul, comes to the rescue. Joe is unusually understanding, and almost too good to be true, both as a husband and as a friend. Ralph wonders, "Have I let him welcome me into his life and then hurt him like this?" (*Mantrap* 283). Joe tells Ralph, as a way of making it seem all right, "No woman that ever lived is worth giving up a real friendship for." (*Mantrap* 269). However, Ralph realizes he has spoiled the paradise of the woods by being led astray by a woman. His concern for Joe and desire to make things right verge on the romantic. Ralph tells him, "we must try to make something big and enduring out of friendship" (*Mantrap* 295) and offers to take Joe to New York and find him a job. Although Ralph means well and his compassion for Joe is admirable, taking a man out of his environment is not a good idea. Joe performs a more noble action, acting drunk and stepping off the train Ralph is taking to New York, because he realizes something that Ralph does not. There is more than one kind of man. Although some men are comfortable with nature and outdoor, physical jobs, others are more comfortable with less physical and more cerebral office work. Joe is not judgmental about this, but accepts it as a fact, something that Ralph, who seems to be caught up in the Rooseveltian idea of man, is much slower to learn.

Babbitt's genuine concern for Paul Riesling, like Prescott's for Joe Easter, indicates Babbitt's depth of character, in that he is able to care deeply about another human being. This love will eventually lead him back to his family, and a better relationship with his children and his wife. This growth of affection Clare Eby sees rightly as a rebellion against "regulation manliness."³⁴ She notes the "compulsion to remain identifiably male [by belonging to some clan or group] prohibits self-realization."³⁵ Although Babbitt moves away from his clan with experiments in free love and socialism, he eventually moves back into the fold of the Good Fellows and solid family men, giving up his individual quest for identity in order to be with his sick wife. However, he has an awareness that he did not have before. He escapes being a stereotypical male because he has gained some self-knowledge.

By the end of their respective novels, George Babbitt and Ralph Prescott may have failed to become stereotypical he-men, but they have succeeded in becoming better human beings. Like other men in novels and short stories of the 1920s, their experience in the wilderness has given them a new perspective. Post–World War I found not only office workers but ex-soldiers looking to nature for solace. Nick Adams in Ernest Hemingway's "Big Two-Hearted River," for example, comes to the wilderness to fish and think after enduring unimaginable violence during the war. And Chaz Windzer, in John Joseph Matthews's *Sundown*, returns to the reservation and Osage land after his time in the military, trying to regain his sense of identity. Their time in the wilderness does not make them into what they would think of as "real" men with swaggering walks and tough attitudes, but instead increases their awareness and compassion. Although Babbitt may say at the end of the novel, "I've never done a single thing I wanted to in my whole life!" (*Babbitt* 401), his realization of the complexities of life and his increased concern for the welfare of his wife and son show that he has changed for the better. Neither he nor Ralph Prescott may be men who are "gallant and wise and well-beloved" (*Babbitt* 102), as Babbitt is to the faery girl of his dreams, but they are finer human beings.

Notes

1. Theodore Roosevelt, "The Strenuous Life," in *The Works of Theodore Roosevelt*. Vol. 12 (New York: Collier, 1900), 4.
2. Taylor Pittman, "The Reaction to Twitter Movement about Masculinity Is Exactly Why It's So Important," *Huffington Post* (September 23, 2015).
3. Robert Bly, *Iron John: A Book about Men* (Reading, MA: Addison-Wesley, 1990), 8, 14.
4. Roosevelt, "Strenuous Life," 5.

5. Andrew Ross notes, "Masculinity, defined from context to context as a set of cultural standards to be observed and emulated, is shaped by social institutions.... All men find it difficult to match up to those standards.... Most, however, actually did suffer from the consequences to varying degrees and fall back upon compensatory fantasies." Andrew Ross, "Wet, Dark, and Low: Eco-Man Evolves from Eco-Woman," *boundary 2* 19, no. 2 (1992): 219.

6. Deborah E. Barker, "Confederate Abjection in D. W. Griffith's Early Civil War Films and Thomas Dixon's *Clansman*," in *Reconstructing Violence: The Southern Rape Complex in Film and Literature* (Baton Rouge: Louisiana State University Press, 2015), 32.

7. John Funchion, *Novel Nostalgias: The Aesthetics of Antagonism in Nineteenth-Century U.S. Literature* (Columbus: Ohio State University Press, 2015), 158.

8. Michael Kimmel, *Manhood in America: A Cultural History* (New York: The Free Press, 1996), 17.

9. Theodore Roosevelt, "Fellow-Feeling as a Political Factor," in *The Works of Theodore Roosevelt*, Vol. 12 (New York: Collier, 1900), 59.

10. Leroy G. Dorsey, "Managing Women's Equality: Theodore Roosevelt, the Frontier Myth, and the Modern Woman," *Rhetoric and Public Affairs* 16, no. 3 (Fall 2013): 425.

11. Aaron Shaheen, "Spencerian Theory and Modern Rites of Passage in John Dos Passos's *Three Soldiers*," *Texas Studies in Literature and Language* 57, no. 2 (2015): 178.

12. Gail Bederman, *Manliness and Civilization: A Cultural History of Gender and Race in the United States, 1880–1917* (Chicago: University of Chicago Press, 1995), 27.

13. See Mark C. Carnes, "Iron John in the Gilded Age," *American Heritage* (Sept. 1993): 37–45; Joe L. Dubbert, "Progressivism and the Masculinity Crisis," in *The American Man*, ed. Elizabeth H. Pleck and Joseph H. Pleck (Englewood Cliffs, NJ: Prentice-Hall, 1980), 303–20; Elizabeth H. Pleck and Joseph H. Pleck, introduction to *The American Man* (Englewood Cliffs, NJ: Prentice-Hall, 1980), 1–49; David G. Pugh, *Sons of Liberty: The Masculine Mind in Nineteenth-Century America* (Westport, CT: Greenwood, 1983); and E. Anthony Rotundo, *American Manhood: Transformations in Masculinity from the Revolution to the Modern Era* (New York: Basic Books, 1993) for discussions of the rise of fraternal organizations at various periods in western civilization, especially in nineteenth- and early twentieth-century America.

14. See Jeffrey P. Hantover, "The Boy Scouts and the Validation of Masculinity," in *The American Man*, ed. Elizabeth H. Pleck and Joseph H. Pleck (Englewood Cliffs, NJ: Prentice-Hall, 1980), 289–93 for information on the increase of women in the office workforce.

15. Rotundo, *American Manhood*, 250.

16. Prescott's trip into the wilderness is based to a certain extent on a trip that Lewis took with his brother Claude to Saskatchewan. Sinclair even told his brother to keep a good record as "this was to be his guide for *Mantrap*." John J. Koblas and Dave Page, introduction to *Sinclair Lewis & Mantrap: The Saskatchewan Trip*, by Claude B. Lewis, ed. John J. Koblas and Dave Page (Madison, WI: Main Street Press, 1985), xv. The diary that Claude kept became *Sinclair Lewis & Mantrap: The Saskatchewan Trip*, published about sixty years after the trip took place.
17. Other male characters of Lewis's go into the wilderness, or at least the country, to escape urban drudgery and dissipation. In *The Prodigal Parents* (1938) Fred Cornplow takes his son into the Canadian wilderness on a canoe trip to try to make a man of him. Martin Arrowsmith goes to the woods at the end of *Arrowsmith* (1925) to set up a laboratory with a friend and escape domestic entrapment. See Glen A. Love, *Babbitt: An American Life* (New York: Twayne, 1993), 63–65, 94 for his view of the wilderness as a form of rehabilitation.
18. Sinclair Lewis, *Babbitt* (New York: Harcourt, Brace, 1922), 24. Subsequent references will be cited parenthetically in the text.
19. Wilson Carey McWilliams, "The Redhead," in *The Idea of Fraternity in America* (Berkeley: University of California Press, 1973), 523.
20. Babbitt's son is named Theodore Roosevelt Babbitt, "whose name resonates with his father's not quite forgotten aspirations toward progressive action and the manly western values." Glen A. Love, "The Western Writings of Sinclair Lewis," in *A Literary History of the West*, ed. Max Westbrook and James H. Maguire (Fort Worth: Texas Christian University Press, 1987), 758.
21. Frederick J. Hoffman, *The Twenties: American Writing in the Postwar Decade*, rev. ed. (New York: The Free Press, 1962), 410.
22. McWilliams, "Redhead," 523.
23. Sinclair Lewis, *Mantrap* (New York: Harcourt, Brace, 1926), 9. Subsequent references will be cited parenthetically in the text.
24. Bederman, *Manliness and Civilization*, 14.
25. George's relationship with Paul is weakened when Paul rejects his friendship after he has tried to kill Zilla. Babbitt feels both depressed and old. Paul had been his college roommate as well as his friend for his entire adult life. Rotundo notes, "in providing love, security, and a sense of being special, these intense attachments gave male youths a substitute for the emotional nurture provided most often in boyhood by a mother" Rotundo, *American Manhood*, 86. Ralph Prescott has also lost his best friend, his mother, to death, and needs to move on to another stage in his life.
26. Pugh, *Sons of Liberty*, 39. Rotundo calls it a return to "boy culture," a concept that arose for middle-class boys in the middle of the nineteenth century: "As a social sphere, it was separate both from the domestic world of women, girls, and small children, and from the public world of men and

commerce." Rotundo, *American Manhood,* 31. Several scouting movements were created in the United States in the early twentieth century: the Woodcraft Indians in 1902, the Sons of Daniel Boone in 1905, and the Boy Scouts of America in 1910. These organizations encouraged an interest in nature, patriotism, and self-reliance. Theodore Roosevelt was a strong supporter of the Boy Scouts.

27. Lewis, despite his cynicism, retained some of these romantic ideas about the wilderness. See Sinclair Lewis, *Minnesota Diary, 1942–46,* ed. George Killough (Moscow, ID: University of Idaho Press, 2000) for trips he took in the mid-1940s to reacquaint himself with nature in his native state.
28. Jonathan Mitchell, *Revisions of the American Adam: Innocence, Identity and Masculinity in Twentieth-Century America* (London: Continuum, 2011), 19, 27–28.
29. Victor J. Seidler, "Rejection, Vulnerability, and Friendship," in *Men's Friendships,* ed. Peter M. Nardi (Newbury Park, CA: Sage, 1992), 27.
30. Mitchell, *American Adam,* 19.
31. Earle Labor and Jeanne Campbell Reesman, *Jack London,* rev. ed. (New York: Twayne, 1994), 25.
32. Robert E. Fleming, "Sinclair Lewis vs. Zane Grey: *Mantrap* as Satirical Western," *MidAmerica* 9 (1982): 125.
33. Sinclair Lewis, *Main Street* (New York: Harcourt, Brace and Howe, 1920), 18.
34. Clare Virginia Eby, "*Babbitt* as Veblenian Critique of Manliness," *American Studies* 34, no. 2 (1993): 9.
35. Ibid., 14.

Kelly Hanson | Performing Haitian History on the Midwestern Stage

The World Premiere of Clarence Cameron White's Modernist Opera *Ouanga*[1]

On June 10, 1949, the opera *Ouanga* (1932) made its world premiere on a modest, midwestern stage in the Central High School auditorium in South Bend, Indiana. The show, set in Haiti and chronicling the rise and fall of the nation's first emperor, Jean Jacques Dessalines (1758–1806), was written by two African American professors, the composer Clarence Cameron White and the writer John F. Matheus. The two men first met in 1924 while teaching at West Virginia State College; they quickly discovered their common interest in telling the story of a "Haitian hero" and decided to work together to "produce an opera entirely for and about Negroes."[2] Over a period of four years between 1928 and 1932, the two men collaborated from afar, with White composing music in Paris and Matheus penning the libretto back home in West Virginia. In 1928, the pair traveled to Haiti to research Haitian culture, music, and sound; as White composed the music, he blended Haitian sounds with traditional elements of French opera, including elaborate ballet dances.[3] When *Ouanga* was finally published in 1932, the opera garnered praise and awards, winning the prestigious Bispham Medal for that year. Despite this initial success, White would labor for the next seventeen years to get the opera staged. He did not succeed until 1949, when the opera received its first full staging after the Harry T. Burleigh Music Association in South Bend, Indiana, chose *Ouanga* for its spring performance.[4]

  This tale of international, collaborative composition serves as a useful introduction to *Ouanga*, a modernist opera that stages the tension between local heritage and transnational modernity. A product of the New Negro (or "Harlem") Renaissance, *Ouanga* invokes the Haitian

Revolution (1791-1804), as well as Dessalines's struggle to build a new nation, in order to celebrate the glorious potential of black sovereignty. The opera's 1949 premiere performance took place in the Midwest, but the opera itself, including its content, storyline, development, and staging, was geographically diverse. Linking contemporary African American efforts to uplift the Negro race to the historic establishment of the Haitian nation state, *Ouanga*'s South Bend production imagined Haiti's revolutionary past as a shared history of sovereignty for black people around the world. Moreover, as a show put on by dozens of performers from the United States and Haiti, the opera positioned the remembrance of this past as a collective endeavor. For African American audiences in South Bend, *Ouanga* constructed a transnational imaginary that linked their local values and struggles to a global experience of race, rooted in a shared history of blackness.

Putting *Ouanga* in Context

Ouanga's retelling of Haiti's revolution and independence created a sense of racial community that was rooted locally but extended beyond national borders. Through this racial invocation, *Ouanga* yoked together two disparate histories and national experiences under the shared experience of race. Still, the circumstances of *Ouanga*'s creation complicated White and Matheus's celebration of sharing in another nation's past: from 1915 to 1934, the United States military occupied Haiti. The U.S. government rationalized the occupation as a benevolent act to help the Haitians clean up their political and economic problems; its public statements cited continuous revolution, political instability, crushing foreign debt, a fledgling economy, and an acute lack of modernized industry and infrastructure as justifications for sending in the marines.[5] As historian Peter James Hudson has argued, however, corporate finance played a significant role in the United States' motivation for occupying Haiti. By 1915, the City Bank of New York (today known as Citibank or Citigroup) held significant investments in the Banque Nationale d'Haiti, and much of the marine presence centered on protecting U.S. assets.[6]

Given the occupation's focus on modernizing Haiti, though, some African Americans viewed the military presence in a positive light. Booker T. Washington, for example, celebrated the occupation as an opportunity for Americans to uplift impoverished Haitians through education.[7] In her 1938 ethnography of Haiti and Jamaica, *Tell My Horse*, Zora Neale Hurston looked back on the arrival of the marines as a prophetic event: "a black plume against the sky ... shall give fright to many at its coming," she wrote of the U.S. warships, "but it shall bring peace to Haiti."[8] Most New Negro artists and intellectuals, however, were deeply critical of the occupation and suspicious of the U.S. government's stated rationales. For many black Americans, the occupation seemed like an attempt to suppress the first independent black nation. In 1920, James Weldon Johnson visited Haiti as part of an NAACP group tasked with investigating claims of marine brutality; he published his findings in the four-part article, "Self-Determining Haiti," a damning exposé that spurred a Congressional investigation.[9]

This historical context forms an important backdrop for *Ouanga*. On the one hand, the opera aimed to celebrate Haiti's history and independence for black audiences in the United States; on the other hand, two American citizens created the opera at the height of the U.S. military occupation of Haiti. Intentionally or not, White and Matheus's opera enacted a cultural imperialism, co-opting Haitian history, music, and sound for U.S. audiences. As Stephanie Leigh Batiste has argued, during the 1930s, African American theatrical performances often participated in cultural appropriation of dominated cultures as a way of claiming belonging within the imperial U.S. nation state. Like other 1930s performances of Haitian history, such as the Federal Theatre Project's 1936 "Voodoo" *Macbeth* or its 1938 *Haiti*, *Ouanga* used sensationalized versions of "voodoo" to quickly signify a primitivism that marked Haiti as backwards and distinctly un-modern.[10]

Yet, I argue here that the Burleigh Music Association's performances of *Ouanga* in South Bend challenged this imperial context. The Indiana production featured Haitian artists and audience members, as well as the blessing of the Haitian embassy. This midwestern performance disrupts tidy understandings of the ways U.S. modernist writers conceived of race. *Ouanga* reveals that transnational exchanges shaped the ways black people in middle America conceptualized and experienced race. Untangling the opera's local and global commitments requires what Jessica Berman has called a "transnational optic" that "shifts our perspective on the forms and commitments of modernism, asking us to recognize the rhetorical action its forms undertake and the continuum of political engagement that undergirds its worldwide emergence."[11] Situating *Ouanga*'s South Bend production transnationally connects the Midwest to the global economic and cultural exchange often associated with coastal and urban areas. In this context, *Ouanga* demonstrates the ways that local and national racial politics are influenced by larger international relationships, imperialist foreign policy, and diasporic history. Lara Putnam has argued that attending to Caribbean modernity forces us to "provincialize" the place of Harlem in the so-called Harlem Renaissance by re-considering the origins of "the black internationalist thinking and organizing" central to black modernist literary production. *Ouanga*'s rich, intercultural exchange calls for a similar approach: provincializing New Negro cultural productions—whether they were made in Harlem, New York, or South Bend, Indiana—illuminates the ways that local and regional racial identities were sculpted in a wider, transnational context.[12]

In the case of *Ouanga*, we must also provincialize midwestern modernity by considering the opera's transnational story and performance, as well as its cultural backdrop, which includes a foreign military occupation, domestic policies enforcing racial segregation, and a regional history of abolitionism. To follow Diana Taylor, who contends that the textual archive and the performatic repertoire transmit different histories, considering *Ouanga* as both an archival text and an historical performance encourages us to re-consider *how* and *where* this work of art was produced, as well as *who* produced it.[13] Even though *Ouanga* premiered in the Midwest and echoed local history in its focus on black self-determination, it cannot be understood as just a midwestern opera. *Ouanga*'s 1949 performance contains a complex act of transnational cultural exchange. Parsing the local, national, and transnational contexts of the opera reveals that the South Bend production of *Ouanga* represented a collaborative, transnational performance of Haitian history. This performance situated the Haitian Revolution and Dessalines's reign as a shared history of black sovereignty for a global black audience.

In order to unpack *Ouanga*'s racial imaginary, the argument that follows first considers *Ouanga*'s story, characters, and religious themes before examining the South Bend performance. This close textual reading helps us better understand the ways that the Burleigh's 1949 production re-cast *Ouanga*'s national racial politics in order to stage a collaborative, transnational performance that claimed Haiti's past as a shared black history. Attending to *Ouanga* through this transnational optic uncovers the opera's global black modernism and its impact on black midwestern identity.

Christianity and Race Pride in *Ouanga*

Ouanga is set in the years immediately following the Haitian Revolution, the only slave rebellion to result in the creation of an independent state. When the real-life Dessalines declared Haitian independence on January 1, 1804, he established the first independent black state in the west. The Haitian Revolution horrified European nations, who profited from the slave trade, and the newly established United States, whose economy was entirely dependent on the labor of enslaved Africans. Historian Michel-Rolph Trouillot argues that the revolution's impact stemmed from the fact that it was "unthinkable even as it happened"[14]; "not even the extreme political left in France or in England had a conceptual frame of reference" for what they saw in the colony of Saint Domingue.[15] In short, Trouillot contends, "the Haitian revolution ... challenged the very framework within which proponents and opponents had examined race, colonialism, and slavery in the Americas."[16] In this way, the Haitian Revolution was not simply a violent war, but a moment in which, to borrow the language of Gayatri Chakravorty Spivak, the subaltern spoke and performed a liberatory act of "epistemic violence" against slavery and white supremacy.[17] The Haitian Revolution constituted a radical epistemic break because it unraveled the west's fundamental understanding of race, citizenship, subjectivity, and basic humanity. For enslaved Africans to rise up in coordinated rebellion, fight against and eventually defeat the most powerful army in the world, and win their freedom and independence from their enslavers was shocking to whites at the time, and remained so well into the twentieth century.

For African Americans, though, the Haitian Revolution and the creation of Haiti represented a powerful history of black self-determination, radical anti-slavery, and freedom. *Ouanga* staged Haiti's early history to celebrate the revolution and its outcome: the establishment of the first independent black state in the west. As Karen M. Bryan notes, "the ex-slave-turned-military leader and emperor represented the new nation as it left colonial domination and struggled to establish an independent state, one that existed on both political and cultural planes. This conflict and its ramifications were of far greater interest [to White and Matheus] than the revolution itself."[18] *Ouanga* presents Dessalines's mission to uplift and Christianize Haiti as part of a larger, noble effort to modernize Haiti and make it economically competitive on the global stage. The play's tragedy hinges on his inability to accomplish this modernization while upholding Haiti's cultural traditions. In this way, the opera concerns itself primarily with the struggles of nation building, a narrative in which present-day black audiences would have seen their own struggles for inclusion and equality in the U.S. nation state.

Ouanga depicts Dessalines's quest for modernization by invoking the values of racial uplift, which would have been familiar to its African American audiences. If racial uplift, as Kevin K. Gaines has defined it, refers to "African Americans' struggles against culturally dominant views of national identity and social order positing the United States as a 'white man's country,'" then performing the history of Haiti, the so-called "black republic," in the elevated form of operatic tragedy served as a way for New Negro artists like White and Matheus to remake U.S. national identity and claim their place in the American nation state.[19] Emphasizing racial uplift through issues like cultural sophistication, hard work, and religious conversion, White and Matheus firmly situated *Ouanga* within the New Negro politics of respectability. In *Ouanga*, Dessalines wants to uplift Haiti through Christianity to make it palatable to white European nations. When he bans *vodou* ceremonies, the townspeople see Dessalines as a tyrant; they murder him for betraying his people. In this way, White and Matheus depict *vodou* as a dark and sinister force that claims the life of a promising young man who sought to lead Haiti to greatness by making it modern, European, and new. By telling Haiti's story in this way, White and Matheus offered their U.S. audiences a critical engagement with New Negro values that problematized uplift, modernity, and the ways in which the "new" of New Negro politics broke with the past.

The central tension of *Ouanga* stems from Dessalines's dual allegiance to the traditional religious practices of the past—represented by his African heritage, *vodou* ceremonies, and the people of Haiti—on the one hand, and the larger white, monarchal, and Christian world, on the other. While Dessalines claims to feel the beating of the drums in his blood, he wants Haiti to move forward and not be pulled back into the past. "On to the light!" he tells Défilée. "On to the cross!"[20] For Dessalines, the light of Christianity offers a way to fully break with the past and experience true freedom. *Vodou,* he believes, enslaves the souls of the people and prevents them from truly investing in Haiti's success. By banning *vodou*, Dessalines believes he is protecting Haiti and helping free his people from tyranny. Positioning *vodou* as a part of the past and his own beliefs as part of the future, Dessalines frames the past as a "relentless" force that must be jettisoned in order to move forward. "'Tis you whose blind misleading lingers on from age barbaric a world thats [sic] gone!" he sings to the Papaloi. "Mine is the new time, yours the old! Yours is the night! My day the future shall unfold!"[21]

But despite his enthusiastic conversion to Christianity, Dessalines has a fraught relationship to *vodou*. "My soul is rent in twain," he cries to Défilée, as he asks her to sing to him "the songs our people crooned in Africa where palm trees sway beneath the drum-shaped moon."[22] Even as he seeks to create a new future for Haiti, he still finds himself drawn back by the beat of the drums and by the closeness he feels to the people of Haiti. "Oh priest!" he cries, trying to win back the support of his people, "I too am linked with Africa. With Africa that claims our minds and fills our blood."[23] Despite this intimate tie to his people, their shared past, the drums, and *vodou* ceremonies, Dessalines attempts to impose his conversion to Christianity on his people. Claiming he is saving them from the tyranny of religion and bringing them into freedom, he sings, "I'll stop the drums—I'll end the 'Ouanga', the 'Ouanga' that would drive us apart—perhaps—For as a snake works its way beneath the ground, the 'Ouanga' would try to coil itself about us and crush our hearts. O God! Save us both from dangers!"[24]

The people of Haiti, however, see this rejection of *vodou* as a rejection of tradition and identity. The priestess Mougali warns the people that Dessalines has abandoned his faith, his lover, and his people.[25] "Death to all who desert the faith!" she yells at his coronation. "Death to him who turns against his loved one.... How well you must remember her who loves you. Behold one victim! Beware!"[26] When Dessalines orders Mougali's execution, the people quickly turn against him. "Murderer!" La Bossal, a former follower, cries when he learns of Mougali's death. "Traitor to your people!"[27] The crowd rebuffs Dessalines's explanations, and puts a *ouanga* curse on him: "Over him whose name we do not call let disturbing forces of the Voodoo fall! Ouanga! Ouanga!" they chant.[28] *Ouanga* makes clear that Dessalines's conversion and subsequent attempts to modernize Haiti not only reject Haiti's gods and traditions but also threaten the people's freedom. By positioning himself against "Ouanga," Dessalines positions himself against Haitian culture and makes himself a threat to Haiti.

Even as *Ouanga* celebrates *vodou* practices and dances, it presents "voodoo" as a dark force that leads the people of Haiti to irrationally murder their leader for not sharing their beliefs. *Ouanga* positions *vodou* rituals as extremist and hints at them involving human sacrifice. While White and Matheus aimed for what they called a "realistic and sympathetic" portrayal of Haitian culture, U.S. audiences who saw the opera viewed the Haitian people as irrational zealots who could not see the positive change Dessalines tried to bring to the country.[29] Reviewing a 1950 performance by the Dra-Mu Opera Company in Philadelphia, the *New York Times* summarized *Ouanga*'s plot thusly: "Dessalines, the first emperor of Haiti, met his fate at the hands of Voodoo fanatics tonight here in the Academy of Music."[30] A program for the same performance informed audiences, "The story of 'Ouanga' is the true story of one man's desperate struggle to bring freedom and Christianity to the people of his native land. It is the story of Dessalines, liberator and first emperor of Haiti, whose love for his country met with tragedy and heartbreak."[31] White himself described the opera as "the story of Haiti during the time of Dessalines, and [it] deals with Haiti's struggle for freedom. It also deals with the triumph of Catholicism over Vodoo [sic] faith of the natives at that time."[32]

In early drafts, White and Matheus overtly positioned Dessalines's battle between old and new as a racialized battle between blackness and whiteness. In a 1931 draft, Défilée accuses Dessalines of being simply an "Imitator of Napoleon" who is "drunk with power." "You are mad to make yourself king on the ashes of your country's ruin," she tells him when he outlaws *vodou* ceremonies.[33] Dessalines responds,

"The drums do move me, but I will be stronger than the drums. I must be. The great white world stretching from ocean to ocean shall not mock us. I will be the king."³⁴ Défilée sees this struggle as his downfall; his soldiers see his interest in white, European culture as Dessalines turning his back on those who stood with him through battle.

Fulfilling Défilée's accusations of betrayal, this early version of Dessalines marries the light-skinned Claire Heureuse without telling Défilée. Leaving his lover for his new wife symbolizes his treacherous abandonment of Haiti, blackness, and the past. This image of Dessalines as an adulterous betrayer did not last for long. In the final script used for live performances, Dessalines had changed dramatically. While he still outlaws *vodou*, Dessalines stays true to Défilée, marrying Claire after he has ended things with his former lover. Moreover, he is motivated by what he thinks is best for Haiti, rather than his ideas about white perception. This later libretto frames Dessalines's engagement with European culture as part of his interest in newness and progress; he wants to move Haiti forward, not backward, and he sees Christian values as the best way to do so. In this final version of the opera, a mistake in judgment—rather than overt dishonesty or betrayal—leads to Dessalines's downfall.

The early drafts of Dessalines's speech offer important context for understanding the final, staged version of *Ouanga*. These drafts make the opera's modernist racial politics explicit and reveal that racial perception framed the ways White and Matheus understood Dessalines and *Ouanga* more broadly. Even though these portions were revised for the final draft, the language of the opera is still infused with an explicit focus on racial representation that makes *Ouanga* an opera about both Haitian and U.S. history. Karen M. Bryan contends that contemporary issues of black nationalism, "race pride," and the New Negro Renaissance all informed Matheus's conception of Dessalines.³⁵ Likewise, as Wallace M. Cheatham notes, White may have been interested in "authentic" Haitian sounds initially, but he ultimately aimed to construct an opera "for and about Negroes."³⁶ At the time of the opera's publication, this concern with politics and social issues made *Ouanga* a hard sell for producers, for as Clare Corbould observes, "most people were not interested in political art"; as a result, "staging productions that challenged racial prejudice was very tricky."³⁷

Still, much of *Ouanga*'s appeal and critical success resulted from its racial politics and representations of black life. White's correspondents lauded *Ouanga* as "the most eloquent speech of the Negro race."[38] "For as long as I can remember," the cellist Marion Cumbo wrote to White in 1949, "you have held the 'light' for the white brothers, so that they could see superior ability and talent and real worth in the black brothers. Continued long life to you Sir, and may your opera 'spread' all over the Metropolitan stage here in N.Y.C. soon."[39] Another correspondent, Martha S. Caeman, wrung her hands about being likely unable to attend the premiere, writing that her desire to attend was partly a result of wanting to "see it and hear it for myself." But, she noted, her attraction to the opera stemmed primarily from "that ever present race pride and hope ... The special joy and stimulation we always get when we see our own excel."[40] In letters seeking future performances, White and his proponents presented *Ouanga* as a sophisticated opera that would bring positive attention to the companies and cities that staged it. One music teacher pitched a production of *Ouanga* to the St. Louis Municipal Opera Association by claiming "such a performance would contribute greatly to the Mayor's program of improvement in race relations and be in keeping with the general national trends in that direction."[41]

Such "race pride" structured the public's response to *Ouanga*, as well as the opera's plot. White and Matheus envisioned Dessalines as a respectable black leader and role model working to unify and modernize Haiti. If White served as a "light" for white folks to see black ability and value, he and Matheus in turn positioned Dessalines as a man who sought to uplift Haiti as a "'light' for the white brothers" to see black talent, ability, and "real worth." In *Ouanga*, Dessalines is a sympathetic character who is assassinated for betraying tradition. White and Matheus's portrayal of Dessalines's story—the fall of a noble, operatic hero cut down in his prime—offered middle-class New Negro audiences a character whose frustrations paralleled their own. In both its narrative and its commercial and artistic success, *Ouanga* appealed to audiences concerned with race pride and racial uplift. The opera's tension between modernity and tradition played out the frustrations of a class of educated men and women who wanted to uplift their race, but found it a constant struggle to shed the past.

Putting *Ouanga* on the World Stage

Despite *Ouanga*'s initial success and critical acclaim when it was first published in 1932, White had difficulty getting his magnum opus staged. In addition to possible roadblocks presented by the opera's racial themes, the Great Depression and war years dried up potential funding for an expensive operatic production, especially one that required an all-black cast; White's desire for the opera's world premiere to take place in Haiti further complicated matters.[42] White claimed that the Haitian people were *Ouanga*'s intended audience, and he went to great lengths to procure tickets for the Haitian ambassador and other diplomats during the world premiere. Yet, *Ouanga* seems to be written with middle-class black audiences in the United States in mind. Even though *Ouanga* was composed in Paris and would eventually make its way to New York at Carnegie Hall and the Metropolitan Opera House, its opening night was more humble.[43] The opera's premiere in a high school auditorium in South Bend, Indiana locates *Ouanga* not in the glitz and glamour of the sleek, urban centers of modernity, but instead in an industrial, midwestern city driven by automobile manufacturing, newly flush with cash from the post-war industrial boom, and simmering with racial tensions. A glut of post-war factory jobs had drawn African American migrants from the South, more than doubling the black population in South Bend between 1940 and 1950.[44] The shifting demographics made local whites uncomfortable, and they met black migrants with scorn.[45]

The Harry T. Burleigh Music Association emerged against this backdrop. Formed by Josephine Curtis in 1933, the Burleigh was created to serve as "a vehicle for African Americans to bond through music and theater, and to give blacks who had studied music a performance venue."[46] Moreover, the Burleigh was designed to push against black musical stereotypes by showcasing the diversity of the black music community. As Cheatham notes, "Curtis wanted to demonstrate that music was universal, that it had no ethnic boundaries."[47] According to former members of the Burleigh, the association was "the only [black] community group in the city (or the state), the sole purpose of which was to perform music."[48] Members of the group hailed from across the Midwest, including performers based in northwest Indiana and Michigan. More than just a local troupe, the Burleigh was considered a significant musical organization for black Midwesterners. Throughout the 1930s and 1940s, the group performed a fall concert and a spring operetta, slowly building an artistic reputation. By 1947, the local paper consistently assigned reporters to review performances. But it was "the premier of Ouanga ... [that] elevated the Burleigh to a new level of distinction."⁴⁹ The Burleigh's 1949 production of *Ouanga* put South Bend, and the Midwest more broadly, on the international opera scene and helped establish the Burleigh Music Association as a skilled professional company, guaranteeing a future of "high-quality performance opportunities for black Hoosiers who would otherwise have been excluded by the barriers of racism."⁵⁰

South Bend's location, however, made it difficult to market the opera and attract the audiences in whom White was interested: Haitian people, wealthy urbanites, and opera aficionados. White's correspondence leading up to *Ouanga*'s midwestern world premiere focused on mobilizing affluent patrons and members of the black middle class throughout the nation to serve as the audience. In early May 1949, White sent out a form notice inviting friends and colleagues from Chicago to New York, and everywhere in between.⁵¹ He targeted music teachers and opera fans, but he focused as well on black educators and teachers at historically black colleges and universities, like Fisk. In response, he received dozens of kind rejections. The location of South Bend was too far away for most coastal city dwellers, and many folks living in nearby small towns simply could not afford the trip. For many who could afford to attend, the trip was too far off of their beaten paths. And even for those who were interested, circumstances prevented them from traveling. Factories throughout the Midwest saw major strikes in 1949; such strikes, one of White's correspondents lamented, "affect[ed] all businesses and professions," and therefore limited the ability of interested audiences to make the trip to South Bend for *Ouanga*'s premiere.⁵²

From a production perspective, it seems, South Bend was attractive only in that it might spur future performances in New York City. "This presentation, we hope, will be attended by persons from New York and Chicago which will interest backers for a metropolitan production and tour," White wrote in 1949.⁵³ Still, though, White felt tied to the Midwest; producing an opera about Haiti in the region where he grew up connected his local, familial history of abolitionism to the diasporic history of Haiti's radical anti-slavery. While White spent his formative years in Washington, DC, and composed much of *Ouanga* while living in Paris, the musician had his own origins in small-town Ohio. "I was practically brought up on the campus of Oberlin College," he remembered in a 1953 interview; he later graduated from the school's music conservatory.[54] White felt deeply rooted in the region's abolitionism; recalling his own family's history, White proudly highlighted his grandfather John H. Scott, "the village-harness maker and a noted abolitionist" and described Oberlin as a place where escaped slaves traveling on the underground railroad sought refuge as they fled to Canada.[55] Staging his magnum opus in nearby Indiana with a local black performance troupe allowed White to connect *Ouanga*'s story of radical anti-slavery and black self-determination to his own family's history of abolitionist activism, as well as to contemporary efforts to improve opportunities for African Americans.

White's pride in his family's history and connection to abolitionism dovetails with a broader midwestern regional identity that traditionally has emphasized progress and freedom. As Andrew Cayton and Susan Gray note, this dominant narrative has had little consideration for the costs of this progress or the unevenness with which Midwesterners experienced freedom.[56] The 1787 Northwest Ordinance, the legislation that established the territory that would become the Midwest, included a ban against slavery in the region. During the early nineteenth century, as White's family history recalls, the underground railroad was active throughout the Midwest, providing safe passage for escaped slaves fleeing to Canada.

Still, in practice, racism was rampant and communities were segregated. The Midwest's very existence rested on the expulsion of Native peoples and the forceful occupation of their land. African Americans living in the Midwest, though legally free, experienced "pervasive hostility" from their white neighbors.[57] In Indiana, this racism was institutionalized well into the twentieth century. During the 1920s, the white supremacist Ku Klux Klan dominated state politics. The Klan took over much of the Republican Party and swept state elections in 1924. In addition to their political and legislative presence, the Klan terrorized local black, Catholic, and immigrant communities with marches, rallies, fliers, and burning crosses. After 1928, the Klan's power waned, and the group officially disbanded following a loss of membership and funds.[58] But the Klan was not the only source of racial terror in Indiana. The racial climate in Indiana during the early twentieth century was toxic and dangerous. In 1930, a mob of white people in Marion, Indiana, lynched two African American teenagers, Thomas Shipp and Abram Smith. For black audiences in South Bend, this local and regional history provided a different context than audiences might have experienced when they saw *Ouanga* in Philadelphia (1950), New Orleans (1955), or New York (1956). Staging and performing an opera about black sovereignty, freedom, and radical anti-slavery in a state recently run by the Ku Klux Klan was a radical act. While White and Matheus's touristy jaunt through Haiti in 1928 positioned *Ouanga* as a distinct product of the U.S. military occupation there, the Burleigh's South Bend performances firmly rooted *Ouanga* in the black, midwestern experience.

Staging an opera like *Ouanga* was a new experience for the Burleigh, which had never performed a full opera before. Being tasked with a world premiere added a further layer of complication, since there were no previous models to draw upon. Many Burleigh regulars sang principal roles, a formidable task given that *Ouanga* had an "involved score with complex orchestration and intricate writing for the voice."[59] To fund the opera, the Burleigh assembled an unlikely group of donors, including a local car dealership, the University of Notre Dame, the Indiana Cab Company, the Welber Foundation, and, most important for this essay, Joseph Charles, who was then the Haitian ambassador to the United States.[60] In addition to the work of the Burleigh and the funding from local businesses, *Ouanga*'s 1949 production depended on Haitian financing and performative labor. Charles attended *Ouanga*'s South Bend performance on its second night and provided a significant portion of the financing. Indeed, as Cheatham notes, Charles's patronage "made the South Bend premier possible," for ticket sales would not have come close to covering the opera's production costs.[61]

Haitians also played central roles in the Burleigh's production of *Ouanga*. The lead singers, Fritz Vincent (Dessalines) and Carmen Malebranche (Défilée), were both Haitian singers and natives of Port-au-Prince.[62] They studied in the United States and eventually made their careers there, with Malibranche also singing Défilée in the 1950 Philadelphia production of *Ouanga* and Vincent going on to perform with the National Negro Opera Company.[63] If, as Stephanie Leigh Batiste has argued, the presence of the "black performing subject" has the potential to disrupt and corrupt the "bare imperialism of primitive and savage performances," then for *Ouanga*, the presence of the black Haitian performing subject doubly disrupted the imperialism and appropriation that turned *vodou* drums and Haitian dances into primitive performances.[64]

This ambivalence marks *Ouanga*'s staging of Haitian history as a series of complicated, transnational performances, financed by U.S. businesses *and* Haitian diplomats, produced by U.S. *and* Haitian bodies, and ultimately consumed by U.S. *and* Haitian audiences. The archival texts of *Ouanga* preserve the residues of this historic collaboration. Rather than further entrenching the lines of power carved by the U.S. occupation—as the opera's plot and focus on racial uplift might suggest—the 1949 performance of *Ouanga* situated the performance of Haitian history as a collective and diasporic endeavor. Despite the limitations of theatrical and operatic productions for enacting political change, *Ouanga*'s transnational creation, cast, audience, and financial backing add an important dimension to an opera that aimed to reshape black cultural memory and conceptions of sovereignty. A story about the struggle for black sovereignty, *Ouanga* enacted this endeavor in its casting and financing. Haitians centrally figured in this performance of Haitian history, making *Ouanga* an example of transnational cooperation in the fight for black self-determination.

Quite the opposite of the tragedy the opera's story conveys, then, *Ouanga* models a transnational performance collaboration that bridges the cultural divides of the U.S. military occupation, which by the 1940s had obscured and distorted Haiti's history for more than two decades. As *Ouanga* went on to future performances in Philadelphia, New Orleans, and New York, this collaborative spirit deflated. The Haitian ambassador no longer served as a financial backer, and Haitian performers did not sing the lead roles. Performances were aimed at wealthy Americans who could afford tickets to Carnegie Hall and the Metropolitan Opera House, and newspapers frequently noted the opera's exotic, "voodoo" dances. Nevertheless, the 1949 performance serves as a model for a transnational black performance that brought together Haitian and U.S. artists, musicians, performers, and politicians to offer New Negro audiences in the Midwest a model of black sovereignty and nationhood. Yet, because these performances are all of the same opera, and presented under the same name, the title *Ouanga* holds within it this geographic and temporal multitude, encapsulating multiple performances, disparate geographic locations, unique local histories, and the contributions of dozens of artists, musicians, and performers.

Focusing on the South Bend premiere through a transnational lens disrupts our understanding of the ways black artists responded to the limitations and expectations encoded in U.S. racial modernity. The black identities and histories *Ouanga* transmits were collaboratively built across national borders. As a New Negro opera celebrating the possibility of black sovereignty, *Ouanga* grated against the U.S. racial divide, segregation, and Jim Crow; as an international opera written by two African American men during the U.S. military occupation of Haiti, it appropriated a foreign culture, flattened racial differences, and reinforced imperialist power structures; but as a performance, *Ouanga* was a transnational collaboration between Haitian and African American performers to create a story that was, in White's words, "for and about Negros."

Acknowledgment

A number of people have helped this article take form. In March 2015, I conducted archival research at the New York Public Library's Schomburg Center for Research in Black Culture. The assistance of Steven G. Fullwood at the Schomburg Center was invaluable; he provided me with finding aids and helped me locate hundreds of documents. I cannot thank Walton Muyumba enough for introducing me to Steven. At IU, Judith Brown, Ed Comentale, Vivian Halloran, and Shane Vogel all read earlier versions of this article; they provided challenging questions, encouraging comments, and pointed critiques of my research in its early and advanced stages. During presentations at the 2016 Caribbean Studies Association Conference (Port-au-Prince, Haiti) and the 2017 Modern Language Association Conference (Philadelphia, PA), my fellow panelists and audience members proved to be generous listeners; their feedback helped me sharpen my argument. Finally, throughout the publication process, Andy Oler has been a thoughtful, patient, and generous editor. Thank you for the opportunity to publish my research in such an excellent collection.

Notes

1. Unless otherwise noted, all archival materials cited in this article are from the Clarence Cameron White Collection (Additions), which is located at the New York Public Library's Schomburg Center for Research in Black Culture in Harlem, New York.
2. John F. Matheus, "My Venture in Libretto Creation," *CLA Journal* (1972): 432; Clarence Cameron White, qtd. in "Opera Premiere Holds Interest," *South Bend Tribune*, June 1, 1949, 16.
3. Wallace M. Cheatham, "Ouanga: South Bend, Indiana, and the Premiere of a 20th-Century American Opera," *Indiana Magazine of History* 100, no. 2 (June 2004): 179.
4. Following the South Bend premiere, *Ouanga* was performed again in October 1950 by the Dra-Mu Opera Troupe in Philadelphia, PA. In 1955, The Xavier Music League staged a performance in New Orleans. The opera finally made its way to New York City in 1956, when The National Negro Opera Company performed it at Carnegie Hall and the Metropolitan Opera House. On the performance history of the opera, see Tim Brooks, *Lost Sounds: Blacks and the Birth of the Recording Industry, 1890–1919* (Champaign: University of Illinois Press), 496, and Perry Watkins, "A Proposed Project for Production & Presentation at the International Bicentennial Exposition under the auspices of The Haitian Government in Port au Prince Haiti," carbon copy of unpublished typescript, Clarence Cameron White Collection (Additions), Box 3, f. 7, "Publicity Materials," 1.
5. The U.S. Marine Corps generally did not provide the labor to build this infrastructure; instead, they used Haiti's outdated *kòve* laws—inherited from the colonial era—to conscript any able-bodied man to perform forced and unpaid labor to repair or rebuild rural roads. For more on the implementation of *kòve* laws, see Kate Ramsey, *Spirits and the Law: Vodou and Power in Haiti* (Chicago: University of Chicago Press, 2011), 118–76.
6. Peter James Hudson, "The National City Bank of New York and Haiti, 1909–1922," *Radical History Review* 115 (Winter 2013): 91–114. On the U.S. occupation of Haiti, see Hans Schmidt, *The United States Occupation of Haiti, 1915–1934* (1971; New Brunswick: Rutgers University Press, 1995); Ramsey, *Spirits and the Law*, 118–76; and Mary Renda, *Taking Haiti: Military Occupation and the Culture of U.S. Imperialism, 1915–1940* (Chapel Hill: University of North Carolina Press, 2001). On the history of U.S.-Haitian political and cultural relations, including the occupation, see Brenda Gayle Plummer, *Haiti and the United States: The Psychological Moment* (Athens, GA: University of Georgia Press, 1992).

7. Booker T. Washington, "On the American Occupation of Haiti," *The New York Age*, October 21, 1915, 1.
8. Zora Neale Hurston, "Tell My Horse: Voodoo and Life in Jamaica and Haiti," in *Zora Neale Hurston: Folklore, Memoirs, and Other Writings* (New York: Library of America, 1995), 331.
9. See James Weldon Johnson, "Self-Determining Haiti: Four articles reprinted from *The Nation* embodying a report of an investigation made for The National Association for the Advancement of Colored People, Together with Official Documents" (New York, The Nation, 1920).
10. Stephanie Leigh Batiste, *Darkening Mirrors: Imperial Representation in Depression-Era African American Performance* (Durham, NC: Duke University Press, 2011), 74–75.
11. Jessica Berman, *Modernist Commitments: Ethics, Politics, and Transnational Modernism* (New York: Columbia University Press, 2012), 9, 31.
12. Lara Putnam, "Provincializing Harlem: The 'Negro Metropolis' as Northern Frontier of a Connected Caribbean," *Modernism/modernity*, 20, no. 3 (September 2013): 471.
13. Diana Taylor, "Acts of Transfer" in *The Archive and the Repertoire: Performing Cultural Memory in the Americas* (Durham, NC: Duke University Press, 2003), 1–52.
14. Michel-Rolph Trouillot, *Silencing the Past: Power and the Production of History* (Boston: Beacon, 1995), 73.
15. Ibid., 82, italics removed from original.
16. Ibid., 82–83.
17. Gayatri Chakravorty Spivak, "Can the Subaltern Speak?" in *Marxism and the Interpretation of Culture*, ed. Cary Nelson and Lawrence Grossberg (Urbana, IL: University of Illinois Press, 1988), 281.
18. Karen M. Bryan, "Clarence Cameron White's *Ouanga!* in the World of the Harlem Renaissance," in *Blackness in Opera*, ed. Naomi Andre and Karen M. Bryan (Champaign, IL: University of Illinois Press: 2012), 121.
19. Kevin K. Gaines, *Uplifting the Race: Black Leadership, Politics, and Culture in the Twentieth Century* (Chapel Hill: University of North Carolina Press, 1997), 14.
20. See John F. Matheus, *Ouanga* Libretto, unpublished typescript, 1939, Bound Teal Spiral, Clarence Cameron White's Personal Copy, Clarence Cameron White Collection (Additions), Box 3, f. 2, "Ouanga Libretto," 13.
21. Ibid., 21.
22. Ibid., 12.
23. Ibid., 21.
24. Ibid., 13.
25. Ibid., 17.
26. Ibid.
27. Ibid., 18.

28. Ibid., 20.
29. Bryan, "White's *Ouanga!*," 116.
30. Untitled typescript compiling quotes from newspaper reviews of the 1950 production, Clarence Cameron White Collection (Additions), Box 3, f. 4, "Publicity Materials—Program October 28 1950."
31. *Ouanga: A Haitian Opera in Three Acts in English*, program, undated, but with publicity materials for the October 8, 1950 performance in Philadelphia, PA, Clarence Cameron White Collection (Additions), Box 3, f. 4, "Publicity Materials."
32. Clarence Cameron White to Benjamin Maloney, February 25, 1949, unpublished letter, Clarence Cameron White papers (Additions), Box 1, f. 24, "Correspondence—General. January-July 1949."
33. John Frederick Matheus, *Ouanga!* libretto, unpublished typescript, 1931, Clarence Cameron White Papers, Microfilm, Box 9, f. 1, Reel 7, Schomburg Center for Research in Black Culture, The New York Public Library, 11.
34. Ibid., 15.
35. Bryan, "White's *Ouanga!*," 129.
36. Cheatham, "Ouanga," 180.
37. Clare Corbould, "At the Feet of Dessalines: Performing Haiti's Revolution During the New Negro Renaissance," in *Beyond Blackface*, ed. W. Fitzhugh Brundage (Chapel Hill: University of North Carolina Press, 2011), 273–74.
38. Edwin Nymovitz to Mary Cardwell Dawson, October 2, 1956, unpublished letter, Clarence Cameron White papers (Additions), Box 1, f. 32, "Correspondence—General. 1956."
39. Marion Cumbo to Clarence Cameron White, May 29, 1949, unpublished letter, Clarence Cameron White Collection (Additions), Box 1, f. 24, "Correspondence—General. January-July 1949," 1.
40. Martha S. Caeman to Clarence Cameron White, May 16, 1949, unpublished letter, Clarence Cameron White Collection (Additions), Box 1, f. 24, "Correspondence—General. January-July 1949," 2.
41. Wirt D. Walton to The St. Louis Municipal Opera Association, July 5, 1949, unpublished letter, Clarence Cameron White Collection (Additions), Box 1, f. 25, "Correspondence—General. July-Dec 1949."
42. In anticipation of the 1949 Bicentennial Exposition of Port-au-Prince, White and theatre producer Perry Watkins proposed that the Haitian Government fund a production of *Ouanga* "in a manner befitting the country and people for whom it was written." See Watkins, "A Proposed Project for Production & Presentation at the International Bicentennial Exposition," 1; and Perry Watkins to Dumarsais Estime, August 4, 1949, unpublished letter, Clarence Cameron White Collection (Additions), Box 1, f. 25, "Correspondence—General. July-Dec 1949."
43. On the South Bend performance, see "Clarence White's 'Ouanga' To Premiere In South Bend," *New York Amsterdam News*, May 21, 1949, 4. See

also the *South Bend Tribune*'s coverage of the performance: "Opera Premier Holds Interest," June 1, 1949, 16; "Ouanga Cast Is Completed," June 9, 1949, 6; "Dancers Featured in Haitian Opera," June 10, 1949, 6; "Opera of Haiti Has Rich Score," June 11, 1949, 16; "Envoy Outlines Haiti's Needs," June 12, 1949, 22.

44. The African American population jumped from 3555 to 8134 between 1940 and 1950. See John Palmer, *South Bend, Crossroads of Commerce* (Charleston, SC: Arcadia, 2003), 135.
45. On the city's changing economy and population booms, see Palmer, *South Bend*, as well as Patrick J. Furlong's entry on South Bend in *The American Midwest: An Interpretive Encyclopedia*, ed. Richard Sisson, Christian Zacher, and Andrew Cayton (Bloomington, IN: Indiana University Press, 2006), 1176–77.
46. Cheatham, "Ouanga," 174.
47. Ibid.
48. Lorene Richardson to Wallace Cheatham, Letter, June 22, 1998, qtd. in Cheatham, "Ouanga," 174 (alterations Cheatham's).
49. Cheatham, "Ouanga," 177.
50. Ibid., 184.
51. Clarence Cameron White, Form Letter to "My dear friend," May 1, 1949, unpublished letter, Clarence Cameron White Collection (Additions), Box 1, f. 24, "Correspondence—General. January-July 1949."
52. Fred Hart Williams to Clarence Cameron White [signed "Fred Hart"], May 13, 1949, unpublished letter, Clarence Cameron White Collection (Additions), Box 1, f. 24, "Correspondence—General. January-July 1949." According to Williams, strikes at the Ford plants in Detroit shut down production throughout the month of May. Newspaper reports show strikes throughout the Midwest in 1949: in South Bend, 7500 workers at Bendix Aviation were on strike for months in the spring and summer of that year; in Chicago, steel plants shuttered during strikes in October; and, during the same month in Dayton, Ohio, the Goodrich tire plant shut down during a thirty-four-day strike. See "Bendix Strike Talks End Up in Confusion: Union Denies Peace Agreement Reached," *Chicago Tribune*, June 16, 1949; "Steel Users Have Supply For 30 Days," *Chicago Daily Tribune*, October 1, 1949, part 2, 7; and "B.F. Goodrich Strike By CIO Workers Ends," *Chicago Daily Tribune*, October 1, 1949, part 2, 7.
53. White to Benjamin Maloney.
54. "Rebirth of an Opera," newspaper clipping dated "7 Mar 1953," Clarence Cameron White Collection (Additions), Box 6, Brown Scrapbook.
55. Ibid.
56. Andrew R. L. Cayton and Susan E. Gray, "The Story of the American Midwest: An Introduction," in *The Identity of the American Midwest: Essays on Regional History*, ed. Andrew R. L. Cayton and Susan E. Gray (Bloomington: Indiana University Press, 2007), 12.

57. Ibid.
58. For more on the Klan's rise to power in 1920s Indiana, see Palmer, *South Bend*, 116–19; *The American Midwest: An Interpretive Encyclopedia*, 724.
59. Gaska qtd. in Cheatham, "Ouanga," 183.
60. Cheatham, "Ouanga," 183.
61. Ibid. For a detailed expense breakdown, see Harry T. Burleigh Music Association, "Ouanga Expenses," unpublished manuscript, Clarence Cameron White (Additions), Box 3, f. 5, "Ouanga Financial Records."
62. Ibid., 182, n.26.
63. Ibid.
64. Batiste, *Darkening Mirrors*, 73.

Kerry Alcorn

Saskatchewan's Midwestern Moment

Education in a Continental, Borderlands Context

In 1907, Walter C. Murray, the freshly minted first president of the newly formed University of Saskatchewan—the sole university in a nascent province only two years old—made the very important, albeit simple, decision to gaze southward rather than eastward for his inspiration. Despite the simplicity of his choice, and the fact that many others in leadership roles across the province would make identical decisions in the years to come, the significance of Murray's decision largely eludes historians of the period. In seeking inspiration and a blueprint for the institution that would, for the next thirty-one years, be synonymous with his name and stature, Walter Murray adhered to the advice of Saskatchewan's former Territorial Premier, F.W.G. Haultain, who advised in 1903 against creating "humble imitations of [universities] in the East."[1]

A decade later, Saskatchewan's Department of Education again gazed southward to apply a very midwestern U.S. approach to consolidate its roughly 4000 school districts. To tackle the challenge the province called upon the acumen of Dr. Harold Foght, an expert in rural education from the Bureau of Education, Washington, DC. Though employed in Washington, Foght was a Midwesterner, the son of Danish immigrants who settled in Nebraska, where he completed his grade schooling. In the early 1900s Foght surveyed state-wide school systems in the Midwest, recommending consolidation of rural schools into municipal districts. In advising the province of Saskatchewan to do the same, Foght legitimated the Department of Education's wish for greater centralized control over provincial schooling. While Foght framed such reforms within the language of "social efficiency," he conveyed a decidedly populist tone in his arguments for consolidation, which appeared in his *Survey* of 1918.[2]

Both Murray's actions and those of the Department of Education betray a penchant for ideas and models emanating from the

U.S. Midwest and Plains. This proclivity, so obvious in Murray, Foght, and others in the fields of higher and grade-school education, was part of a larger cultural transfer northward from the U.S. Midwest and Plains into the province of Saskatchewan in the early twentieth century. Indeed, the evolution of Saskatchewan in the first three decades of the twentieth century is best interpreted within a continental, midwestern American process of development.

The essay that follows first establishes the province of Saskatchewan, from its formation in 1905 until roughly the 1930s, as an extension of the U.S. Midwest and Plains. In this period culture moved freely across the forty-ninth parallel, but mostly northward from the United States into the Canadian prairies. Within the northern portion of this borderlands region the development of higher education at the University of Saskatchewan, and grade-school education, is best understood within a larger cultural transfer from the U.S. Midwest and Plains into Saskatchewan. This transfer occurred largely in resistance to the "back-eastern conservatism" of Ontario and Canada's eastern provinces.[3]

Saskatchewan within a Midwestern Context

Any traveler crossing the forty-ninth parallel west of the Ontario–Minnesota border quickly determines that boundary's arbitrariness and artificiality. It bifurcates a single physical and natural environment, albeit one with a slightly shorter growing season northward. This environmental affinity sustained a north-south cultural affinity within a midwestern continental region spanning the international border. The so-called "end" to the American frontier in the late 1890s and the subsequent settlement of what Canadians identified as the "last best west" (what became Saskatchewan and Alberta) produce an extension of the U.S. Midwest and Plains regions into these provinces. The large-scale pattern of settlement into Saskatchewan from 1896 to 1924 mirrored that of the U.S. Midwest and Plains some twenty years prior. This two-decade developmental lag to the north persists in a host of areas, especially in agriculture and education, but equally so at the deeper level of political culture and culture largely conceived.[4] The end result is a Saskatchewan political culture that is populist and moralistic and, like its midwestern cousins, resistant to the east.

I have argued previously, in *Border Crossings*, that U.S. Midwest and Plains culture migrated northward into Saskatchewan in the first three decades of the twentieth century along a host of avenues. These include Saskatchewan residents pursuing higher education in a few leading U.S. universities and returning home with very American sensibilities on several matters; the free flow of publications like the *Grain Grower's Guide* (Canadian) and *Leader* (U.S.) across the border; the movement of U.S. organizations, like the Grange and The Farmer's Union, into the province as more Americans settled there; the practice of Saskatchewanians taking "sociological tours"[5] to the Midwest to bring U.S. solutions to western Canadian problems; and inviting U.S. experts to Saskatchewan to provide guidance on issues and problems endemic to both locales. Not surprisingly, however, such cultural transfer was dependent upon the immigration of large numbers of Americans into Saskatchewan in a continuing pursuit of free land in the "last best west."

The exact number of U.S. citizens who settled in Saskatchewan between 1896 and 1930 is difficult to pinpoint. In 1916, Harold Foght estimated that 28 percent of Saskatchewan residents—approximately 87,000—were one-time U.S. residents.[6] By 1931, the number lay between 200,000 and 300,000.[7] The majority of Americans who ultimately settled in Saskatchewan and Alberta originated from the Dakotas, Iowa, Michigan, Minnesota, and Wisconsin.[8] The foremost U.S. historian of the Canadian Plains, Paul Sharp, extends these origins to include Kansas, Missouri, Montana, and Utah.[9]

For American political scientist Daniel J. Elazar, these states historically conveyed a moralistic political subculture. Elazar's moralistic political subculture tempers the interests of the individual with those of the community. Governmental intervention in the lives of its citizens is not preferred but at times warranted. Politics remains a concern for every citizen, with every citizen involved in the life of the commonwealth: "By virtue of its fundamental outlook, the moralistic political culture creates a greater commitment to active government intervention in the economic and social life of the community."[10]

Coupled with this moralistic undertone is a populism that fosters a rural population that resists conservative, and in U.S. and Canadian contexts, back-eastern influences. Sharp captures this anti-eastern sentiment that spanned the forty-ninth parallel:

The western Canadian farmer who protested against a high tariff, trusts and combines, and "money power" in 1911 did so in the best Jeffersonian tradition. His protests were rooted in the same soil of Lockean thought and evangelical Protestantism and sprang from the same grievances that had produced the Grange, the Farmers' Alliance, and Populism in the United States. His crusade coincided with and sought the same fundamental objectives as the Farmers' Union, the Society of Equity, Robert M. LaFollette's "Progressivism," and Woodrow Wilson's "New Freedom." This was no accident. The impact of monopolistic consolidation of Canadian industry hit the prairie farmer with such force during these years that in self-defence he turned to reforms similar to those advocated by American muckrakers and reformers in their "quest for social justice."[11]

On both sides of the forty-ninth parallel, then, there existed hostility in the west toward the east. The east epitomized the money interests, or plutocracy—those newly wealthy who gained their fortunes, it was believed, by corruption or graft, often on the backs of the working class or, in the case of the continental Midwest, farmers. These plutocrats were represented by the great eastern corporations, like the railroad companies or manufacturing associations, and by fabulously wealthy businessmen like Andrew Carnegie, J. P. Morgan, and John D. Rockefeller.[12] Within this moralistic, populist, midwestern borderland—a borderland characterized by western antipathy toward the east—parallel systems of education would develop, where the main difference would be the two-decade lag in the north.

Walter Murray and Saskatchewan's "Culture of Emulation"[13]

Upon heading west to Saskatchewan in 1908, President Murray left a promising position at Dalhousie University in Halifax, Nova Scotia. With Murray holding his doctorate from the University of Edinburgh and having served on Dalhousie's faculty, and with his closest colleague and confidant, Sir Robert Falconer, sitting as President of the University of Toronto, one anticipates Murray's university would replicate those from across the Atlantic, as did most from Ontario eastward. Instead, Murray chose to leave behind the denominational struggles plaguing Canada's universities back east. Arthur Morton credits F.W.G. Haultain, the then territorial Premier of the Northwest Territories, with first acknowledging that Saskatchewan needed a university different from Canada's East. "Too often the institutions of the West have been humble imitations of those in the East. But Haultain's mind was too virile, and his decisions grew too much out of his own experience and knowledge, for him to follow slavishly the example of the older sections of Canada."[14] Early in his tenure as president, Murray advised his board of governors that a trip southward was needed to visit "some of the universities to the south whose problems are similar to those of Saskatchewan."[15] What Murray and his group found in the U.S. Midwest and Plains would serve as the blueprint for his University of Saskatchewan.

Murray's and his colleagues' 1908 sociological tour stopped first in Winnipeg at the University of Manitoba, visited several universities in Ontario, then headed south. In the U.S. Midwest the trio visited the state universities of Illinois, Indiana, Iowa, Michigan, Minnesota, Missouri, and Wisconsin. Upon their return to Saskatchewan, they stopped at Washington University in St. Louis and the University of Chicago.[16] The extent to which this first trip southward influenced Murray and the evolution of his university cannot be overstated.

The first key imitation was the adoption of the "Collegiate Gothic" architectural style, first witnessed by Murray and his two travelling companions at Washington University in St. Louis, Missouri. All three were struck by its beauty, and when they learned it existed at Princeton University, they quickly decided it was right for Saskatchewan.

In that initial sociological tour to the U.S. Midwest, Murray and company found much to adapt to the Canadian prairies. At the helm of each state university sat a powerful president who personified the institution he led. Whether it was A. Ross Hill at Missouri or Charles Van Hise at Wisconsin, Murray found the president the unquestioned head of the institution. Some historians of higher education, like Clark Kerr, ascribe the role of "giant" to the university president, while others, like Clyde Barrow, see the president as a "corporate head."[17]

In Murray, Saskatchewan had both. Furthermore, the administrative structure he replicated at Saskatchewan bore U.S. roots in both form and function. As new colleges emerged in the early decades of the University of Saskatchewan, each gained a dean, with departments soon following. "Branch offices" quickly germinated throughout the province in the form of Junior Colleges, with seven in existence by 1929. Murray favored the creation of these colleges as feeders to his university, not as competitors.[18] His pursuit of a corporate-style campus, patterned after many state universities in the United States, is entirely reasonable when one considers his direct involvement in one of two large U.S. philanthropic organizations: the Carnegie Foundation for the Advancement of Teaching (CFAT). Both it, and the other American philanthropic institution, Rockefeller's General Education Board, granted funding to those institutions that adhered to its strict, corporate-like model.

As Jeffrey Brison reminds us, "Concerns for efficiency and scientific management always dictated Carnegie and Rockefeller approaches to reforming and/or creating educational infrastructure."[19] Murray became a member of the board of governors for the CFAT in 1919 and served as vice-chair of the board from 1922 through 1924 and chair in 1934–1935.[20] Murray used his position within the CFAT to guide the evolution of higher education in Saskatchewan in several ways, including meeting the criteria to warrant funding from Carnegie; gaining meagre funding to support specific programs at the University of Saskatchewan; and guaranteeing efficiency prevailed across the province by ensuring there was no duplication of programming. Such dutiful service to the corporate ideal, articulated by the CFAT, ensured the University of Saskatchewan's and Murray's pre-eminence in higher education across Saskatchewan.

While the administrative structure of the university quickly expanded, Murray maintained complete control over virtually all aspects of its development, including the hiring of new faculty. Such practices were in keeping with Murray's colleagues south of the border. What some perceived as Murray's "dictatorial" manner led to a "crisis of loyalty" in 1919, when a handful of faculty accused Murray of misappropriating funds and governing the university with an iron fist. An inquiry soon followed, resulting in the immediate dismissal of the "gang of four" and Murray suffering a nervous breakdown. Identical to high-profile dismissals at U.S. campuses, this crisis of loyalty confirmed the limits of academic freedom at the University of Saskatchewan and that professors were employees of the university.[21]

Premier Haultain was not alone in his belief that Saskatchewan needed to look southward for inspiration rather than eastward. In 1908, the Canadian-born President of the University of Missouri, A. Ross Hill, advised Murray, when seeking to hire faculty for his campus, to find Canadians who completed their studies in the United States and "know something of the conditions in the Middle West especially."[22] Where possible, Murray complied with Hill's advice. Given that higher education in Canada remained in its infancy, Murray filled a significant number of faculty positions with graduates from U.S. campuses, most notably in agriculture, the academic cornerstone to Saskatoon's campus. The College of Agriculture's first Dean, W.J. Rutherford, came to Saskatchewan having taught at Iowa State College in Ames. Saskatchewan's decorated agricultural engineer, Evan Hardy, born in Sioux Falls, South Dakota, completed his doctorate at Ames. By 1929, CFAT reported that eighteen of thirty-one doctorates among science faculty, and twenty-seven of sixty-one across campus, were earned at American institutions.[23] Murray's faculty hires adhered to President Hill's suggestion—they knew something of the Middle West.

Once hired at Saskatchewan, it became common for professors "knowing something of the Middle West" to return there, frequently, during their tenure to continue their research, thereby ensuring the ongoing cultural transfer across the continental Midwest. For example, Dean Rutherford made frequent sociological tours to the Midwest, including Minnesota in 1915, and Minnesota, Wisconsin, and Illinois in 1918. Evan Hardy, likewise, took sabbatical in 1929, visiting Minnesota, Michigan, Michigan State, Wisconsin, and Cornell, in addition to the campus located at Guelph, Ontario.[24] Moreover, scholars like Hardy often created Saskatchewan chapters of U.S. organizations on Saskatchewan's campus, like the American Society of Agricultural Engineers, which met regularly during Hardy's extended tenure.

Easily the most significant midwestern influence on the University of Saskatchewan came from Murray's emulation of the University of Wisconsin and its "Wisconsin Idea." Writing in 1908, following his return from the United States, Murray commented, "In Wisconsin they [the three sociological tourists] saw an admirable example of a University whose watchword is service of the State. In the University of that State there is a happy blending of the best of the old and the new—a harmonious combination of the Liberal Arts and Pure Sciences with the Sciences applied to Agriculture and the Professions."[25]

Writing to his long-time friend, President Falconer of Toronto, in 1930, Murray made clear his deference to Wisconsin:

> Perhaps the greatest contribution from American sources is the larger conception of the purpose and scope of a State University—the conception of it as the scientific arm of the state for Research, for carrying the benefits of Science to all and sundry in the state, and for the supply of information to Legislative assemblies and their Executives.
>
> To Saskatchewan Wisconsin appeared in 1908 as an excellent example of this kind of University as contrasted with the Oxford type—a place for Liberal Culture and preparation for the Learned professions.[26]

Veysey articulates that the "Wisconsin Idea" enabled two key reforms within American higher education. The first injected the expert in society's technical and social planning within government, thereby carving out an important role for the academician in everyday life. The second placed the university in service to the entire state and took higher education directly to the people, wherever they were. This democratization of higher education saw the expansion of vocational and professional schools, especially in the realms of agriculture and engineering. Such service universities became particularly prevalent in the midwestern heartland during this period.[27] Murray embraced both these reforms wholeheartedly as he nurtured his fledgling university.

Central to the University of Wisconsin's service to the state was its location in the state capital, Madison. In making his case to the province regarding the University of Saskatchewan's role, Murray anticipated that because the university should serve the province, its location was paramount and must be sited in the provincial capital, Regina. In 1909 he stated, "The greatest reason is the service the University can render the State. Wisconsin, we were told, renders its state three to five times more service than the Universities which are distant from their capitals. Last year Wisconsin had 41 professors serving the state in various capacities, some in three or four, and nearly all gratuitously."[28] Murray and others expected the board of governors to agree on Regina as the location for the University of Saskatchewan. His voice, however, was only one of nine voting members on the board. The vote regarding location was held on April 9, 1909, and in one of the best-kept secrets ever maintained in the province (the vote tally was neither officially recorded nor revealed), Saskatoon won over Regina. Though Murray's wishes were officially ignored on this occasion—one of very few instances when this was true—his desire to establish a Wisconsin-like model on the South Saskatchewan River proceeded unabated.

Foremost within Murray's execution of the "Wisconsin Idea" was to make the College of Agriculture the centerpiece to his campus. While he failed to convince decision-makers to locate the university in Regina, once Saskatoon became the campus site, Murray labored to ensure that the agricultural station be housed there, not in the countryside, which was customary in other Canadian universities, like the Ontario Agricultural College located in Guelph, Ontario—an affiliate of the University of Toronto. In making his case for a unified campus in his first President's Report, Murray cited Wisconsin, Illinois, Missouri, and Minnesota as strong examples, and added an argument from President Snyder of the Michigan Agricultural Station.[29] This time, Murray succeeded in his request, and a unified campus ensued. In 1910, the Extensions Department began its work across the province. From that point forward, the vocational components to the University of Saskatchewan took shape, with the College of Law established in 1912, Pharmacy in 1913, Business in 1914, Engineering in 1916, and Household Science in 1928.[30]

At Saskatchewan, President Murray consistently identified his university in relation to universities in the U.S. Midwest. While Wisconsin sat preeminent among these universities, others, like Michigan, Minnesota, and Missouri, also figured prominently. Among Canadian universities from the east, he found problems: "Nearly every University has suffered because short views were taken in the beginning. It is true that fifty years ago it was well-nigh impossible to forecast the extent of the growth of a progressive University. McGill, Toronto, Queen's, Dalhousie and Manitoba are notorious examples of overcrowding."[31] Especially in the formative years of the University of Saskatchewan, it was the universities of the U.S. Midwest to which President Murray turned as a model, and eastern Canadian campuses from which he turned away.[32]

Education "Rooted to the Soil": Harold Foght and the Midwestern Rural School

While President Murray persisted with his "culture of emulation" at Saskatchewan, heeding President Hill's advice to seek guidance from those with knowledge of the Middle West, the province's Department of Education pursued similar inspiration for its system of grade schools. Indeed, the period beginning in 1916 through the 1920s signals a high water mark in midwestern U.S. influence in Saskatchewan schooling, starting with the arrival in the province of the American expert on rural schools, Harold Foght. On loan from the U.S. Bureau of Education in Washington, DC, Foght came with an extensive resume in relation to writing about, surveying, and reforming U.S. rural schools. Though other academics, including Elwood Cubberley and Mabel Carney, gained greater notoriety following publication of their studies of the American rural school, Foght's *The American Rural School* was the first book-length account of the evolving rural school, and arguably the most comprehensive and passionate defense of rural life maintained through rural schools.[33]

Within this borderland, agrarian, rural environment, this populist crusader devoted himself to preserving the golden age of rural American life—a life he witnessed already eroding south of the border, wrought by eastern winds of industrialization and urbanization. Upon arriving in Saskatchewan in 1916, Foght attempted to preempt this decline in Saskatchewan through a very midwestern solution to the "rural school problem." In the consolidated rural school, Foght envisioned the sustenance of rural life through education "rooted to the soil."[34]

Foght clearly articulated his arguments for consolidating rural schools in many works, most notably in the numerous surveys he conducted while working for the U.S. government. While Foght's *Survey* of Saskatchewan schools was the first of its kind in Canada, the survey movement itself was ubiquitous throughout the United

States, particularly among midwestern states. As recently as 1915, Foght campaigned to preserve rural life through consolidating rural schools in Minnesota.[35] In its Preface, Foght commended the state for its early commitment: "Perhaps no other State has been quite as successful as Minnesota in establishing a system of schools intended to meet the demands of modern rural life."[36] While the title to Foght's study of Minnesotan rural schools suggests a devotion to efficiency, his arguments go beyond the language of the day to a much greater calling for rural schools, that is, the preservation of rural life:

> Its schoolmen and legislators recognize that preparation for life in rural communities can be given in schools specially organized to meet rural needs. The one-teacher schools of the State are, on the average, as efficient as those in other States; but they have proved unable to meet the needs of modern farming in preparing the children for practical and contented lives on the soil.... Most important of all, the men who are responsible for the [school district] reorganization have kept well in mind that the new schools must be rooted firmly in the soil.[37]

Moreover, Foght's analysis of rural school consolidation is firmly rooted within the midwestern experience. In Foght's estimation, across the Midwest, states struggled to unearth a more satisfactory unit for school organization, often failing due to the "plea for local democracy and home rule" from the local citizenry. This was particularly prominent within smaller districts. Minnesota, however, was an exception to the typical midwestern state, for the large, undivided districts and unorganized territories located in northern Minnesota were most easily consolidated. "The larger the unit, apparently, the easier it is to consolidate schools."[38]

Though the eponymous title to Foght's book-length analysis centered around the *American* rural school, for its author the American rural school was best exemplified among consolidated Midwest and Plains rural schools. Here, in the states of Ohio, Indiana, Kansas, and Illinois, rural schools most readily met the aim of consolidation: restoring the ancient principle of "equal rights for all."[39] Though he referred to southern and Massachusetts districts as examples of consolidation,

Foght clearly intimates a pro-western stance. Particularly when one layers his work on consolidation in Minnesota over his previous examination of the midwestern school, his pro-western perspective crystallizes:

> The people in many parts of Minnesota are wide-awake to the great waste of the small school. They are beginning to realize that even where the one-teacher school is modern in architecture, is well kept, and in charge of a well-paid teacher, it cannot fully meet the demands of modern country life. Even under the most favourable circumstances the school cannot approximate the work that it should do, *viz*, prepare the boys and girls of the community for satisfied, well-rewarded living on the country soil.[40]

The importance of this point cannot be overstated, for it was this change in circumstances for the rural student that consolidation, systemically, and Foght, personally, sought to remedy. Over time the rural school had suffered relative to the village or town school from industrialization and urbanization, so much so that free schooling had lost its original purpose. "In order to re-establish this educational equality [equal rights to all] it becomes necessary to give the twelve million boys and girls living in the rural communities just as thorough a preparation in school for their life work as we are now offering city children. Consolidation of rural schools is the practical remedy, and wherever given a fair trial it has proved conclusively that just as good, just as thorough-going schools may be made to flourish in the beneficent rural environment as in the city."[41] This sentiment, one expects, convinced Saskatchewan policymakers that this American, populist crusader must come to Saskatchewan—a province that in 1916 was 70 percent "rural-minded," and its system of schools fragmented and inefficient.[42] Clearly, both the government of Saskatchewan and its newfound American expert viewed the province as part of a midwestern borderland whose problems warranted midwestern solutions.

Foght's language of fairness and equality was firmly engrained in Saskatchewan prior to his arrival. In 1910, Foght deemed the rural school problem emanated from "spasmodic attendance," poor interest among students, frequently changing teachers, and a curriculum that catered to the urbanite.[43] In 1913, one Saskatchewan school inspector agreed: "The evils of the present system are short term schools, involving a constant change of teachers; and teachers badly prepared for their work."[44] A similar statement in 1914 echoed Foght's concern from the Midwest: "This is regrettable both from the point of view of the state and that of the rural school child. Has the rural school child the right to ask the state to furnish him with educational facilities equal to those provided for the urban child?"[45]

Foght's passionate, populist rhetoric was also well received in the province. In 1910 he wrote, "City life is terribly devitalizing. In its artificial, hot-house atmosphere the human organism literally starves and early deteriorates. Into this life, then, our best country boys and girls are thrown annually by the hundreds of thousands—their manifest destiny to reinforce the ebbing vitality of city life. The infusion of the sturdy country stock into the city assures a continuation of city prosperity and progress. But at what awful cost!"[46] In Saskatchewan, another inspector wrote in 1913, "The chief nation-builders of the province are the pioneers on the frontier. After all the hardship that they must endure, is it fair to penalize their children, condemning them to a meagre education, whilst the children of the city made great by their labor have every educational advantage?"[47]

By the time Foght's *Survey* was published in 1918, his pro-western, populist bent (made clear in *The American Rural School*) had blossomed into an anti-eastern lament. Given his midwestern heritage, recent success of the Non-Partisan League in North Dakota in 1916, unparalleled third-party successes of Teddy Roosevelt between 1910 and 1920, and the fact that he wrote for a rural, populist audience in Saskatchewan, one can forgive Foght's self-assuredness in the Introduction to his *Survey*: "Saskatchewan, in common with the other prairie provinces of Canada, is dominated by people of progressive type—forward looking people, who have shown a striking determination to escape the hindering influence of back-eastern conservatism by taking action before their educational institutions shall become afflicted with inertness, resulting in failure to respond to the changing life of their democratic civilisation."[48] That a U.S. expert could draw such a conclusion is made possible from his 1915 study of rural schools in Ontario. There, he found farmers to be "conservative[s who] cling tenaciously to the old ways."[49]

Foght's greatest testament to his populist, anti-eastern stance, however, comes when discussing the Saskatchewan curriculum. Here, he clearly includes Saskatchewan in a continental, midwestern region:

> The high schools and collegiate institutes of Saskatchewan offer almost exclusively the traditional course of study of the eastern provinces and the eastern states of the American union. Economic, social, and civic demands are only beginning to make themselves felt. Agriculture, the one great industrial interest of the province, fills a relatively unimportant role as compared with Latin and mathematics. The high schools of Saskatchewan are meeting the needs of one small group of boys and girls who are going to college or into teaching; they are neglecting the large mass of boys and girls who most need high school education in a democracy.[50]

In addition to recommending a more pragmatic curriculum for the rural school student, Foght argued that consolidation equalized opportunities for rural students relative to those from the city or town. By sharing the wealth of any rural municipality, rural students were guaranteed stronger teachers, extended terms, well-maintained schools, and more sustained schoolwork.[51] In this way, rural life was preserved through consolidated rural schools.

While Saskatchewan policymakers welcomed Foght's recommendations and attempted to enact them in the decade following his *Survey*, resistance in the province paralleled that in the U.S. Midwest, emanating from the single segment of the population Foght sought most to serve: rural people. Local control over local institutions—central to a populist and moralistic ideology—carried the day in Saskatchewan in much the same fashion as in many midwestern states. The only difference is the duration of the resistance. In states like Minnesota and the Dakotas, local control gave way to centralized control in the early part of the century, whereas in Saskatchewan this was not the case until 1944 with the election of the Cooperative Commonwealth Federation (CCF).

In *Border Crossings* I attribute this to a deeper penetration of moralistic and populist political culture into Saskatchewan relative to the U.S. Midwest and Plains. More recent scholarship, however, leads me to conclude these divergent paths to rural school consolidation may instead reflect different strains of what Laura Grattan describes as *aspirational democratic populism* operating simultaneously within this borderland.[52] Says Grattan: "Populism ... animate[s] the usually dormant ideal of popular sovereignty, by mobilizing the aspirations of ordinary people to exert a degree of power over their everyday lives and their collective fate. To aspire means to yearn for something out of reach."[53] Paradoxically, Foght sought to do right by rural people, but did so from the perspective of a policy elite, without reference to what the people themselves desired or aspired to.

Essentially, Foght's elite, technocratic aspirations for "the people" saw rural life guaranteed through consolidated, municipal schools. He was a devoted reformer of the sort David Tyack and Larry Cuban describe as an "administrative progressive."[54] Like other administrative progressives, Foght was convinced that changing how rural school districts were organized, always through consolidating small, rural districts into larger, municipal districts, would prove the most effective way to equalize opportunities for rural students relative to urban students. State systems of education across the Midwest, including those Foght "surveyed," like Minnesota and Missouri, were increasingly successful at achieving consolidation at the time Foght arrived in Saskatchewan in 1916. For Foght, centralized control through consolidation was always intended to improve rural education and thereby improve rural life.

For rural people themselves, however, democratic aspirations were inextricably preserved through what Saskatchewan political scientist John C. Courtney describes as an ideology of local control.[55] Furthermore, the eminent American political sociologist Seymour Martin Lipset, who conducted his doctoral research within Saskatchewan's cooperative commonwealth in the 1940s,[56] found very high levels of democratic participation among the province's farmers. Simply put, Saskatchewan rural folk maintained control over those institutions closest to them. Surrendering one's school-age youth to a distant municipal school ran contrary to this expectation.

Conclusion

To a large degree Walter Murray and Harold Foght were populist allies in Saskatchewan's Midwestern Moment, although there is no record the two ever met. Each acted to preserve the rural nature of Saskatchewan: Murray through utilizing the "Wisconsin Idea" in his service-oriented, people's university; and Foght, through attempting to consolidate 4000 rural schools and provide, for the majority of grade school students, education "rooted to the soil." Each gained his midwestern perspective through divergent avenues: Foght, most obviously, was a Midwesterner himself, having spent his professional life working on behalf of rural schooling, while Murray acquired his ethos vicariously through his sociological tour of several midwestern campuses (most notably Wisconsin's) in 1908 and by adhering to the advice of his many colleagues from across the continental borderland. Ultimately, each acknowledged that provincial problems were best resolved through continental solutions. This seems entirely fitting given both the cultural and natural affinities that made Saskatchewan an extension of the U.S. Midwest and Plains.

Such a south-to-north interpretation runs contrary to "standard" histories of Canadian prairie development, where Saskatchewan is typically viewed as part of an east-to-west flow of culture emanating from the province of Ontario.[57] A continental, borderlands perspective, first envisioned by American historian Paul Sharp in the 1950s, more accurately captures Saskatchewan's early cultural roots—roots that betray an aversion to back-eastern conservatism and an affinity for midwestern solutions to continental problems. Following a decade-long natural disaster in the 1930s, World War II, and the election of a democratic socialist provincial government in 1944, Saskatchewan's first Midwestern Moment passed, giving way to a Canadian political culture that diverges substantially from its U.S. cousins. Recent events on both sides of the forty-ninth parallel, however, including an oil boom and subsequent bust, increasing demands for indigenous people's control over the land and its resources, and farm crises of various forms, leads one to consider whether a second Saskatchewan "Midwestern Moment" beckons.

Notes

1. Arthur S. Morton, *Saskatchewan: The Making of a University* (Toronto: University of Toronto Press, 1959), 59.

2. Harold W. Foght, *A Survey of Education in the Province of Saskatchewan, Canada* (Regina: King's Printer, 1918). See also, Harold W. Foght, *The American Rural School: Its Characteristics, Its Future and Its Problems* (New York: Macmillan, 1910).
3. Kerry Alcorn, *Border Crossings: US Culture and Education in Saskatchewan, 1905–1907* (Montreal: McGill-Queen's University Press, 2013).
4. William H. Sewell, Jr., "The Concept(s) of Culture," in *Beyond the Cultural Turn: New Directions in the Study of Society and Culture*, ed. Victoria E. Bonnell and Lynn Hunt (Berkeley: University of California Press, 1999), 35–61; William H. Sewell, Jr., *Work and Revolution in France: The Language of Labor from the Old Regime to 1848* (New York: Cambridge University Press, 1980). I meld Sewell's conception of culture, which consists of *meanings* and *practice*, often as exposed through *language*, with Daniel J. Elazar's description of a US *moralistic* political subculture in Daniel J. Elazar, *American Federalism: A View from the States* (New York: Thomas Y. Crowell Co., 1966).
5. Daniel T. Rodgers coined the term "sociological tour" in Daniel T. Rodgers, *Atlantic Crossings: Social Politics in a Political Age* (Cambridge, MA: Belknap Press, 1998).
6. This equalled 87,000 Saskatchewan residents. Foght, *Survey*, 13.
7. Alcorn, *Border Crossings*, 21.
8. Robert Bruce Shepard, "American Influence on the Settlement and Development of the Canadian Plains," unpublished dissertation (University of Regina, 1994), 6–7.
9. Paul F. Sharp, *The Agrarian Revolt in Western Canada: A Survey Showing American Parallels* (Winnipeg: Hignell Printing, 1997), 5.
10. Elazar, *American Federalism*, 118–19.
11. Sharp, *Agrarian Revolt*, 40.
12. Alcorn, *Border Crossings*, 45–48.
13. Here I make a play on the title of David O. Levine, *The American College and the Culture of Aspiration, 1915–1940* (Ithaca, NY: Cornell University Press, 1986).
14. Morton, *Saskatchewan*, 59.
15. Ibid., 37.
16. Alcorn, *Border Crossings*, 193, n. 64.
17. Clark Kerr, *The Uses of the University* (Cambridge, MA: Harvard University Press, 2001), 25; Clyde Barrow, *Universities and the Capitalist State: Corporate Liberalism and the Reconstruction of American Higher Education* (Madison: University of Wisconsin Press, 1990).
18. David R. Murray and Robert Murray, *The Prairie Builder: Walter Murray of Saskatchewan* (Edmonton: NeWest Press, 1984), 81.
19. Jeffrey D. Brison, *Rockefeller, Carnegie, and Canada: American Philanthropy and the Arts and Letters in Canada* (Montreal: McGill-Queen's University Press, 2005), 49.

20. Murray and Murray, *The Prairie Builder*, 180.
21. See Alcorn, *Border Crossings*, 132–34, on the "gang of four."
22. Letter from A. Ross Hill to Walter C. Murray, September 8, 1908, University of Saskatchewan Archives, Jean Murray Collection, A.IV.82.
23. Howard J. Savage, "Supplementary Memorandum on the U of S," October 15, 1928, 13, University of Saskatchewan Archives, President's Office fonds, Walter C. Murray fonds, B, vol. 21.
24. Letter from Dean Rutherford to President Murray, November 15, 1915, 5; Letter from Dean Rutherford to President Murray, November 28, 1918, 1–2, in University of Saskatchewan Archives, College of Agriculture, (I) Dean's Correspondence, A. Reports to the President, 1912–1928.
25. Walter C. Murray, "Report of the President, 1908–1909," 2. http://www.usask.ca/archives/history/president1-report.php?css=plain. Retrieved July 24, 2007.
26. Letter from Walter Murray to Robert Falconer, February 22, 1930, quoted in Michael Hayden, *Seeking a Balance: The University of Saskatchewan, 1907–1982* (Vancouver: University of British Columbia Press, 1983), 35.
27. Lawrence R. Veysey, *The Emergence of the American University* (Chicago: University of Chicago Press, 1970), 108–09.
28. Walter C. Murray, "Report respecting the principles which determine the location of a University," Regina, Sask., January 29, 1909, 8, University of Saskatchewan Archives, Jean Murray Collection, A. IV, 82.
29. Alcorn, *Border Crossings*, 134–36.
30. Ibid., 138–39.
31. Murray, "Report of the President, 1908–1909," 6.
32. Alcorn, *Border Crossings*, 139.
33. Cubberley's book, Elwood Cubberley, *Rural Life and Education: A Study of the Rural School Problem as a Phase of the Rural-Life Problem* (Boston: Houghton Mifflin, 1914), was completed while he was a professor at Stanford University. Carney completed Mabel Carney, *Country Life and the Country School: A Study of the Agencies of Rural Progress and of the Social Relationship of the School to the Country Community* (Chicago: Row, Peterson, and Company, 1912) shortly before she joined the faculty at Teacher's College, Columbia University.
34. See Foght, *The American Rural School*; Alcorn, *Border Crossings*, 107–16.
35. H.W. Foght, *The Rural School System of Minnesota: A Study in School Efficiency* (Washington, DC: Government Printing Office, 1915).
36. Ibid., 6.
37. Ibid., 7.
38. Ibid., 11.
39. Foght, *The American Rural School*, 302. Ohio (partial consolidation); Indiana (complete consolidation): Kansas (village type of consolidation); Illinois (purely rural type of consolidation). Foght highlights these examples in 315–25.

40. Foght, *The Rural School System of Minnesota*, 28.
41. Foght, *The American Rural School*, 303.
42. See Foght, *Survey*, 77, for a breakdown of rural vs. urban students.
43. Foght, *The American Rural School*, 304.
44. *Annual Report of the Department of Education of the Province of Saskatchewan, 1913*, 62.
45. *Annual Report, 1914*, 63.
46. Foght, *The American Rural School*, 16–17.
47. *Annual Report, 1913*, 62.
48. Foght, *Survey*, 5.
49. Harold Waldstein Foght, *The School System of Ontario with Special Reference to the Rural Schools* (Washington, DC: Government Printing Office, 1915), 47.
50. Foght, *Survey*, 88
51. Ibid., 29.
52. Laura Grattan, *Populism's Power: Radical Grassroots Democracy in America* (New York: Oxford University Press, 2016).
53. Ibid., 40.
54. David B. Tyack and Larry Cuban, *Tinkering Toward Utopia: A Century of Public School Reform* (Cambridge, MA: Harvard University Press, 1974).
55. John C. Courtney, "The Ideology of Local Control: A Reply," in *Education and Social Policy: Local Control of Education*, ed. C.A. Bowers, Ian Housego, and Doris Dyke, eds. (New York: Random House, 1970), 47–48.
56. Seymour Martin Lipset, *Agrarian Socialism: The Cooperative Commonwealth Federation in Saskatchewan (A Study in Political Sociology)* (Berkeley: University of California Press, 1971), 32–33.
57. I sustain this argument throughout *Border Crossings*.

Contributors

Kerry Alcorn is an independent scholar who lives and works in Saskatoon, Saskatchewan, Canada. He completed his PhD in Educational Policy Studies from the University of Kentucky and is the author of *Border Crossings: US Culture and Education in Saskatchewan, 1905–1937*, published by McGill Queen's University Press in 2013.

Wayne Anderson is a lecturer in the Rhetoric Department at the University of Iowa. A lifelong Midwesterner, he grew up on his family's century farm in southwestern Minnesota, received his BA in History and English from Luther College in Iowa, and earned his MA and PhD degrees in American Studies from the University of Iowa. He has taught classes on persuasive speaking and writing, business rhetoric, American cultural history, and rural history. His research focuses primarily on portrayals of the Midwest in popular culture, and he regularly presents his work at the annual Agricultural History Society conference.

Camden Burd is a PhD candidate in the Department of History at the University of Rochester. He currently holds an Andrew W. Mellon Fellowship for the Digital Humanities. He speaks, writes, and publishes on American Environmental History.

Owen Cantrell studies nineteenth-century American literature and its relationship to labor in American culture. Cantrell has published on midwestern literature in *MidAmerica* and on Bruce Springsteen and folk music in the collection *Bruce Springsteen and Popular Music: Rhetoric, Memorial, and Contemporary Culture*. He is currently an assistant professor at Perimeter College at Georgia State University in Alpharetta, Georgia.

Kelly Hanson is a lecturer in Communication Skills at Indiana University's Kelley School of Business. She received her PhD in English from Indiana University. Her research focuses on the construction of race in early twentieth-century American literature through a transnational lens. She has published work on rock music and theatrical performance in the journal *Theatre Survey*. Currently, she is working on a book manuscript that explores the links between modernism, race, and military occupations.

Jonathon Josten is a high school Drama and English teacher at Kalama High School. He has been published in the *Middle West Review*, *Epiphany*, *USA Today College*, and elsewhere. He holds an MA (Literature and Culture) from Oregon State University. His thesis project focused on September 11 and midwestern authors. Prior to Oregon State, he attended two rival schools to earn an MEd from the University of Sioux Falls and a BA (English; Theatre) from Augustana University. He currently lives in Vancouver, Washington, with his wife and two kids.

Jordan Lea Ludwig was born, raised, and educated in her beloved home state of Iowa, and has always had a special interest in local writers and poets. She currently lives in Dubuque, Iowa, where she works as an editor for educational publisher Great River Learning. This is her first published essay.

After nearly twenty years at the North Central campus of Purdue University, **Bob Mellin** is now a semi-retired English adjunct at Saint Xavier University. His publications and presentations concerning the Midwest have focused on Indiana authors such as Gene Stratton-Porter, Thomas Rogers, Edwin Way Teale, and Kurt Vonnegut; he has also presented work concerning the creation of the Indiana Dunes State Park and National Lakeshore as experiments in social justice.

Jim O'Loughlin is Associate Professor of English in the Department of Languages & Literatures at the University of Northern Iowa. He is the editor of *Discovered Poems of James Hearst* (Final Thursday Press), coordinator of the James Hearst Digital Archive (http://hearstarchive.uni.edu), and author of the flash fiction collection, *Dean Dean Dean Dean* (Twelve Winters Press).

Sally E. Parry is Associate Dean in the College of Arts and Sciences at Illinois State University and Professor of English. She has served as the Executive Director of the Sinclair Lewis Society and editor of the *Sinclair Lewis Society Newsletter* for over twenty-five years. She is the editor of two short story collections: *Go East, Young Man: Sinclair Lewis on Class in America* and *The Minnesota Stories of Sinclair Lewis*. In addition, she and Robert L. McLaughlin are the authors of *We'll Always Have the Movies: American Cinema during World War II* and are at work on a companion volume on Broadway theater during the war.

Patrick C. Riley earned a bachelor's degree in political science and an MPA degree in economic development from the University of Illinois at Chicago (UIC) and a master's degree in political sociology and statistical analysis from the University of Chicago. He has served as the project and research director for the Chicago Democracy Project since 1999.

Yi-chin Shih is Associate Professor in the Department of English Language and Culture at Tamkang University, Taiwan (R.O.C.). Her interests in research include modern drama and cultural studies. Her articles have appeared in *The Explicator*, *CLCWeb: Comparative Literature and Culture*, *NTU Humanitas Taiwanica*, and other publications. She is also the author of *How Timberlake Wertenbaker Constructs New Forms of Gender in Her History Plays: Exposing the Power Relations between the Sexes* (2012).

Nora Pat Small grew up in northern Illinois, served as the architectural historian for the state of Kansas in the SHPO office, and has taught in the History department at Eastern Illinois University for twenty-two years. She earned degrees from the University of Delaware (BA Art History), University of Virginia (Master of Architectural History with certificate in Historic Preservation), and Boston University (PhD in American and New England Studies). She has an abiding interest in the vernacular built environment of the early American republic, and in the preservation stories and histories associated therewith.

Michelle Story-Stewart earned a bachelor's degree in economics from Northwestern University, a master's degree in economics from the

University of Illinois at Chicago (UIC), and a doctorate in Public Policy Analysis/Urban Planning and Policy from UIC. She has nearly twenty years of professional experience in community development, including providing technical assistance for neighborhood revitalization.

Kimberly Wilmot Voss is a tenured associate professor at the University of Central Florida (PhD, Maryland). Her most recent book is *Women Politicking Politely: Advancing Feminism in the 1960s and 1970s* (Lexington Books, 2017). She is also the author of *The Food Section: Newspaper Women and the Culinary Community* (Rowman & Littlefield, 2014) and a co-author of *Mad Men & Working Women: Feminist Perspectives on Historical Power, Resistance and Otherness* (Peter Lang, 2014 & 2016). She has published more than forty articles about women and media history. Her upcoming book is *Celebrating Soft News: Re-evaluating Women's Page Journalism in the Post-World War II Era*.

Seretha D. Williams is Professor of English and Women's and Gender Studies at Augusta University. Her research interests include African and African American literature and the Black Arts Movement. She is the co-editor of *Afterimages of Slavery: Essays on Appearances in Recent American Films, Literature, Television and Other Media* (2012) and the author of articles on Margaret Walker and Langston Hughes.

www.ingramcontent.com/pod-product-compliance
Lightning Source LLC
Chambersburg PA
CBHW030051100526
44591CB00008B/107